THE DUTCH REPUBLIC
AND THE AMERICAN REVOLUTION

Series XXIX   No. 2

JOHNS HOPKINS UNIVERSITY STUDIES

IN

HISTORICAL AND POLITICAL SCIENCE

Under the Direction of the

Departments of History, Political Economy, and
Political Science

THE DUTCH REPUBLIC

AND THE AMERICAN REVOLUTION

BY

FRIEDRICH EDLER, M.DIPL., PH.D.

AMS PRESS

NEW YORK

Reprinted from the edition of 1911,Baltimore

First AMS EDITION published 1971

Manufactured in the United States of America

International Standard Book Number:0-404-02246-4

Library of Congress Number:78-149686

AMS PRESS INC.
NEW YORK, N.Y. 10003

CONTENTS.

PREFACE.

Nearly all phases of the American Revolution have been carefully investigated. This is, to some extent, true also of the influence which European powers exercised upon its development. Little attention, however, has been paid to the important part which the United Provinces of the Netherlands played in the contest. Their aid to the Americans, though mostly clandestine, or indirect, and often based upon selfish principles, was nevertheless remarkably effective. Some Dutch historians, like Colenbrander and Blok, have at some length dealt with the relation of the United Provinces to the young American commonwealth. They did so, however, when writing the history of their own country, and consequently considered matters entirely from a Dutch point of view. In America no complete account of the assistance given by the Netherlands to the Revolution has been written. It seemed, therefore, desirable to add this missing link.

While the subject is presented in this essay chiefly from a diplomatic standpoint, matters of political economy, as the commercial and financial relations between the two republics, have not been neglected. Consideration is also given to military and naval affairs. A discussion, however, in how far the governmental system of the United States is derived from Dutch sources was deemed beyond the scope of this monograph and consequently omitted.[1]

The material needed for a thorough study of the subject was found in the United States. The archives of Europe have been—and are still being—searched by Americans for

---

[1] This question has been repeatedly treated. See: Douglas Campbell, The Puritan in England, Holland, and America; William Elliot Griffis, The Influence of the Netherlands in the Making of the English Commonwealth and the American Republic, and other writings of the same author on Holland; Henry William Elson, History of the United States of America, Chapter "Colonization—New York."

everything connected with the history of their country. Copies made abroad are easily accessible at public libraries in the United States. The archives of the Netherlands, England, France, and Prussia are thus literally brought to the door of the student in America: Sparks' collection of transcripts in the library of Harvard University, Bancroft's similar collection in the New York Public Library, Sparks' Dutch Papers in the library of Cornell University, and Stevens' Dutch Papers in the Library of Congress, together with the published and unpublished manuscripts in the possession of the Department of State at Washington, furnished most of the information for this monograph.

In conclusion I wish to express my sincere thanks to Professor J. Franklin Jameson, Professor William Ray Manning, and Dr. William Elliot Griffis for their valuable suggestions and kind assistance and to my wife who for many months helped me in the tedious work of arranging notes and preparing the manuscript.

THE DUTCH REPUBLIC AND THE AMERICAN REVOLUTION.

CHAPTER I.

THE UNITED PROVINCES AT THE BEGINNING OF THE AMERICAN REVOLUTION.

"All Europe is for us," wrote the American commissioners at Paris in 1777.[1] This had been true even in the earlier stages of the struggle between England and her American colonies, though perhaps less known. It was the outcome of the British policy of the last two decades, which had resulted in the isolation of England in Europe.[2] France had been compelled to accept most humiliating conditions from England in the treaty of Paris of 1763, ceding thereby Canada, the island of Cape Breton, and her African possessions on the river Senegal. In India property and territories were restored to their ancient limits, but the French were to send thither no more troops and consequently lost all influence. Naturally France was looking for an opportunity to retrieve these losses, to wipe out the disgrace, and to pay England back in her own coin. Her attitude was fully understood in England. "A dismemberment of the British empire," wrote a prominent Englishman of the time, "was an idea that now offered itself to her [the French] councils, in all the splendor of well-founded expectation. To deprive

---

[1] Benjamin Franklin and Silas Deane to the Committee of Secret Correspondence, April 9, 1777 (Wharton, The Revolutionary Diplomatic Correspondence of the United States, II; 287).

[2] "Every nation in Europe wishes to see Britain humbled, having all in their turns been offended by her insolence, which in prosperity, she is apt to discover on all occasions" (Benjamin Franklin and Silas Deane to the Committee of Secret Correspondence, March 12, 1777, in Wharton, II, 289).

an ancient enemy of his hereditary possessions, to strip a victorious rival of his most valuable conquests, was too brilliant a temptation for ambition and inveteracy to resist."[1] It cannot be surprising, then, that the efforts of the Thirteen Colonies to gain independence from their mother country had been watched with interest and sympathy by the French government from the beginning.

Another European state which had been greatly offended by the treaty of Paris in 1763 was Prussia, now at the height of its prosperity and power. Frederick the Great concluded, in 1756, the Convention of Westminster with England, and the latter was his only ally during the greater part of the Seven Years' War; but when Bute replaced Pitt in the English cabinet, British policy changed. All the provisions of the Convention were broken successively by England. The subsidies to Frederick were discontinued, and a separate peace was concluded with France (that of Paris in 1763) without even guaranteeing the Prussian dominions as had been stipulated by the Convention.[2] The consequence was that Frederick conceived a strong hatred for England in general and Bute in particular, which he later transferred to Lord North. Though the Prussian king, from political reasons, abstained from taking part openly with the Americans against England, he strongly sympathized with them and assisted them indirectly in many ways. In later chapters will be shown his efforts to influence the Dutch Republic against her old ally, Great Britain.

Still a third power was anxious, if not to avenge offences committed by England, yet to recover former losses. Spain, at the end of the Spanish succession war, had ceded to England the island of Minorca and her stronghold Gibraltar, the key to the Mediterranean.[3] Everything tending to

---

[1] John Andrews, Two additional Letters to His Excellency the Count Welderen, 1781, p. 37.

[2] France had occupied the Rhenish provinces of Cleve, Geldern, and Moers. England, in 1763, left France at liberty to surrender them to Austria or return them to Prussia (Petersdorff, Friedrich der Grosse, 451).

[3] By the treaty of Utrecht in 1713.

weaken England was afterwards welcome to Spain, since Great Britain's embarrassment would open the prospect for gaining back those two important possessions. Hence, she joined the enemies of England during the Seven Years' War. Her efforts to get back Gibraltar and Minorca failed; and in the Peace of Paris of 1763 she was compelled to cede Florida to Great Britain, although the latter power returned to her Cuba and the Philippines, while France gave Louisiana by way of compensation for Florida. Spanish hostility to England continued.

The rest of Europe was more or less indifferent with regard to the gigantic struggle just begun by the American colonies against their mother country. There was only one power which at this period was allied with England by commercial and political treaties. The attitude of the United Provinces of the Netherlands at the beginning of the American Revolution was an important problem. While France, Prussia, and Spain were governed by the will of their kings only, the United Provinces formed a republic in which party spirit ruled.[1] There were two large political classes, the

---

[1] The form of government in the United Provinces was very complicated, and in order to make the proceedings there during the revolutionary period comprehensible, a short outline of their constitution is desirable.

The United Provinces consisted of the following seven provinces: Holland, Zealand, Utrecht, Guelderland, Overyssel, Groningen, and Friesland. These states differed greatly in size, situation, and general tendencies, some being maritime, others inland provinces; some Protestant, others Catholic; some democratic like Friesland, others aristocratic like Holland (Griffis, Brave Little Holland, 3). Having formed their confederation at Utrecht in 1579, they had been united for almost two hundred years.

The president or stadtholder (since 1751 William V of Orange) stood nominally at the head of the government and held the offices of captain-general and admiral-general, in which capacity he had the supreme command over all the military and naval forces of the Republic, but he could not declare war or conclude peace. As grand-admiral he presided over the admiralties—councils which not only had charge of the administration of the navy but also had the direction of the custom-house. Only a few offices could be filled by the states, the disposal of the rest belonging to the stadtholder. This was a powerful means for putting the magistrates, especially those of the cities, under obligations to him and for attaching to his person such men as were looking for positions. The stadtholder was the first member of the Council of State and was privileged to

partisans of the stadtholder or English party and the anti-stadtholder or Anti-Orange party, also called the French party or Patriots.[1]   These two groups were contending with

---

be present at the sessions and take part in the deliberations of the States General at his discretion, and also to make propositions to them.   In several provinces, as Holland, Guelderland, Utrecht, and Zealand, he was president of the body of nobles.   William V was, by a resolution of the States General in 1749, made also governor-general and supreme director of the companies of the East and West Indies, and possessed as such considerable power, being represented in their chambers and appointing their directors.

The main part of the sovereignty of the Dutch Republic was, however, vested in a senate of sovereign states or States General, in which each state or province, large or small, carried one vote (Griffis, Brave Little Holland, 2).   The States General declared war and made peace, and their resolutions were decisive for the Republic. They appointed ambassadors and ministers to foreign courts, also instructing them and receiving their reports, which as a rule were directed to the griffier, that is to say, secretary of the States General.   Diplomatic officials reported also to the stadtholder.   All treaties, alliances, and conventions were negotiated and ratified in the name of the States General, after having been communicated to and ratified by the assemblies of the several provinces, since the deputies had to submit the subjects under consideration to their provinces before voting on them in the States General.   It was, however, often not clear in what cases either a majority or absolute unanimity was necessary.   The foreign ambassadors and ministers at the Hague were accredited to the States General.   A few were also accredited to the stadtholder.   The presidency of the States General changed weekly, the deputies of the provinces occupying this office in rotation (Wharton, IV, 88 ff.; Fitzmaurice, Life of William, Earl of Shelburne, 113).   The assemblies of the separate states or provinces were composed of the nobles and of the deputies of the cities within the provincial boundaries.

The cities formed almost independent republics within the state. At the head of each were placed as chief executives the burgo-masters, who belonged also to the great council consisting of the burgomasters and the councilors.   The regencies, composed of the burgomasters, councilors, and schepens (judges), appointed the deputies to the provincial assemblies, the large cities sending as such two burgomasters, two schepens or two councilors, and one pensionary.   The minister, or secretary, of a city was called pensionary; he stood under the authority of the burgomasters (Wharton, V, 99).

The prime minister or secretary of the States of Holland, who was practically also the foreign minister of the Republic, had the official title of Grand Pensionary and was a very influential man, as the province of Holland could be considered half the nation.   In fact, his power was greater than that of the stadtholder.   The resolutions of the assembly of Holland were more or less decisive for the other provinces (Wharton, V, 686, 687; Fitzmaurice, Shelburne, 113).

[1] Schlözer, Ludwig Ernst, Herzog zu Braunschweig und Lüneburg, 76–82.

each other bitterly, but being at this juncture about equally divided, neither obtained absolute supremacy.

At the head of the Orange party was the stadtholder, William V. Since his mother, Princess Anne of England, had always remained more attached to her native country than to the United Provinces, it was natural that her son too should have a personal affection for that country. The partisans of France in the Netherlands having strong republican tendencies, he saw in England the power which alone could fortify his position, and his attachment to Great Britain was therefore based rather on selfish motives than on patriotic considerations. His wife was Wilhelmine, niece of King Frederick II of Prussia, and she shared, to some degree, her uncle's inclination toward France. Since William V was irresolute[1] and of a weak character, though good natured, there is no doubt that Wilhelmine would have succeeded in causing her husband to seek closer connections with the court of France. Her influence was, however, counterbalanced by that of Duke Louis Ernest of Brunswick, the prince's former tutor and constant adviser, who was an ardent English partisan. The duke is said to have been endowed with extraordinary intelligence, with which, however, he combined an ambitious and intriguing character. He could never during his long residence in the United Provinces accommodate himself to the spirit of the Dutch,[2] and the consequence was that, forsaken by the Orange party and violently attacked by the Patriots, he was finally compelled to leave the Republic. In the period under consideration he had, however, still great influence upon the affairs of the country. Subsequent research[3] has exonerated him from the serious charges made against him, and it seemed that he served as a kind of a scapegoat for the political sins of both parties. He was principally accused of having kept the young prince in ignorance of the affairs

---

[1] Wharton, I, 449.
[2] Davies, History of Holland and the Dutch Nation, III, 440.
[3] Schlözer, Braunschweig; Nijhoff, De Hertog van Brunswijk. Both books were written for the purpose of defending the duke.

of the Republic, and of having arranged while his tutor a secret agreement (Acte van Consulentschap) with William, according to which the latter was bound to ask the duke's advice in all affairs of importance. The Prince of Orange himself confessed once to Maillebois that his military instruction had been such as to make him a corporal, and he might as well have added that in civil matters too he was scarcely able to hold a subaltern's position,[1] but, according to what has become known of the prince's capacities, this does not speak against Duke Louis. As to the Acte van Consulentschap, Brunswick, aware of the young stadtholder's lack of intelligence, firmness, and energy, thought such a measure necessary for the welfare of the country. His conduct can therefore not be attributed wholly to ambitious aims.

Of the provinces, some like Zealand and Guelderland, where the prince had large possessions, were almost wholly for the English cause, while others, especially the province of Holland, and the large towns (Amsterdam at their head) inclined toward France and the American colonies. The Patriots counted in their number the rich merchants and craftsmen of the country, and also many of the laboring classes, most of whom adhered to the Orangists. A religious sect, the Mennonites, also belonged to this party.[2] The aristocrats, who had much influence at the court, were traditionally and as a consequence of their preference for the French manner of living and thinking members of the French party. While the English minister to the States General, Sir Joseph Yorke, was tempestuous and overbearing, the French envoy, Duc de la Vauguyon, won, by his courtesy and tact, the social circles of the aristocrats. French at that time was still the court language, and French literature was much read among the more refined classes of the people throughout Europe.[3]

---

[1] Colenbrander, De Patriottentijd, Hoofzakelijk naar buitenlandsche bescheiden, I, 78.
[2] Schlözer, Braunschweig, 76–82.
[3] Wharton, I, 449.

At the outbreak of war between England and her colonies the English partisans in the United Provinces sympathized, of course, with Great Britain; on the other hand, the French party, like France herself, with the colonies, though not yet openly. The Dutch population in general watched with interest the exertions of the Americans for liberty, as they saw in that struggle a certain analogy to their own defection from Spain, which originated, like the American Revolution, partly in the unwillingness of the dependent provinces or colonies to be taxed by their mother country.

For the Dutch foreign policy there was, at the beginning of the American Revolution, only one course, that of remaining neutral. The United Provinces were not in a state of effective defence, either on land or on sea. They were far less prepared for an offensive war, their navy not being strong enough to give the slightest prospect of success in a naval contest with England, nor their army sufficient in numbers, compared with the military forces of the surrounding countries, to assist England on the continent, in case the war should spread over Europe. There was another reason why the Republic should keep out of the war. The Dutch were the great carriers of the world, transmitting the products of Europe to all parts of the earth, and vice versa, and would remain such so long as they were neutrals; but from the instant they should become involved in the war, their ships would be liable to seizure by the other belligerents, and their commerce and navigation must decline accordingly. The attitude of the masses of the Dutch at the outbreak of the English-American war was, consequently, in general friendly to the cause of the rebelling colonies,[1] while the interests of the country as understood by those who were in any way connected with commerce and navigation—and that was the great majority of the population—did not allow armed assistance. Great Britain was too formidable a naval adversary for the small republic in her present defenceless condition to cope with, and the

---

[1] Davies, History of Holland, III, 445.

Dutch were fully aware of the fact that the destruction of their navy meant the ruin of their country. "Strictest neutrality" must therefore be their political motto. It will be seen in the course of this essay how great a service the Dutch rendered to the American cause by not taking an active part in the war until it was well nigh decided in favor of the American arms. The following chapter will show the first official efforts of the United Provinces to remain neutral.

CHAPTER II.

The Dutch as Neutrals.

Though the government of the United Provinces, at the beginning of the Anglo-American war, was neutral, with a tendency on the part of the stadtholder to oblige England whenever possible, it could not prevent agents of the American colonies as well as of France from carrying on secret negotiations on Dutch ground. Sir Joseph Yorke, the English ambassador at the Hague, reported, in April, 1776, confidentially to Lord Suffolk that a friend had shown him a letter of very suspicious contents, which had been intercepted at the post-office.[1] It was from Abbé Desnoyers, the French chargé d'affaires at the Hague, and directed to Count de Vergennes, the foreign minister in Paris, dated April 16. It revealed the fact that a certain person calling himself an Englishman and living in the United Provinces, but not at the Hague, was corresponding with Dr. Benjamin Franklin, then chairman of the committee of secret correspondence in Philadelphia. The com-

---

[1] Yorke to Suffolk, April 19, 1776 (Letters and extracts from the correspondence of Sir Joseph Yorke, in the library of Harvard University, Sparks MSS., LXXII).

The United Provinces followed the practice of other countries at that time of having the letters of foreign ministers clandestinely opened at the post-office and copied. A special official then deciphered them. This was not so very difficult, since being appointed for this particular purpose, he was apt to find the key to the ciphers. In this way the reports of the French as well as of the Prussian minister were copied at the Hague, and also those of the Prussian envoy at the court of St. James, who sent his letters to Berlin by way of the United Provinces. The reports of the English envoy could not be intercepted as he had them safely delivered on board the ships (at Hellevoetsluis) which carried them over to England. The copies circulated among the Grand Pensionary of the States of Holland, the register or griffier of the States General, and the Prince of Orange. Griffier Fagel, who was an ardent English partisan, communicated them to the English minister (Colenbrander, Patriottentijd, I, 118–119).

mittee had transmitted full powers to that person, adding instructions with data regarding the present state and disposition of the colonies. The American agent had called upon Desnoyers to propose, on behalf of the colonies, closer connections between the two powers. France might become the mediator of the quarrel, or open her ports to the colonies and be received in theirs. The French chargé submitted the matter to the French court, stating that the American agent was ready to confer with the French authorities.

In May, Sir Joseph Yorke was able to send a second confidential report on this subject to Lord Suffolk, enclosing another extract from a letter to Count de Vergennes from the Abbé Desnoyers, in which the latter gave an account of an interview with the American correspondent. Desnoyers had informed the agent that Louis XVI could not accept the propositions of Congress, but that the vessels of all nations, including those of England, were free to enter the French ports, and that no difference would be made between England and her colonies in that respect. Only the carrying of contraband goods and the enlistment of soldiers were prohibited. Sir Joseph expressed his surprise at this attitude of the French court and added that it would be a good lesson for His Majesty's deluded and rebellious subjects, but feared that it would only result in confirming Dr. Franklin in his determination to continue the struggle for independence.[1]

Later in the year Ambassador Yorke reported again to Lord Suffolk regarding these negotiations between the American colonies and France. The correspondent of the American committee had repeated his propositions to Desnoyers, and the latter had informed his court of the interview. From the contents of the chargé's letter it appeared that the attitude of the King of France had not changed and that the agent had received no further instructions from America.[2] A few days later, Yorke wrote

---

[1] Yorke to Suffolk, May 24, 1776 (Sparks MSS., LXXII; Colenbrander, Patriottentijd, I, 119).
[2] Yorke to Suffolk, August 2, 1776 (Sparks MSS., LXXII).

less cheerfully to Lord Suffolk concerning the conduct of France and also that of the Dutch Republic. He had been informed of an utterance of Desnoyers to the effect that the latter wished the troubles between England and her colonies to continue a little longer in order that Great Britain might be reduced to a state as weak as that of France. The United Provinces shared this hope, but from different motives, commercial advantage being their main reason.[1]

In the course of the year 1776 France had become more decided in her hostility toward England and in her sympathy for the colonies. It was henceforth essential for her to draw the Dutch Republic away from Great Britain, and to attach it more closely to herself for reasons which were partly of a commercial, but more of a strategical nature. In case of a war with England, if the Dutch Republic should be the latter's ally, France would have to close her ports to the Dutch ships. This action would deprive her of the very means of carrying on the hostilities effectively, since the United Provinces were the chief sources of French naval stores and provisions. At the same time she would have to engage her army either to defend her northern boundaries against the United Provinces or to invade the latter. Part of her navy would be required to hold the Dutch forces in check. It was thus of utmost importance for France to have the United Provinces at least neutral neighbors. On July 7, 1776, Count de Vergennes read a memorandum in the French council on the new situation, laying out a plan to be pursued by France in the controversy between England and her colonies. He recommended an effective French propaganda in the United Provinces to stir up the republican party, which France had neglected. He would also profit by the thirst for riches with which the Dutch were imbued individually by letting them enjoy a neutrality which would become a source of wealth for them.[2] To carry out this policy a new French ambassador was appointed for the

---

[1] Yorke to Suffolk, August 13, 1776 (Sparks MSS., LXXII).
[2] Doniol, Histoire de la Participation de la France à l'Etablissement des Etats-Unis d'Amérique, I, 528.

vacant post at the Hague, the Duc de la Vauguyon.[1] The choice was a very lucky one from the French standpoint. His talents for accomplishing the task set him were extraordinary. He succeeded in causing the authorities to follow his suggestions so that the Republic became, in the end, utterly dependent on France. Following his instructions, he aroused in commercial circles the greed for gain and among the regents the love of power, at the same time somewhat discrediting the stadtholder in order to isolate him and to paralyze his influence; but he took care to do this in an inconspicuous manner. The main field of his activity in the United Provinces was the province of Holland and especially the city of Amsterdam, with the regents of which he was soon in close connection. However, in the beginning, he avoided conferring with the leaders of the French party as he thought it dangerous to show his cards too quickly.[2] Even his personality was highly fitted for his mission, and won him many friends in the Republic. He is said to have differed much from the average Frenchman of his class at that time, being neither frivolous nor skeptical and not making any efforts to appear a witty man.[3] These qualities counted greatly in the eyes of the stern and plain Dutch natives. Furthermore his figure was more of the Dutch than of the French type.[4]

The English colonies in America declared their independence on July 4, 1776. This bold step was received with hearty applause in Europe. The news of the declaration arrived in the United Provinces toward the end of August, 1776, and caused there much rejoicing. Only the partisans of England were greatly depressed. Yorke declared that

[1] Paul François de Quelen, Duc de la Vauguyon, was appointed minister to the States General in December, 1776, being then a little over thirty years old. He was a favorite of Louis XVI, his father having been the latter's tutor (Colenbrander, Patriottentijd, I, 120–121).

[2] Nijhoff, Brunswijk, 156.

[3] Colenbrander, Patriottentijd, I, 121.

[4] In a letter to Lord Eden, dated December 24, 1776, Sir Joseph Yorke speaks of Vauguyon as being "of the right cut for this Embassy, being as *squab* as anything in Holland" (Colenbrander, Patriottentijd, I, 121, note).

he could not help thinking such a step would be advantageous to the English government, for the hot heads amongst the Americans, who had gone too far to hope for pardon, had probably carried this point in the Congress by main force, in the hope, by breaking down the bridge behind them, of drawing the others along with them into the mire. In this light, he said, it was looked upon by reasonable people in the United Provinces.[1]

While the English ambassador at the Hague and the partisans of Great Britain thus faintly tried to console themselves with the supposition that the Declaration of Independence had been forced upon the colonies by "hot heads," and was therefore not due to general conviction, the French charge, Desnoyers,[2] sent a report to his government which is of special interest, since it dealt with public opinion in the Netherlands regarding the independence of America and the expectations which the Dutch connected with it. The Dutch flattered themselves that the independence of the English colonies would open to them a new source of commerce and wealth. The Dutch had always been very observant of the American contest, having once themselves possessed considerable portions of North America, where a large number of their nation still subsisted, preserving the customs and religion of the United Provinces. The Dutch at home would willingly aid their American kindred, who would as willingly reunite themselves with the mother country. The act of independence, he continued, was going to occupy greatly the minds of those among the Dutch who thought it possible to assist the Americans in making their revolution as successful as had been the Dutch revolution against Spain. Jealous of the commerce of other countries, the United Provinces, he thought, would not wish any nation to be ahead of them in the friendship of a new

---

[1] Yorke to Eden, August 23, 1776 (Sparks MSS., LXXII).
[2] The Duc de la Vauguyon arrived at the Hague in December, 1776. Desnoyers wrote to Vergennes on December 17, 1776, that he expected Vauguyon's arrival daily, and that his duty as chargé d'affaires would then be ended (Sparks MSS., LXXXII).

nation of such vast economic possibilities, and one which in the time of peace would multiply as the sand.[1]

The French were, however, still apprehensive that English influence might predominate in the United Provinces and that the neutrality of the Dutch would give way to an armed assistance of England. The French ambassador was suspicious as to the recent zeal of the Prince of Orange in naval matters, noticing also that the stadtholder revealed his sympathy for Great Britain more and more. He had heard, besides, of a marriage project between the Prince of Wales and the stadtholder's daughter. The prospect of such a union was said to have been opened to William V by his envoy at the court of St. James, Count van Welderen. The latter, then on leave at the Hague, had just been in conference with Sir Joseph Yorke.[2] At this conjuncture, the French government took into consideration a renewal of the treaty of commerce of 1739 with the Dutch Republic, but Count de Vergennes rejected this project because the treaty would give advantages, as before, only to the Dutch. On the other hand, it would not cause the ties existing between England and the United Provinces to cease. Furthermore he did not deem such a treaty necessary for attaching the United Provinces to France because it was well known to the Dutch that France desired their neutrality; and this was so advantageous to the Republic.[3] The ambassador, Vauguyon, was, however, instructed by Count de Vergennes to assure the friends of France in the United Provinces that Louis XVI was taking a special interest in the prosperity of the Republic and that the Patriots would always find sufficient support in France to counterbalance the influence and the aims of England.[4]

In the meantime the colonies in America had not remained inactive regarding the appointment of representatives in

---

[1] Desnoyers to Vergennes, September 10, 1776 (Sparks MSS., LXXXIII).
[2] Vauguyon to Vergennes, August 1, 1777 (Sparks MSS., LXXXII).
[3] Vergennes to Vauguyon, August 3, 1777 (ibid.).
[4] Same to same, August 7, 1777 (ibid.).

Europe. Soon after the committee of secret correspondence had been formed in 1775, with Benjamin Franklin as
its chairman, a resolution was passed appointing C. W. F.
Dumas at the Hague[1] its correspondent in the United Provinces. Silas Deane[2] of Connecticut was elected by Congress
as American business agent in Paris and Franklin,[3] then in
his seventieth year, as commissioner to France. Arthur
Lee, Franklin's successor in England after the latter's departure in the spring of 1775, had in the same year been
appointed secret agent of the committee of secret correspondence in London, and was elected in October, 1776,
commissioner of Congress to the court of France as a sub-
stitute for Mr. Jefferson, who had not accepted that office.[4]

Dumas owed his appointment to Dr. Franklin, with whom
he had become acquainted during a stay of the latter in the
United Provinces at the beginning of the American Revolution. Franklin, noticing Dumas' strong love of liberty
and his devotion to the American cause, did not hesitate
to propose him as secret correspondent to Congress. A
prominent Dutchman (van der Capellen) wrote to Livingston in 1779 that Dumas was devoted with heart and soul
to the cause of the Thirteen States, to which he had rendered important services.[5] Francis Wharton says of Dumas:
" It will be seen by M. Dumas' correspondence that his services were unremitting, assiduous, and important, and performed with a singular devotedness to the interests of the
United States, and with a warm and undeviating attachment to the rights and liberties for which they were con-

---

[1] " Charles William Frederick Dumas . . . was a native of
Switzerland, but he passed a large portion of his life in Holland,
chiefly employed as a man of letters. He was a man of deep learning, versed in the ancient classics, and skilled in several modern
languages, a warm friend of liberty, and an early defender of the
American cause. About the year 1770, or a little later, he published
an edition of Vattel, with a long preface and notes, which were
marked with his liberal sentiments " (Wharton, I, 603).
[2] In February, 1776 (ibid., I, 559).
[3] On September 27, 1776 (ibid., I, 473).
[4] Ibid., I, 517.
[5] Beaufort, Brieven van en aan Joan Derck van der Capellen van
de Poll, 114.

tending."[1]   When Arthur Lee was elected secret agent in
London, Franklin referred him (on December 12, 1775) to
Dumas, to whom the committee of secret correspondence
had sent detailed information regarding the American affairs.
Dumas, Franklin wrote, would also transmit Lee's letters
to the committee via the Dutch island St. Eustatia, in case
Lee should not be able to send them more directly.[2]   When
Deane left America to enter upon his duties as the commercial agent of Congress in France, Franklin recommended
him also to Dumas, instructing Deane to inform the latter
of everything of interest that had happened in America.[3]
Soon after Deane's arrival at Paris a correspondence between the two began, and Deane expressed to Dumas his
desire of visiting the United Provinces as a private gentleman.   In a letter, dated August 18, 1776, Deane gave this
interesting account of the American policy regarding the
United Provinces to Dumas :—

" It is the policy of the United Provinces of Holland to be neuter
to every attention. The United Colonies only wish them to keep
steady to their only true system of policy in the present case; and
give me leave to say that a reflection on their former struggles must
show them in what point of light the Americans are to be considered. The United Colonies ask no aid or alliances. Let Britain
court every, even the most petty and mercenary, power in Europe,
the United Colonies only ask for what nature surely entitles all
men to, a free and uninterrupted commerce and exchange of the
superfluities of one country for those of another, and the first power
in Europe which takes advantage of the present favorable occasion
must exceed every other in commerce."[4]

Though Dumas used every means for keeping his activity
for the American Congress a secret, it was not long before
Sir Joseph Yorke discovered it. He informed Lord Suffolk
confidentially that one Macintosh was certainly in correspondence with America, but that Dumas must be regarded,
properly speaking, as the agent of Congress.[5] Lord Suffolk,
however, seemed to have additional intelligence of American
agitation in the United Provinces, for he wrote to Sir Joseph

[1] Wharton, I, 603.
[2] Wharton, II, 63; R. H. Lee, Life of Arthur Lee, I, 53.
[3] Wharton, II, 82.
[4] Wharton, II, 128.
[5] Yorke to Suffolk, September 17, 1776 (Sparks MSS., LXXII).

soon afterwards that he had reason to believe Alexander Foster from Philadelphia to be the American agent at Amsterdam and William Hodge at Rotterdam.[1] With all these French and American influences in the United Provinces known to the English ambassador it is surprising that he could say in a letter to W. Eden that the rebels were losing friends every day, which was the fate of those going down.[2] When Yorke learned of Silas Deane's intention to visit the United Provinces, he warned the government at the Hague that neither the treaties existing between England and the Republic nor the friendly relations entertained by them could allow such rebel visitors in the United Provinces.[3]

While the agents of three countries were thus busy in the United Provinces trying to move the Dutch according to the special interests of their respective governments, the Republic pursued officially the policy of neutrality. In February, 1775, Sir Joseph Yorke had presented a memorandum to the States General, in which he announced that the English colonies in America had risen in rebellion against his master, who would find means to bring his subjects back to their duty. For this purpose the king thought it necessary that the rebels should not receive, under the pretext of commerce, anything that might nourish the insurrection. Yorke asked then in the name of George III that the States General, without delay, take such measures as they deemed proper for preventing the inhabitants of the United Provinces from exporting arms and munitions of war to the West Indies beyond what was bona fide necessary for the use of the Dutch colonies. He observed that the temporary inconveniences caused by this prohibition would be small; it was, however, the only means for preserving harmony between the two countries and for avoiding disagreements, which must result from a different conduct.[4]

---

[1] Suffolk to Yorke, November 29, 1776 (Sparks MSS., LXXII).
[2] Yorke to Eden, December 24, 1776 (ibid.).
[3] Yorke to Suffolk, July 15, 1777 (ibid.).
[4] Yorke's memorandum, February 27, 1775 (Sparks MSS., CIII; Bancroft MSS., America, Holland, and England).

The States General, thereupon, passed a resolution in March, in which they expressed their desire of maintaining the liberty only of the bona fide commerce and navigation, and of checking any abuses which might possibly be made of that freedom to the disadvantage of the English crown. They prohibited, for a period of six months, the export of arms, gunpowder, and other munitions of war in English vessels or ships carrying the English flag.[1] Ships of other nations, including those belonging to subjects of the States General, were forbidden to export such goods during the same period, unless with express permission of the competent admiralty. At the same time the admiralties were to be instructed to permit such goods to be exported only when the sender should declare under oath that he had no knowledge, directly or indirectly, of the arms or ammunition being sent to places situated in the dominions of Great Britain in America. The Dutch colonies in the West Indies were to receive the same orders concerning the export of contraband from there. The States General declared that this was the utmost that they could do without violating the freedom of commerce and navigation; they trusted therefore that this resolution would meet with the approbation of the king.

The States General then issued detailed orders for the Republic. All export of munitions of war, gunpowder, cannon, guns and balls, in ships domiciled in the English dominions was forbidden provisionally for a period of six months under fine not only of the confiscation of the arms and ammunition found in those vessels, but in addition of one thousand guilders to be paid by the skipper, his vessel being confiscated in case of non-payment. For the loading of such goods in other vessels, including Dutch, permission by the competent admiralty was prescribed. For contravention of the latter regulation the same fine as before was fixed. The admiralties were instructed according to the

---

[1] This was, of course, aimed chiefly at the Americans, who were at this period still considered English subjects. Not yet possessing a flag of their own, they were using the same colors as the mother country.

resolution. The West Indies Company, the Society of Surinam, and the Administration of the Berbice were asked to issue the same orders for the colonies under their management, the fine to be fixed according to the circumstances of the colonies and the permission for Dutch ships and those of other nationality to be given by the competent governments or authorities of the colonies.[1]

George III, through his ambassador at the Hague, declared his satisfaction with the neutrality of the United Provinces as expressed by the resolution of the States General of March 20, 1775. As the term of the prohibition of the export of contraband would expire in the month of September, 1775, Yorke presented, in August, another memorandum to the States General asking for a prolongation of the term,[2] which was granted for one year by a resolution of the States General of August 18.[3] Similar resolutions, each for one year, were passed by them, on October 10, 1776—after Yorke had made strong representations that the previous measures had been absolutely ineffective[4] —and again on November 3, 1777.[5]

The French chargé d'affaires, Abbé Desnoyers, reported these declarations of neutrality to Count de Vergennes on September 24, 1776. He had heard, he wrote, of a memorial of the English ambassador requesting the renewal of the prohibition of the export of contraband to the revolting colonies. After stating the previous decrees for that purpose he continued that the language held by the Dutch in these resolutions seemed rather curious, when compared with their subsequent leniency as to facts. It was almost proved, he said, that they had contributed to raising the confidence of the colonies in declaring their independence, while

---

[1] Resolution of the States General, March 20, 1775 (Bancroft MSS.; Groot Placaatboek, IX, 107).

[2] Yorke's memoranda of April 7, 1775, and August 8, 1775 (Bancroft MSS.; Sparks MSS., CIII).

[3] Resolution of the States General, August 18, 1775 (Sparks MSS., CIII).

[4] Yorke, October 1, 1776 (Bancroft MSS.; Sparks MSS., CIII). Below, p. 41.

[5] Groot Placaatboek, IX, 107.

at the same time they had furnished the English ministry with packets and store ships. The Republic had quickly seized the opportunity for this double game at sea and found it profitable, both financially and politically. But he thought the United Provinces would sooner or later be compelled to take some part in the controversy. If the court of Vienna should then be inclined to encroach upon the Dutch boundaries or commerce, the embarrassment of the United Provinces would become very great. The adjustment of England with her colonies, Desnoyers said, could consequently not be very agreeable intelligence for the majority of the Dutch. This adjustment, after the American Declaration of Independence, appeared to many people impossible, but, he said, might perhaps be the more easily effected on that very account.[1]

It is not quite clear from this letter which way Desnoyers wished the Dutch to turn. Apparently he was not aware of the policy of the French government decided upon in the course of the year 1776, according to which the neutrality of the United Provinces was greatly desired by France, but at the same time a secret or indirect support of the American colonies by the Dutch could only be agreeable to her.

While these declarations of neutrality were in favor of the English, another decision of the Dutch government in a neutral direction was certainly very pleasing to the colonies, that is, the quasi refusal to send the Scotch brigade to England.[2]

In November, 1775, William V informed the States General of George III's desire transmitted to the stadtholder in the preceding October of borrowing the brigade[3] during

---

[1] Desnoyers to Vergennes, September 24, 1776 (Sparks MSS., LXXXIII).

[2] Pfister, Die amerikanische Revolution, I, 298.

[3] One of the main reasons why the Scotch regiments were left in the United Provinces and why their recruiting in Scotland was formerly not only permitted but facilitated was probably that they formed a small army at the disposal of the English kings, especially the Stuarts, for emergency use whenever Parliament would not grant the raising of one (Colenbrander, Patriottentijd, I, 115).

the rebellion of the colonies in America. Since England was making war against her own colonies and outside of Europe, the treaty with the United Provinces of 1678 was not available, and she could not ask for the six thousand auxiliaries stipulated by that treaty.[1] Neither could the lending of the Scotch brigade be demanded on account of the treaty but merely on the ground of the friendly relations existing between the two governments. According to tradition, it is true, the brigade was at England's disposal whenever she wanted it, but since Great Britain had forbidden the recruiting of the brigade in Scotland the obligation of the United Provinces to adhere to the tradition on her part had ceased. It seems that England foresaw the difficulties created by her request and that, according to a note in the diary of the Duke of Brunswick, the whole transaction was only a political trick of Lord North, who thought he might be enabled by a refusal of the Dutch to persuade Parliament of the necessity of hiring foreign troops.[2]

George III, in return for the loan of the brigade, offered to replace the latter by an equal number of Hanoverian troops, or to pay the expenses for levying the same number of national Dutch troops. The States General were furthermore to have the choice of either recalling the brigade or leaving it to Great Britain at the conclusion of the war. In the case of the recall of the brigade, George III would again grant permission for recruiting in Scotland.[3] The States General referred the proposition to the provinces, four of which (Guelderland, Friesland, Overyssel and Groningen) immediately gave their consent to the transfer of

---

[1] Nijhoff says (Brunswijk, 145) that William V was immediately willing, "om die complaisance aan den koning van Engeland te bewijzen, als of het afstaan van circa 6000 man troepen als een zaak van beleefdheid kon worden aangemerkt." As only the lending of the brigade, counting scarcely more than a thousand men, was and could be in question, Nijhoff seems to be mistaken here. See also Colenbrander, Patriottentijd, I, 116, note 1.

[2] Nijhoff, Brunswijk, 148, footnote.

[3] Ferguson, Papers illustrating the History of the Scots Brigade in the Service of the United Netherlands, II, 396.

the Scotch brigade. The attitude of Zealand and Utrecht has not become known. Holland, though Yorke had asked for an answer within a month,[1] came to a resolution only in February, 1776, accepting then England's offer, under conditions which made the acceptance equal to a refusal. She required that permission to recruit in Scotland must be restored after the brigade should return to the United Provinces; that England should bear all the expenses of transport from the Republic and back, as well as the pay of the brigade during its absence from the Netherlands and the cost of replacing it by foreign troops; and finally that the brigade should in no case be employed either wholly or partly outside Great Britain's possessions in Europe.[2]

These conditions were accepted by the States General on April 5, 1776.[3] The last condition especially was a great disappointment to George III, since he wanted to employ the brigade, according to a statement by Yorke, against the American colonies.[4] A few days later, on April 8, the Prince of Orange, who had corresponded privately and directly with George III, made known that the King of England had sent him an autograph letter thanking him for his good offices and announcing that he would accept the conditions which the prince had communicated to him as the opinion of the States General, in case he should be in a position to renew his request.[5]

Though the United Provinces had given in these transactions a strong proof of their neutrality, what was more important was the fact, revealed in the course of the debates, that the relations between England and the United Prov-

---

[1] Colenbrander, Patriottentijd, I, 116.
[2] Ferguson, Scots Brigade, II, 397; Colenbrander, Patriottentijd, I, 116.
[3] Secret Resolution of the States General, 1776 (Sparks MSS., CIII).
[4] Brunswick to William V, September 24, 1775 (Nijhoff, Brunswijk, 144, footnote).
[5] Mrs. Fairchild states (Francis Adriaan van der Kemp, 38) that when the brigade was at last lent to the king, it was upon the condition that it should not be used outside of Europe. This seems to be a mistake, as the brigade, in fact, was never lent to George III.

inces had become rather cool while the sympathy for the American colonies had greatly increased. Amsterdam had even considered the proposition of selling the Scotch brigade to England as if aiming at the severance of all relations with Great Britain.[1] The Duke of Brunswick was indignant at the English request and, though an English partisan himself, was violently opposed to granting it. In his opinion, England, knowing the unwillingness of the States General to increase the Dutch army, ought not to have asked for a measure which would have diminished the number and the strength of the Dutch military forces and therefore weakened the resistance of the Republic to France. He had no faith in either raising the number of Dutch national troops or hiring foreigners. The former would not be granted by the States General. On the other hand, it would be difficult to subject all those foreign troops to the military and civil laws of the Republic, and they would therefore endanger the safety of the state.[2]

Most remarkable were the proceedings in the States of Overyssel, owing to the opposition of van der Capellen van de Poll,[3] who was destined to become the great leader of the Dutch Patriots and the man to whom the United States

---

[1] Ferguson, Scots Brigade, II, 397.

[2] Brunswick to Prince of Orange, January 30, 1776 (Nijhoff, Brunswijk, 292).

[3] Joan Derk van der Capellen van de (or "tot den") Poll was born on November 2, 1741, as the eldest son of Frederich J. van der Capellen, major of infantry. He was anxious to enter the Ridderschap and the Upper House of the States of Zutphen, province of Guelderland, but was not admitted, failing to fulfill the requirements. Van der Capellen then turned to the province of Overyssel. His birth and his possession of a knightly estate, "that of Bredenhorst" (later exchanged for that of Poll), qualified him there, and with the support of the stadtholder he was admitted as regent into the Ridderschap of Overyssel on October 22, 1772. By the study of English philosophy and statecraft he was imbued with liberal principles and ideas, which brought about his determination to establish an open and declared opposition; this he thought of the utmost importance for the maintenance of a constitution in which, like the Dutch, a great dose of monarchy entered. Carrying out this plan, he drew upon him the hatred of the English faction and the indignation of the stadtholder, who recognized too late that he had assisted an opponent in becoming a regent (Fairchild, van der Kemp, 30–35; Beaufort, Brieven van der Capellen, 87).

owe gratitude for his courageous support of the cause of
the Revolution at a time when no one dared to plead openly
in the United Provinces for American independence and
when the success of the rebellion was very problematic.[1]
On December 16, 1775, he violently opposed in a now
famous speech before the States of Overyssel the lending
of the Scotch brigade to Great Britain. He declared, whatever might be the fate of the American colonies, he would
always regard it as a glory and an honor to have openly protected, in his public character, their cause which he regarded
as that of all the human kind. It was absolutely necessary
for the Republic, he said, to keep strictest neutrality during
the controversy of Great Britain with her colonies, since it
was the duty of the United Provinces to restore their own
commerce and agriculture which had greatly declined.
Therefore if the Republic were going to give assistance to
England, the same must be given also to the Americans.
Besides the conduct of England was not such as to cause
the United Provinces to break with a peaceful neighbor,
France, who was the natural friend of the Republic. Hideous as this unnatural war between brothers was, in which,
according to the newspapers, even barbarians declined to
interfere, it would be more hideous if this should be done
by a people who once themselves had been slaves and had
borne the name of rebels, but most hideous of all must it be
regarded if assistance should be given against the Americans, who, a brave nation, deserved the respect of all the
world, and who defended unfalteringly the rights which as
men they had received from God Almighty and not from
England.[2]

Van der Capellen was bold enough to have this speech
printed and distributed, causing thereby a great sensation.
The States of Overyssel, on March 14, 1777, removed his
"Avis" from their records, declaring that it was not conceived in decent terms, and soon afterwards arranged his

---

[1] Beaufort, Brieven van der Capellen, 61, 63.
[2] Vaterlandsche Historie (Wagenaar's Vaterlandsche Historie,
continued), XXV, 55–57.

dismissal as a regent. In America van der Capellen won many friends and admirers by his brave defence of the American cause, as is proved by the letters which he re- that of the President and members of Congress;[1] and from Governor Trumbull of Connecticut in his own name and that of the President and members of Congress;[2] and from Franklin and others. Van der Capellen's courage did not fail to impress the majority of the Dutch; his attachment to America and his conduct in the affair of the Scotch brigade made him dear to his fellow-citizens.[2]

Another important act of neutrality of the Dutch was the keeping open of their ports to American vessels. Ambassador Yorke had frequent conferences with the heads of the Republic on the subject of closing the Dutch ports in all parts of the world to vessels of the American colonies, but the United Provinces declined.[3]

The passage of foreign troops in British pay through the United Provinces for embarkation to America was, however, not denied. Sir Joseph Yorke presented a memorandum to the States General on February 23, 1776, in which he stated that England had concluded a treaty with the Prince of Hesse-Cassel by which the latter was obliged to furnish a regiment of infantry for English service. This regiment was to be sent down the rivers, Main and Rhine, to the Dutch frontier, and permission was asked to let it pass through the Dutch territory without molestation. The regiment would observe the most exact discipline, and everything for its passage would be paid in cash. In a similar English memorandum of February 17, 1777, free passage was requested again for Hessian troops with their arms and baggage from the Dutch frontier to Dort or Willemstadt, and for about thirteen hundred men of Anspach with their field artillery.[4]

---

[1] Fairchild, van der Kemp, 36–39.
[2] Beaufort, Brieven van der Capellen, 59.
[3] Desnoyers to Vergennes, October 11 and 22, 1776 (Sparks MSS., LXXXII).
[4] Bancroft MSS., America, Holland, and England.

While the United Provinces indirectly assisted England by allowing this passage of troops, they, in a similar affair, acted in favor of the Americans, restoring, thereby, their neutrality. The Republic employed in her service two regiments of the Prince of Waldeck, which George III was very anxious to obtain against the American colonies. Sir Joseph Yorke, therefore, in concert with the griffier of the States General, Fagel, and the chiefs of the English party, had many interviews with principal members of the Republic on this subject. The Prince of Waldeck, of course, as owner of the regiments, was asked for this cession too, but replied that he would first communicate the proposition to the States General. He would accept it only if the United Provinces should not increase the compensation for the regiments.[1] Yorke thought that the States General would never grant such an increase, and that the regiments would consequently pass over into the English service. He was, however, mistaken. The States General voted in favor of the retention of the regiments on the conditions of the Prince of Waldeck.[2]

As an act of neutrality must also be considered the renewal by the States General of the placaat of 1756. According to this resolution pirates appearing in Dutch waters, or privateers entering any of the Dutch ports without showing colors and not being able to produce legal commissions, were liable to be seized and prosecuted. All the Dutch admiralties were immediately informed accordingly and instructed to put the law in force at once.[3] Though the

---

[1] "Augmenter la capitulation." It is uncertain whether this means "increase the contract money," or "renew the contract" by which the regiments had passed into the service of the United Provinces. Probably the first, since Yorke—apparently in view of the Dutch parsimony—did not expect the States General to grant it. The renewal of the capitulation could scarcely have been considered extraordinary by him.

[2] Vauguyon to Vergennes, July, 1777 (Sparks MSS., LXXXII).

[3] Yorke to Suffolk, May 6, 1777 (Sparks MSS., LXXII).

The interesting episode of a man-of-war constructed by the Dutch for the United States should be mentioned. The American commissioners in Paris succeeded in having a frigate built for the United States at Amsterdam in 1777. She was a very large vessel,

Dutch government thus gave in many ways proof of its earnest desire to be strictly neutral, the court of St. James was by no means satisfied with the conduct of the Dutch, as will be seen in the next chapter.

---

carrying thirty 24-pounders on one deck, and almost equalled a ship of the line in appearance. Unfortunately difficulties arose about the equipping and manning of the vessel in the neutral Dutch Republic. The commissioners were also lacking funds. They resolved therefore to sell the frigate to the King of France (Franklin, Deane, and Lee to the Committee of Foreign Affairs, November 30, 1777, in Wharton, II, 433). Louis XVI, on his part, ceded the "Indian," as the frigate was called, to the Chevalier Luxembourg. In 1780 Alexander Gillon, a merchant from South Carolina, rented the vessel for his state and renamed her "South Carolina." He sailed from Amsterdam in July, 1780, but did not arrive at Philadelphia until May 28, 1782. The "South Carolina" was put to sea again in December of the same year, but was chased and captured by an English squadron soon after she had left the Capes of Delaware. Luxembourg, as had been stipulated by contract, demanded 300,000 livres for this loss. His claim was settled only on December 21, 1814, when the state of South Carolina made a final payment of $28,894 to the heirs of the Chevalier Luxembourg (C. O. Paullin, The Navy of the American Revolution, 264, 304, 436-440).

CHAPTER III.

English Complaints.

Though George III, in 1775, had expressed his satisfaction with the Dutch proclamation prohibiting contraband trade with North America,[1] the sentiments of the English authorities soon changed. Sir Joseph Yorke wrote to Lord Suffolk in the following year that he was glad to receive from Sir William Gordon an ordinance, in terms very friendly to his Majesty, just published by the government of Brussels prohibiting the exportation of arms and ammunition, which he would take care to publish in the United Provinces as worthy of imitation. "I stated," the ambassador said in another letter to his government, "the strong proof of friendship lately given by the King of Portugal, and proved more or less, that every Power in Europe had gone further than the Republic."[2] Still it was apparently not so much the wording of the Dutch declaration that displeased Great Britain as it was the failure to enforce it.[3] According to the law of nations it was then, just as to-day, considered a breach of neutrality, and formed a casus belli, for a state to furnish arms and other contraband goods to belligerents. If, however, private citizens engaged in such commerce, they did not involve their country in any breach of neutrality but ran the risk of losing their goods.[4] In the case of the subjects of the States General, it did not make any difference that the latter had issued special regu-

---

[1] Above, p. 27.
[2] Yorke to Suffolk, April 30, 1776; same to same, August 6, 1776 (Sparks MSS., LXXII).
[3] The admiralties were apparently not very strict in the observance of the regulations (Colenbrander, Patriottentijd, I, 115; Jameson, "St. Eustatius in the American Revolution," American Historical Review, July, 1903, p. 687).
[4] Wharton, I, 453.

lations. Dutch citizens violating the contraband laws of their country were subject to the punishment provided for such transgressions, yet the status of the Dutch government with reference to Great Britain was not changed thereby. The English were, therefore, as far as the law of nations was concerned, not justified in making the contraband trade of Dutch merchants the subject of violent reproaches to the Republic.

There were many ways in which the Dutch merchants were able to evade the regulations of the States General. As it was forbidden to export contraband to the American colonies the Dutch carried their goods first to some French port where the goods passed nominally into the possession of the French. This manipulation was even sometimes performed in mid ocean, American and Dutch vessels exchanging their cargoes. In 1777 the Grand Pensionary of Holland, at the instigation of Sir Joseph Yorke, had these manoeuvres on the high sea investigated. The ambassador, reporting the result to his government, said that the fact of illicit trade seemed clearly proved by this inquiry, however with the difference that Frenchmen assisted in the collusion to cover the Dutch, and that papers were given to mask the transaction and prevent the law from taking effect.[1] A more frequent means of making the ordinances ineffective was to send the contraband goods to the Dutch West Indies, especially the island of St. Eustatia, whence American vessels carried them to the colonies. It seems that in the beginning of the war only comparatively few American merchant vessels ventured as far as the coast of the Dutch Republic. They usually unloaded their cargoes at French or Spanish ports where Dutch vessels received the American goods in exchange for contraband brought from the United Provinces. Sir Joseph Yorke observed ironically that the Dutch merchants ought to become anti-American, not out of good will to England,

---

[1] Yorke to Suffolk, November 25 and 28, 1777 (Sparks MSS., LXXII).

but from jealousy in seeing the American trade, owing to the greater facility of the voyage, pour into French and Spanish ports instead of theirs.[1] Another trade in which the Dutch merchants were engaged might have been considered unlawful, that is, the commercial intermediacy between England and her revolting colonies. To such violations, however, Great Britain closed her eyes. The English ambassador wrote to Lord Suffolk in 1776 that the English manufacturers conveyed their goods to America through the United Provinces. He added that he did not expect to see a stop put to it and that he was not insisting upon the prohibition of any other branch of contraband than warlike stores.[2] No wonder then that Dutch commerce and navigation reached a height during the American Revolution which had never been attained before. England was losing accordingly. The high marine insurance, sometimes as high as 35 per cent., for English goods destined for the West Indies was almost prohibitive. Many of the Dutch who had never thought of engaging in the commerce with distant countries now took their share in the American trade. It was as if a gold-mine had been opened for Dutch commerce.[3] A regular trade intercourse between America and the United Provinces, especially Amsterdam, had been established, according to the French chargé d'affaires, Abbé Desnoyers, as early as 1776. He informed the foreign minister in France that the "independents of the English colonies" seemed to have a very regular intercourse with Amsterdam, that some of them were actually there and purchased great quanti-

---

[1] Yorke to Suffolk, December 24, 1776, and Yorke to Eden, December 27, 1776 (Sparks MSS., LXXII).

[2] Yorke to Suffolk, December 3, 1776 (Sparks MSS., LXXII).
The French, too, replaced English navigation to a great extent at this period (Arthur Lee to the Committee of Foreign Affairs, September 9, 1777, in Wharton, II, 391–392).

[3] On the flourishing of Dutch commerce and navigation see: Kampen, Verkorte Geschiedenis der Nederlanden, II, 290; Dumas to the American Commissioners, June 19, 23, 26, 1778 (Lee's MSS. in the library of Harvard University, IV, No. 156); Vaterlandsche Historie, XXV, 58.

ties of goods for ready cash. A large quantity of ducats recently coined at Dordrecht he supposed to be intended also for the American agents.[1]

To what extent contraband trade was carried on between the United Provinces and America may be judged from reports of the English ambassador at the Hague to his government. In April, 1776, he wrote that within two days 850 barrels or 85,000 pounds of gunpowder had been shipped from Amsterdam to France. He concluded that those shipments must be for America since never before, even in times of war, had so much gunpowder been shipped from Amsterdam.[2] Orders for powder continuing to arrive from France, Yorke was confirmed in his opinion that since all those consignments were certainly destined for the American colonies, there must be means for eluding the ordinances. "In short," he wrote to Suffolk, "this is the first and almost sole market for the Rebels, tho' conducted from hence thro' so many different channels to conceal it, and to endeavour to have it appear that other countries are equal sharers with them in this mischievous commerce."[3] The reason why the Dutch engaged so much in this dangerous trade was that they obtained very high prices in America, an inducement which few merchants were able to resist. As one of the most considerable Dutch traders to North America Sir Joseph Yorke mentioned the house of Crommelin. In his opinion all attempts to stop that illegal trade would be without results since future attempts could not be prevented when the profits were so great.[4] He said that gunpowder brought a profit of more than 120 per cent. at St. Eustatia.[5] According to a statement of one R. Irvine in Rotterdam these profits were even larger. Gunpowder taken from the United Provinces to St. Eustatia and sold there had yielded 230 Dutch florins (or guilders)

---

[1] Desnoyers to Vergennes, September 10, 1776 (Sparks MSS., LXXXIII).
[2] Yorke to Suffolk, April 30, 1776 (Sparks MSS., LXXII).
[3] Same to same, August 9, 1776 (ibid.).
[4] Same to same, March 22, 1776 (ibid.).
[5] Same to same, April 2, 1776 (ibid.).

per cwt., that is, 46 Dutch stivers or 4s. 2d. sterling a pound, while the price in the United Provinces was only from 40 to 42 guilders per cwt. or about 9d. sterling a pound. These exorbitant profits, together with the facility of obtaining permission for the export of powder in their own bottoms, he said, would induce the Dutch merchants to run all risks. They could afford to lose two cargoes out of three and still make considerable profits. Powder was therefore exported in every possible disguise, in tea chests, rice barrels, etc., so that, in case of search, the powder would not be found by a superficial inspection of the cargo. Irvine stated further that not fewer than eighteen Dutch vessels, laden with powder and ammunition for the American market, had sailed from Amsterdam for St. Eustatia, between the first of January and the middle of May, 1776.[1]

Under these circumstances the anger of the English at the conditions existing in the United Provinces and Yorke's despair are comprehensible. In August, 1776, Sir Joseph wrote to Lord Suffolk that should the unhappy situation in America be by any accident prolonged, it appeared to him that the surest, indeed the only, way to act with the Republic was to determine what Great Britain had the right to require of a nation styling itself friend and ally, to communicate it previously in friendship to the stadtholder and the ministers, and to make a formal demand to the States General, requiring a speedy answer; letting it be known at the same time, that, in case of a refusal, His Majesty would be under the necessity of taking measures for his own security. He expressed his hope that such a step would not dissatisfy the reasonable and well intentioned; from others England could expect nothing voluntarily which would run counter to their private interest. The ambassador proposed then that Great Britain should request of the States General

---

[1] Irvine to Suffolk, May 14, 1776 (Sparks MSS., LXXII).

How profitable European trade with the American colonies was and how it could be carried on with comparatively small risk we learn also from the letter of Arthur Lee to von der Schulenburg of June 7, 1777 (Wharton, II, 330).

that the term of the Dutch proclamation expiring in September of the same year might be prolonged. He suggested also that an " amplification " should be demanded, having experienced the inefficiency of prohibitions, dependent on the oaths of brokers who were only proxies for merchants.[1] Yorke's suggestion fell on fertile soil in England. About a month later he received instructions from his government directing him to submit a memorial to the Dutch authorities, in which not only the renewal of the prohibitory edict, expiring on the 20th of September, was requested but more efficient measures demanded for suppressing the smuggling to the American colonies.[2]

Yorke's memorial, delivered on September 17, in execution of this direction, was received rather coolly by the States General. They replied that they could not extend the prohibitions beyond what had been done already. Every individual was at liberty to hazard his fortune in commerce. Besides, making their prescriptions more severe might result in keeping their own colonies from receiving the necessary supplies, and Great Britain could not expect the United Provinces to prepare the ruin of their own colonies.[3] The English, not satisfied with this answer, were at a loss what to do to check the Dutch contraband trade to America. Sir Joseph Yorke thought that means might be found to restrain that trade. As an effective measure he proposed to inform the United Provinces that, in case they should continue their present attitude, orders would be sent to Bengal not to let them bring home any saltpeter, since they made such bad use of their gunpowder.[4] Lord Suffolk suggested that all doubt and embarrassment could be avoided if the States General would not allow the exportation of larger military stores to the Dutch West Indies than had been

---

[1] Yorke to Suffolk, August 6, 1776 (Sparks MSS., LXXII).
[2] Suffolk to Yorke, September 13, 1776 (ibid.).
[3] Desnoyers to Vergennes, October 7, 1776 (Sparks MSS., LXXXIII).
The proclamation of the United Provinces was renewed by the resolution of October 10, 1776.
[4] Yorke to Eden, October 25, 1776 (Sparks MSS., LXXII).

sent annually upon an average of some years preceding the American Revolution.[1] Sir Joseph Yorke approved of such a measure, and hinted that if it should be rejected, the necessity might be urged of confiscating all the powder found in Dutch vessels sailing for the settlements of the United Provinces, unless its use for the Dutch possessions could be proved.[2] In fact, the ambassador warned the Prince of Orange as head of the West India Company to prevent all extraordinary exportations of military stores to the Dutch territories both in Africa and the West Indies.

Ever since the beginning of the Revolutionary War the chief intercourse between the United Provinces (as well as other European countries) and the American colonies had been effected by way of St. Eustatia.[3] This Dutch island therefore soon attracted the attention of the British government. According to Yorke's observations it was the rendezvous of everything and everybody that was meant to be conveyed clandestinely to the continent of America.[4] Be-

---

[1] Suffolk to Yorke, October 22, 1776 (Sparks MSS., LXXII).
[2] Yorke to Suffolk, October 29, 1776 (ibid.).
[3] The following discussion of St. Eustatia and the part the island played in the American Revolution is almost wholly based upon Dr. J. Franklin Jameson's most excellent and exhaustive monograph, "St. Eustatius in the American Revolution," in the American Historical Review, July, 1903, p. 683 ff. For the sake of conciseness references are mostly given only where sources besides Dr. Jameson were consulted or, in a few instances, where the details of this essay exceed Dr. Jameson's data.
[4] Yorke to Eden, May 14, 1776 (Sparks MSS., LXXII).
Besides St. Eustatia, of the Lesser Antilles the islands of Curaçao, Bonaire, Aruba, Saba and St. Martin belonged to the United Provinces. St. Eustatia—an island of an area less than seven square miles—was little more than a mass of barren rocks and had almost no production of its own (at the time of the American Revolution it did not produce more than six hundred barrels of sugar a year). The same was true of the other islands except perhaps St. Martin. The only Dutch colonies in America which had a production of any importance were those in Guiana, called after the rivers on which they were situated Surinam, Essequibo, Demerari, and Berbice (Wild, Die Niederlande, II, 320; Gazette de Leyde, April 6, 1781, p. 7); see also Hansard, The Parliamentary History of England, XXII, 220, 221.
Geographical lexicons call this island "St. Eustatius," but since all documents of this period name it Eustatia, that form is used in this paper. Similarly, the contemporary spellings "Doggersbank," "Demerari," and "Trinconomale" are used.

ing a free port, it became during the American Revolution the store house for goods of all nations. Here the English bought the products of America, and the Americans the manufactures of England; here, after France had joined the war, the British merchants met the planters from the French West Indian islands; and here, finally, was the chief market where the Americans obtained their military stores. After the outbreak of war between France and England many planters and merchants of the British West Indian islands, especially of St. Kitts—also called St. Christopher—stored their goods at St. Eustatia to secure them from capture by the French. The whole island was one vast store house, equally useful to friend and foe.[1] Still the English government, anxious to suppress the rebellion in North America, regarded · St. Eustatia in a different light. Report after report arrived at London of the numerous and large purchases of arms and ammunition effected by the Americans on that island. The principal agent in the business was said to be Mr. Isaac van Dam, a Dutch resident of St. Eustatia. It was learned that in one instance he had sent 4000 pounds of gunpowder on board a Virginia vessel to North Carolina in support of the rebellion; then he was found to have sent £2000 sterling to France for the purchase of powder to be sent to St. Eustatia for transmission to the American colonies. Harrison sent 6000 pounds of powder from Martinique, and then 14,100 pounds more from St. Eustatia. Of these 10,000 were shipped to Charleston; the rest, to Philadelphia.[2] Later a single vessel is said to have exported 49,-000 pounds.[3] Sir Joseph Yorke was directed to express to the States General the dissatisfaction of George III and to give them to understand that they must not be surprised if the English men-of-war in the vicinity of St. Eustatia henceforth should show more vigilance and less reserve.[4]

---

[1] Hannay, Rodney, 151–152.
[2] Maryland Archives, XI, 494; XII, 171, 268, 332, 423; Force, American Archives, fourth ser., VI, 612, 905; fifth ser., I, 1025; II, 965; III, 513; Jameson, St. Eustatius, 688.
[3] August 2, 1776 (Sparks MSS., LXXII).
[4] Suffolk to Yorke, April 12, 1776; Yorke to Suffolk, April 19, 1776 (Sparks MSS., LXXII).

Thereupon the States General assured Sir Joseph of their disapproval of such illegal proceedings on the part of their subjects. When Yorke reported this answer to London, he could inform his superiors at the same time of the death of van Dam, who had made a declaration before his death that the consignments of contraband to North Carolina had been effected on the account of French merchants.[1] St. Eustatia was now guarded by the English in such a way that it became almost impossible to enter even the necessary provisions for the inhabitants of the island. This caused great indignation in the United Provinces, and some Anti-Orangists even proposed to blockade, in return, the residence of the British ambassador at the Hague.[2]

The governor of St. Eustatia, Johannes de Graaf, had been appointed in the middle of the year 1776, his predecessor being thought by Great Britain to have favored the contraband trade. It was soon evident that the new governor did no better. " This day the Port of Statia is opened without reserve to all American vessels, and I find that the salutes of their armed vessels are returned at St. Croix as well as at Statia," wrote Captain Colpoys to Vice-Admiral Young from Basseterre, St. Christopher, on November 27, 1776.[3] Yorke had also intimated to the Dutch authorities that de Graaf should be cautioned. This was done by the direction of the Prince of Orange. Still the exportation of contraband was continued at Amsterdam with the same zeal.[4] But, on October 22, Yorke could write to his government that the contraband trade to the West Indies was suspended at present, occasioned, as he believed, by the late " glad tidings " from Long Island.[5] In January of the

---

[1] Yorke to Suffolk, May 31, 1776 (Sparks MSS., LXXII).
[2] Desnoyers to Vergennes, October 8, 1776 (Sparks MSS., LXXXII).
[3] Sparks MSS., LXXII (following a letter of Yorke to W. Eden, dated March 7, 1777).
[4] Yorke to Suffolk, September 10, 1776 (Sparks MSS., LXXII).
[5] Yorke to Suffolk, October 22, 1776 (Sparks MSS., LXXII).
The " glad tidings from Long Island " were the news of the disaster of the Americans at Brooklyn Heights when Sullivan and Lord Stirling (William Alexander) with some eleven hundred men were taken prisoner by General Howe on August 27, 1776.

following year, 1777, de Graaf complained to the directors of the West India Company about the conduct of English vessels. British men-of-war, he wrote, were cruising daily in the roads of St. Eustatia, seizing, even under the cannon of the fortress, vessels intending to enter or leaving the port. The island must therefore almost be considered blockaded and its commerce would be ruined. He asked to be instructed as to what course he should pursue since he was anxious to avoid everything that could give to Great Britain the slightest pretence for a complaint. Though the Dutch, he said, were perfectly entitled to repulse the British aggressions by force, prudence must persuade the island to suffer the hostilities, owing to want of sufficient means. This would, however, be very hard and disadvantageous for St. Eustatia.[1] Yet the hardships thus pictured by de Graaf were only the preliminaries of greater troubles which the English had in store for the governor and the inhabitants of the island.

In February, Sir Joseph Yorke received a letter from his government, informing him of a " flagrant insult offered to His Majesty's colours, in the public honour paid by the principal Dutch fort [St. Eustatia] to a Rebel brigantine carrying the flag of the Rebel Congress." This offence, the missive stated, was not only proved by a letter of President Greathead of St. Christopher, but was uncontradicted by de Graaf's answer to it. The ambassador was then directed to demand of the States General a formal disavowal of the salute, and the immediate dismissal and recall of de Graaf. The King of England would not allow the United Provinces to amuse him with assurances, and he would, therefore, instantly give orders for such measures as he thought "due to the interests and dignity" of his crown.[2]

---

[1] Gouverneur de St. Eustache aux directeurs de la Compagnie des Indes occidentales, January 28, 1777 (Sparks MSS., LXXXII).

[2] Suffolk to Yorke, February 14, 1777 (Sparks MSS., LXXII; Colenbrander, Patriottentijd, I, 124).

The salute of the " Andrew Doria " by Fort Orange, on November 16, 1776, has been claimed to be the first salute to the American flag abroad (Bancroft, History of the United States, IX, 293;

On the following day the Lords of Admiralty in London were instructed to give

"immediate orders to the Commander in Chief of His Majesty's ships and vessels at the Leeward Islands to station proper cruizers off the harbour of St. Eustatia, and to direct their commanders to search all Dutch ships and vessels going into and coming out of the said harbours, and to send such of them as shall be found to have any arms, ammunition, clothing, or materials for clothing on board, into some of His Majesty's ports within the limits of the command of the said Commander in Chief . . . , to be detained there until further orders."[1]

On February 21, Yorke delivered a memorandum to the States General according to his instructions. He declared that the complaints were based on authentic documents (which he appended to his note), as Their High Mightinesses would admit after perusal. De Graaf, besides having allowed an unlimited commerce with the Americans, had neglected his duty to such a degree as to allow an American pirate to take an English vessel almost within reach (presqu'à la portée) of the cannon of his island. To crown his insult to the British nation and all the powers of Europe, he had caused the fortress of St. Eustatia to answer the salute of a ship carrying the rebel flag. Yorke continued that all the friendly representations which the president of the neighboring island of St. Christopher had made to de Graaf had been answered by the latter in a most vague and unsatisfactory manner. The Dutch governor had even refused to enter into a discussion with or give an explanation to a member of the King's Council of St. Christopher, who

B. F. Prescott, The Stars and Stripes: The Flag of the United States of America; When, Where and by Whom was it first Saluted? [Concord, 1876]; Dr. W. E. Griffis, "Where our Flag was first saluted," New England Magazine, n. s., VIII, 576). Still, in a letter dated October 27, 1776, and sent from the Danish island of St. Croix to Vice-Admiral Young, it is said of an American schooner, which had departed two days before with a small cargo of powder: "But my astonishment was great to find such a Commerce countenanced by the Government here. The vessel went out under American Colours, saluted the Fort and had the compliment returned the same as if she had been an English or Danish ship" (Letter of October 27, 1776, in Bancroft MSS.; Jameson, St. Eustatius, 691).

[1] Suffolk to the Lords of Admiralty, February 15, 1777 (Sparks MSS., LXXII).

had been sent by President Greathead to St. Eustatia for
that express purpose. The ambassador then stated the demands of his king and concluded, citing verbally from his
instructions, that satisfaction must be given.[1]

The first enclosure with the memorandum was a letter of
President Greathead to Governor de Graaf, dated December
17, 1776. Greathead wrote that although the rebel colonies
had been said for some time to be receiving protection at
St. Eustatia, he had not previously complained about this.
He could, however, not remain silent longer, because authentic reports had verified these rumors. Not only had
provisions and military stores been furnished the Americans
daily and openly by inhabitants of the island, but even
armed vessels had sailed from St. Eustatia with the avowed
intention of making prizes of ships and property of peaceful and loyal English subjects. He referred in particular
to the sloop " Baltimore Hero," which, carrying the flag of
the Continental Congress, had on November 21 attacked
and seized under the cannon of St. Eustatia a brigantine
and her cargo. The brigantine, belonging to one McCon-
nell, an English subject living on the island of Dominica, had
been on her way from St. Christopher to St. Eustatia. The
American sloop returned afterwards to the roads of St.
Eustatia, enjoying there apparently every protection. Greathead stated further that the American armed vessel, "Andrew Doria " (Captain Robinson), flying the rebel flag, had
entered the roads of St. Eustatia about the middle of November and saluted Fort Orange by 13 guns, which were
answered by the fort in the solemn way that was due to
the flags of independent and sovereign states. The " Andrew
Doria " had thereupon been suffered to take on board gunpowder and other articles of war as well as provisions for
the use of the American army. The Americans having
usurped their power, their armed ships were to be con-

---

[1] Yorke's memorandum, February 21, 1777 (Bancroft MSS.,
America, Holland and England; Sparks MSS., LXXXII; Vater-
landsche Historie, XXV, 111; Sparks Dutch Papers; Stevens
Papers in the Library of Congress).

sidered pirate vessels. To the disgrace of all public faith
and national honor it had been left for a Dutch colony
avowedly to assist the Americans in their treason, and to
become the protectors of their buccaneering. It was a
fortress of Their High Mightinesses which first recognized
the American colors, until now unknown in the catalogue
of national flags. Greathead, in conclusion, demanded full
satisfaction for the insult offered by Fort Orange to His
Britannic Majesty's flag, also effective means to prevent a
repetition of such incidents, and an indemnity for the pirate
act of the "Baltimore Hero" together with an exemplary
punishment of the culprits. The president of St. Christopher sent Mr. Stanley, member of the King's Council and
Solicitor General, to present the complaint to Governor de
Graaf and to wait for an answer.

De Graaf asked in his reply of December 23 (forming
the second appendix to Yorke's memorial) for authentic
proofs and witnesses of the alleged daily and open furnishing of contraband to the Americans, since he was prohibited
by his commission as well as the laws of his country to
prosecute persons without plaintiff and witnesses, or to
condemn them without evidence. The governor rejected
the accusation of having protected and furthered piracy, and
he denied therefore his obligation to give indemnity in the
case of the "Baltimore Hero." He said that he knew himself to be free of partiality and that he must not be expected to disturb the commerce and navigation of St.
Eustatia and of the Dutch nation. He flattered himself
that he was able to justify his attitude toward the American
vessel "Andrew Doria." No one on earth, he declared, but
his superiors was entitled to call him to account for acts
of administration effected by him.

Greathead, on December 26 (Yorke's appendix No.
three), expressed his disapproval of de Graaf's conduct as
not in conformity with the treaties existing between Great
Britain and the United Provinces, and informed the governor of his intention to lay the matter before his royal master.

Appendix four, dated December 16, 1776, contained an affidavit of a certain James Fraser and others before John Stanley, member of the King's Council of St. Christopher and Solicitor General of the British Leeward islands in America. The "Andrew Doria" had according to this affidavit been saluted by Fort Orange on or about November 16, 1776. The American vessel was said to have fired eleven guns and the fort nine. The witnesses stated that they had learned that the commandant of the fort had hesitated to answer the salute, but that the governor had ordered him to do so.

In appendix five, dated December 9, 1776, was presented the affidavit of one Matthew Murray, who had deposed that he sailed from St. Christopher to St. Eustatia about December 1, 1776. When their boat arrived in the waters of St. Eustatia by the side of a sloop, a fellow passenger of Murray's (whose name, however, no one on board had heard before), exclaimed: "You may all know now, who I am. I am "constapel" (gunner?) of the sloop called the "Baltimore Hero," an American privateer, the same which, some days ago, captured the Irish brig off St. Eustatia!" To the memorandum was also appended the affidavit of one John Trottman, a sailor who had deserted from the "Andrew Doria." He declared that the American vessel had sailed for St. Eustatia with the intention of buying there clothes and other necessities for the American army.[1]

Yorke, evidently self-complacent, reported that he had executed the orders of His Majesty the King. He stated that he had informed the Prince of Orange and the Duke of Brunswick of what had happened, and that both had been highly surprised, since they had received no news of such transactions. They disavowed the proceedings of the governor of St. Eustatia, and Yorke said he had no doubt that the States General would do the same and give every satisfaction possible.[2] The Prince of Orange and the Duke

---

[1] Sparks Dutch Papers.
[2] Yorke to Suffolk, February 21, 1777 (Sparks MSS., LXXII).

4

of Brunswick were certainly surprised at what they heard concerning de Graaf, but they were more indignant at Yorke's language and that of his government. Brunswick wrote to the stadtholder that Yorke's note to the States General was certainly the most arrogant missive ever transmitted to a sovereign. The threat expressed by the King of England in the conclusion of the memorandum was an insult as well as an injustice to the Republic. The latter could not comply wtih the king's demands as long as she desired to be considered a sovereign and independent state. What made the matter worse, the duke said, was the verbal declaration of the English ambassador to the States General that he would be recalled in case satisfaction could not be given within three weeks. England's contempt for the Republic was evident.[1] The duke was far from defending the conduct of the governor of St. Eustatia; on the contrary, he was of opinion that de Graaf should be called upon to justify his conduct, and that, in case the accusations were found to be true, England ought to be given satisfaction. The honor and dignity of the Republic required, however, that such satisfaction should be denied until the accused had been heard. It was the duty of the Republic to be firm on this occasion, and to take measures for the protection of her commerce and her ports. The duke hinted that the court of St. James had taken this step only in order to justify her searching and seizing of Dutch vessels.[2]

---

[1] Yorke, who had represented Great Britain in the Netherlands since 1751, was apparently not the right representative of his country there under the circumstances. He was always inclined to carry matters to extremes, and offended continually the national feelings of the Dutch by the imperious manner in which he carried out his instructions. As early as 1769 the Duke of Brunswick wrote to the stadtholder that the way in which Yorke treated things was always very disagreeable, and that so long as he (Yorke) was at the Hague England would never be of any service to the United Provinces. It would therefore be desirable in the interest of the stadtholder and the whole country that Yorke should be removed. According to the Dutch envoy at the court of St. James, Count van Welderen, Yorke was the greatest enemy of the Republic (Nijhoff, Brunswijk, 142). In the present case Yorke seems to have been less guilty of arrogance, since he used in the memorial apparently the terms of his instructions.

[2] Nijhoff, Brunswijk, 149–152.

Yorke was unconcerned about the indignation which his memorandum roused throughout the United Provinces. "Had any other Governor of any other Power done the same," he wrote to W. Eden, "we should have done wrong not to have exacted the same satisfaction." Sir Joseph Yorke thought it would become public more easily in the United Provinces than anywhere else and would be a good lesson for other powers. He informed Lord Suffolk confidentially that the memorial had raised a violent fermentation through the country, that the exchange was alarmed and the people in general frightened. Since his note was a categorical demand and did not imply a negotiation, he expected that it would be complied with.[1]

Before an answer was given to the ambassador's memorial, the States General received, through the West India Company, a letter from de Graaf, written at St. Eustatia on January 28, 1777, in which he reported that the English brigantine "May," skipper William Taylor, had been captured by the armed American bark "Baltimore Hero," commanded by Thomas Waters, between St. Christopher and St. Eustatia on November 21, 1776, and sent to Maryland. The owners of the "May," merchants of the island of Dominica, complained about it to Thomas Shirley, the governor of Dominica, and to James Young, the Vice-Admiral of the English squadron at Antigua, stating that the "Baltimore Hero" was fitted out at St. Eustatia and partly belonged to residents of that island. They applied for indemnity to de Graaf. The "Baltimore Hero," the governor stated further, had stayed at St. Eustatia from November 11 to 20, 1776, neither importing nor exporting anything, except taking with her some necessary provisions and water. On December 2 the bark returned to St. Eustatia. Though no complaints had been received then, de Graaf questioned Waters why he had taken the "May," whether his vessel was fitted out at St. Eustatia, and whether she belonged wholly or in part to merchants there. Waters thereupon

---

[1] Yorke to Eden, March 7, 1777 (Sparks MSS., LXXII).

showed his commission from Maryland, issued by the Council of Safety, John Hancock, President, declaring under oath that his ship had not been fitted out at St. Eustatia and was not owned by residents of that island. De Graaf concluded by stating that at St. Eustatia no American war vessel had been received and saluted, but only merchant vessels.[1]

Yorke, having learned of de Graaf's report, informed his government of it. Sir Joseph said that the governor endeavored to justify himself by stating that it was a merchant vessel which had been saluted, and not a war vessel; but all impartial people condemned him. The ambassador also announced that the Dutch minister at the court of St. James was to deliver a resolution regarding St. Eustatia to the British government.[2] This was true. The States General, indignant at the English ambassador's offensive language, resolved to have their answer to his memorial delivered to the British government not through him, but through Count Welderen. The latter accordingly conveyed to George III the complaints of the States General at the reproaches expressed in Yorke's memorial and at the threatening tone of the latter, which were unacceptable to a sovereign and independent state, but above all inadmissible between neighbors united by the ties of good harmony and of mutual friendship. De Graaf, Welderen continued, had been instructed to come home in order to answer the charges pending against him. The governor was also to give an account of all that had come to his cognizance concerning the American colonies and their ships ever since he had taken over the command of the island. The States General would not hesitate to disavow acts of their officials which might in the least be construed to be a recognition of the sovereignty and independence of the American colonies. The Dutch governor and commanders in the West Indian colonies had again re-

---

[1] Missive van Representant en Bewindhebberen der Westindische Compagnie, March 22, 1777 (Sparks Dutch Papers; Stevens Papers in the Library of Congress).
[2] Yorke to Suffolk, March 25, 1777 (Sparks MSS., LXXII).

ceived instructions from the States General to observe strictly the orders and regulations against the exportation of military stores to the American colonies.[1]

Three days after van Welderen had handed this memorial to Lord Suffolk for transmission to the English king, the orders of February 15 to the Lords of the Admiralty were revoked, and the latter instructed to return to the government of St. Eustatia such Dutch vessels as were seized and detained merely in consequence of those orders.[2] On April 10, Lord Suffolk handed to Count van Welderen the king's answer. It was a declaration that George III could not consider the English memorandum of February 21 contrary to the respect which sovereign and independent states owed to each other. His Majesty was pleased that the States General had complied with his request in recalling their governor and renewing to the Dutch governors and commanders in the West Indies the orders concerning contraband trade.[3]

The British answer was not well received in the United Provinces. Burgomaster Temminck of Amsterdam was said to have been very much vexed that Count Welderen accepted Lord Suffolk's note without criticizing it. Governor de Graaf was not to be recalled definitely, as stated by the English note, but he was only to return in order to explain his conduct. Temminck did not doubt that de Graaf would be able to justify his actions and in that case it would be impossible not to send him back to his island. Yorke too does not seem to have been convinced, at this time, of the reliability and adequacy of the material which he had transmitted to the States General as evidence of de Graaf's offences. He asked his government now for additional proofs, especially for particulars from the accounts—sent from St. Christopher—of smuggling at St. Eustatia.

Governor de Graaf became apparently henceforth more

---

[1] Count van Welderen's memorial, March 26, 1777 (Bancroft MSS., America, Holland, and England; Sparks MSS., CIII; Stevens Papers in the Library of Congress).

[2] Above, p. 46. Suffolk to the Lords of the Admiralty, March 29, 1777 (Sparks MSS., LXXII).

[3] Suffolk to Welderen, April 10, 1777 (Bancroft MSS., America, Holland, and England; Sparks MSS., CIII).

severe in the supervision of the commercial transactions at
St. Eustatia. Some residents of the island, according to
Yorke, submitted a petition to the directors of the West
India Company, complaining of de Graaf's severity in visiting their vessels. They said they were not able to export
the smallest quantity of powder or other military stores for
their own use, and they requested therefore that the governor be removed. The States General, however, did not give
credit to their complaints,[1] and it is possible that this petition
was recognized as a political manoeuvre in connection with
de Graaf's temporary recall. Another cause of the ruin of
the trade of St. Eustatia was, as Yorke informed his government, the long credit granted to the North American colonies by St. Eustatia merchants. He added that de Graaf
continued to salute the Americans that stole into the port,
but according to his regulation of honors, with two guns less
than the king's ships. The latter, Yorke concluded, no
longer saluted the port.[2]

The St. Eustatia incident formed a good object lesson for
the United Provinces. They saw what they had to expect
from Great Britain, and awakened to the fact of their own
weakness, and the danger threatening their commerce and
navigation. The result was a new impulse to increase the
Dutch navy. The province of Holland especially asked for
the fitting out of a squadron to be sent as convoy to the
West Indies, and urged contributions by the other provinces
for the building of twenty-four new ships of the line. In
May, 1778, the last province gave her consent to this
measure.[3]

---

[1] Yorke to Eden, April 25, 1777 (Sparks MSS., LXXII); Resolution of the States General, April 24, 1777 (Sparks MSS., CIII).
Yorke wrote, however, to Lord Suffolk, May 2, 1777, that the petition was not the work of inhabitants of St. Eustatia, but was drawn
and signed by a number of masters of vessels navigating to the
Dutch West Indies (Sparks MSS., LXXII).

[2] Yorke to Eden, July 4, 1777 (Sparks MSS., LXXII).

[3] Colenbrander, Patriottentijd, I, 126.

According to Franklin and Deane, the States General immediately
ordered twenty-six men-of-war to be put upon the stocks (Franklin
and Deane to the Committee of Secret Correspondence, March 12,
1777, in Wharton, II, 289). The commissioners were apparently
mistaken regarding the exact number of ships to be built.

In August, 1777, the directors of the West India Company again presented to the States General a letter from de Graaf (dated June 30, 1777). This time he requested to be excused from coming over to Europe. By such a precipitate departure from St. Eustatia, his family affairs and private business would greatly suffer. He thought furthermore that the voyage was too dangerous now, since the hurricane season had begun. His body being still weak from a recent illness, he feared too that his health would be injured by a stay in Europe during the winter. In addition to his former report he mentioned some details of the incidents which had caused such violent accusations against him. Fort Orange, he declared, answered the salute of the "Andrew Doria," as a merchant vessel, according to a long established custom of the island, with two guns less than she had fired. The return of the salute of such ships was merely an act of courtesy, in which no attention was paid to their nationality. The answering of the salute of the "Andrew Doria" did not therefore imply the recognition of the independence of North America. Relative to the commerce with North America effected by American vessels, de Graaf explained that St. Eustatia had to rely upon that country for her necessary provisions, as flour, bread, Indian corn, rice, salted fish, etc.; as well as timber for houses, barrels, etc. Ever since he had taken over the command of the island he considered it his duty not to disturb this commerce. Besides, he had never received any orders from his superiors to do so. That this trade had increased, as Great Britain pretended, was contrary to facts. The danger attending American navigation since the beginning of the Revolution was too great to allow extensive trade on their part. As to the exportation of contraband to North America, he said, he was conscious of having complied as strictly with the regulations issued by the States General as was in his power. In cases where the least suspicion of an illegal exportation existed, the cargo of the vessels in question was examined. He had now even appointed a sworn examiner to visit all American vessels at their arrival as well as their departure, in order not only to prevent the exportation of contraband but also the manning and equipping of the vessels. Of course, there were always men who would violate the laws, or find ways and means to evade them. Since this had happened at all times and places, no reproach could be cast upon him for such transgressions. With reference to the taking of an English vessel near the fortress of St. Eustatia, the governor declared that this was not done within the range of the cannon of the island. It had therefore not been more in his power to prevent the capture than if the latter had taken place off the coast of Africa.[1] In October the States General resolved finally not to comply with de Graaf's request to be excused from coming to the United Provinces.[2]

The governor of St. Eustatia addressed a serious complaint to the Dutch West India Company on June 28, 1777, which was laid before the States General. The English man-of-war "Seaford" had seized and taken to the island of Antigua two Dutch vessels, which had set sail at St. Eustatia for Zealand on the day before. James Young, the commander of the English squadron in the West Indies, had tried to justify the capture by stating that the "Watergeus," one of the Dutch vessels, had on board products of the British American colonies in rebellion, previously imported into St. Eustatia. This was contrary to a recent act of Parliament, forbidding all commerce and intercourse with the North American colonies. The other ship, the "Hoop," was accused of having had on board gunpowder and ammunition. Young had also complained about the conduct of one van Bibber at St. Eustatia, said to be an agent of the

---

[1] Missive van Bewindhebberen der Westindische Compagnie, August 27, 1777 (Sparks Dutch Papers; Stevens Papers in the Library of Congress).

[2] Resolution of the States General, October 6, 1777 (Sparks MSS., CIII). Yorke called de Graaf the "dirty governor of that nest of smugglers" (Yorke to Suffolk, private, September 24, 1777, in Sparks MSS., LXXII).

American Congress.[1] Van Bibber was consequently arrested by the governor, but when de Graaf asked for evidence against him Young replied that the only proof he had was the deposition before the court of the Vice-Admiralty at Antigua of one George Rall. The latter was the commander of a small American privateer called "Jenny" which had been taken by Captain Colpoys. Rall had declared that van Bibber, the American agent, had sent several men on board the "Jenny" from other American vessels, then at St. Eustatia. Bibber had subsequently ordered him to pursue a sloop, domiciled at Antigua, which had shortly before left St. Eustatia, laden with cotton, cloth, etc. These proceedings, Rall stated also, had been public and were in no way prevented by the government of the island. Abraham van Bibber, interrogated upon these charges before the assembly of St. Eustatia, asserted that he had not furnished people to the "Jenny," nor given orders to Rall, except that he should bring up his prizes at Martinique. Although Young could not furnish sufficient evidence or witnesses, van Bibber was continued in custody. He seized, however, an opportunity to escape from St. Eustatia. De Graaf informed Vice-Admiral Young that the "Watergeus" had sailed from St. Eustatia for the port of Middleburg, province of Zealand, with products of America and the West Indies, and that the "Hoop" was returning to Flushing with 1750 barrels of gunpowder and three barrels of flint which could not be sold at St. Eustatia. He demanded the

---

[1] Abraham van Bibber was the agent of the state of Maryland at St. Eustatia as early as March, 1776, taking care of cargoes sent or underwritten by that state. Later in the year van Bibber of St. Eustatia and Richard Harrison of Maryland formed a co-partnership. They solicited from the Virginia Committee a portion of their custom (Maryland Archives, XI, 266, 442, 443, 494, 501, 555; Force, American Archives, fourth series, VI, 905; manuscript letters of March 11, 23, 28, June 14, July 25, August 15, 1776, in the Virginia Archives; Jameson, St. Eustatius, 685). Van Bibber claimed to be on the best of terms with Governor de Graaf, and urged the Maryland Council to send all their vessels to St. Eustatia rather than to any other island (Force, American Archives, fifth series, II, 180; III, 513, 759; Jameson, St. Eustatius, 690, 691; Maryland Archives, XII, 423, 456).

immediate release of the two ships and their cargoes and
an indemnity for costs and damages, caused by the seizure
and detention of the vessels. De Graaf asked if the admiral
could think that the United Provinces would permit commerce and navigation from one Dutch possession to the
other to be disturbed in such a way as long as the Republic
formed an independent and sovereign state.[1]

The proposition of the province of Holland to send a
squadron as convoy to the West Indies was now at last
approved by the States General. Originally it was intended
to despatch about twenty vessels, but it was not found possible to man more than eight. They set sail in December,
under the command of Vice-Admiral Count van Bylandt,
under strict orders to protect only the legal trade.[2] In
April of the following year (1778) Count van Bylandt sent
home a confidential report on the condition of St. Eustatia.
It showed to what degree the United Provinces had neglected
the defence of their West Indian possessions. Bylandt informed the States General also of hostilities committed by
English privateers on the river Demerari, and of his intention to despatch a man-of-war there. British privateers
even anchored at St. Eustatia, under the pretext of being
compelled to do so for want of provisions. They did not
stay long in the harbor but cruised afterwards in the neigh-
borhood of the island. Bylandt emphasized the necessity
of putting St. Eustatia in a position of defence which would
enable her to maintain herself against an enemy for some
time and to protect her flourishing trade. Many complaints
were presented to him by inhabitants of the island about the
governor. According to these people the latter acted arbi-
trarily in the administration of St. Eustatia. The assembly
of the island, consisting of one chairman (Capitein der

---

[1] Missive van Bewindhebberen der Westindische Compagnie, August 26, 1777 (Sparks Dutch Papers; Stevens Papers in the Library
of Congress).
[2] According to Yorke, however, most of the ships had sailed without convoy (Yorke to Suffolk, December 23, 1777, in Sparks MSS.,
LXXII). The squadron remained at or near St. Eustatia until the
year 1779 (Colenbrander, Patriottentijd, I, 125).

Burgerije) and four councillors, was wholly in the hands of de Graaf. The governor was rich, being owner of a number of farms and holding mortgages on many others. This resulted in making many people dependent on him, so much the more as he had given several important administrative offices to relatives of his.[1] That Count Bylandt was not only a good sea-captain, but also a diplomat, may be concluded from the fact that the English were satisfied with his conduct.[2] The British as well as the French ambassador at the Hague had predicted trouble when the sending of a convoy to the West Indies was considered by the Provinces.[3] His position was difficult, but during his whole stay at St. Eustatia no conflict of any significance occurred.

In accordance with the resolutions of the States General of March 21 and October 6, 1777, de Graaf sailed for the United Provinces in order to answer the charges brought against him by Yorke. Two directors of the West India Company had been instructed by the States General to examine de Graaf. After his arrival in July, 1778, he was directed to answer in writing the following three charges: Did he admit the equipping of American vessels at St.

---

[1] Secret Resolution of the States General, June 4, 1778 (Sparks MSS., CIII; Sparks Dutch Papers; Stevens Papers in the Library of Congress).

[2] Yorke to Suffolk, August 25 and 28, 1778 (Sparks MSS., LXXII). Lord Macartney, governor of Grenada, thought, however, that "to see a man of Count Byland's Birth and Quality receive aboard his Flag Ship the Masters of Rebel Privateers with all the attention and civility due to their equals in regular service excites one's pity and contempt" (Jameson, St. Eustatius, 694).

[3] "A party at Amsterdam are endeavouring to push the States to give convoy to the West-Indian trade, which will be plunging into all the inconveniences and squabbles of the last War, and therefore I hope this Government will be too prudent to give into, for I make no scruples to tell them as my private opinion, that England can never suffer such a trade to be so cover'd, when the proofs of the ill use made of our indulgence are so notorious" (Yorke, September 24, 1777). "Il n'est pas douteux que malgré la protection des vaisseaux de guerre, les Anglois voudront continuer de visiter les navires marchands. On m'assure même que M. Yorke l'a positivement déclaré, et il me paroit alors impossible d'éviter de part et d'autre des actes violents" (Vauguyon, October 31, 1777, in Colenbrander, Patriottentijd, I, 125, 126, footnote).

Eustatia? Did he allow, almost under the cannon of the island, the capture of an English vessel by an American pirate? Did he permit his fortress to return the salute of a vessel carrying the American flag?

In addition de Graaf was to state everything that had come to his knowledge, during his stay at St. Eustatia, concerning the American colonies and their vessels.[1] The governor answered with a very interesting report covering, appendixes included, about 340 printed folio pages. He said in general, only much more in detail, what he had stated already in his previous reports. His defence was exceedingly clever and convincing. The West India Company submitted his missive to the States General, informing them that, after careful examination, they had nothing to add to his report, except that in their opinion the United Provinces had more cause to complain about the conduct of Great Britain than the latter about that of the Republic. The two directors of the West India Company finally recommended de Graaf to the protection of the States General, expressing their hope that the latter would also find the governor innocent. De Graaf's report was then examined by the several provinces. Holland made a lengthy resolution in favor of the governor, instructing their deputies to the States General accordingly.[2] A petition of de Graaf to be allowed to return to his post[3] was finally complied with by the States General and he went back to St. Eustatia.[4]

---

[1] Bicker and Warrin (directors of the West India Company) to the States General, March 23, 1779 (Sparks Dutch Papers; Stevens Papers in the Library of Congress; "blue book" in possession of Dr. W. E. Griffis, Ithaca, N. Y.; Jameson, St. Eustatius, 692, note 1).

[2] Extract, Resolution of States of Holland and Westfriesland, August 6, 1779 (Sparks Dutch Papers).

[3] De Graaf to the States General, June 18, 1779 (Sparks Dutch Papers).

[4] "De Graaf went out again as governor, and conducted himself so acceptably to the Americans that two of their privateers were named after him and his lady; and his portrait, presented sixty years afterward by an American citizen grateful for the 'first salute,' hangs in the New Hampshire state-house [it was copied in

In concluding this discussion of the St. Eustatia controversy it may be mentioned that the commerce between the United States and the United Provinces was carried on more and more directly now. Thulemeier, Frederick the Great's envoy at the Hague, reported to his master in the beginning of the year 1778 that the commerce of the United States with St. Eustatia had almost ceased. The proximity of the English fleets was too great a danger for the Americans. The Dutch established their offices at Bordeaux and other French ports. In July of the following year, he informed the king that the commerce of the Republic with North America became larger every day. No less than ten vessels, equipped by Congress, were lying in the harbor of Amsterdam. An American agent by the name of "la Serre" resided there, without, however, being recognized by the regents. Still the contraband trade with the United States was decreasing because the establishment of factories by the Americans had made considerable progress. They were therefore less dependent on Europe for their gunpowder, ammunition, and other warlike articles.[1] Sir Joseph Yorke from time to time also sent reports to his home government, to the effect that commerce with St. Eustatia was reduced. From other sources, however, we may conclude that there was rather a continuous increase. John Adams, after his return from his first mission to Europe, wrote in a letter to the President of Congress, "From the success of several enterprises by the way of St. Eustatia it seems that the trade between the two countries [United States and United Provinces] is likely to

---

Surinam from a painting owned there by de Graaf's grandson]. Of his defense no more need now be said than that an observance of neutrality which gave to the one belligerent such absolute contentment and to the other such unqualified dissatisfaction can hardly have been perfect" (Jameson, St. Eustatius, 695).

[1] Thulemeier to Frederick II, January 16, 1778, July 23 and September 28, 1779 (Bancroft MSS., Prussia and Holland). Thulemeier apparently misspelled the name of the American agent and, no doubt, meant Stephen Sayre, who, according to Ambassador Yorke, was in Amsterdam in 1779. Sayre was a disreputable character (Wharton, Introduction, sec. 146, 150, 192 ff.).

increase, and possibly Congress may think it expedient to
send a minister there [to the United Provinces]."[1] Vice-
Admiral Bylandt stated in the journal which he kept during
his command at St. Eustatia in 1778–1779 that 3182 vessels
sailed from the island during the thirteen months of his
stay there.[2] It was said that in 1779 more than 12,000
hogsheads of tobacco and 1,500,000 ounces of indigo were
shipped to St. Eustatia from North America, in exchange
for naval supplies and other goods from Europe.[3]

Besides the Dutch contraband trade and the conduct
of the governor of St. Eustatia, another incident aroused
the anger of the English against the United Provinces,
furnishing a pretext for serious reproaches on the part of
Great Britain later. This was the admission of the American sea-captain John Paul Jones with English prizes to the
Dutch waters.

On October 4, 1779, Jones appeared at the Texel and
anchored there with the English vessels " Serapis " and
" Comtesse de Scarborough " which he had taken in the
North Sea. His ships were flying the American flag. As
soon as Sir Joseph Yorke learned of this, he called upon
the Prince of Orange. The latter told him that he had given
immediate orders to take no notice of the American flag.
He hoped, besides, that the Dutch authorities might be able
to oblige Jones to leave immediately with his prizes. Yorke
replied that the treaties between England and the United
Provinces would require more than that. The prince was,
however, of the opinion that American ships coming in
with prizes would all have French commissions and colors,[4]
and that it would therefore be difficult to act against those
vessels. The president of the States General, to whom

---

[1] John Adams to the President of Congress, August 4, 1779 (C.
F. Adams, The Works of John Adams, III, 282).

[2] Jameson, St. Eustatius, 686; De Jonge, Geschiedenis van het
Nederlandsche Zeewezen, IV, 384.

[3] Nieuwe Nederlandsche Jaerboeken, 1781, p. 794 (Jameson, St.
Eustatius, 686).

[4] In the previous year (1778) France had joined the war against
England.

Yorke also applied, answered at first evasively that the States General had no official information of the incident yet, and were therefore at present unable to take any steps in the matter. A few days later the president informed the ambassador, however, that the affair had been brought to the knowledge of the States General, but that it was complicated in so far as the American captain would probably produce a French commission. While Yorke's previous appeals had been informal, he submitted an official memorial to the States General on October 8, after some conferences with Duke Louis. Sir Joseph claimed that Jones was a rebel and pirate, because the revolting colonies had no power to issue legal commissions. Yorke therefore demanded the restoration to Great Britain of the two vessels with their officers and crews. He even tried to have Jones arrested. The High Bailiff, Mr. Dedel, declared, however, that he was not authorized to effect the arrest, unless evidence and affidavits of robberies or demands of money were presented to him against Jones. Since the ambassador was not able to comply with these requirements, his attempt failed.[1] After a request by Jones and repeated appeals by Yorke, the States General authorized the admiralty at Amsterdam to have sick and wounded on board of Jones'·ships taken on shore and cared for.[2]

Otherwise the Dutch government was still inactive. Yorke wrote home that the Dutch were puzzled to the highest degree, and, foreseeing dangers and difficulties on all sides, they did nothing at all. The ambassador said he looked upon the Jones incident as a lucky circumstance. The captain had come to Amsterdam and was insulted when he appeared in the coffee houses. Yorke thought therefore

[1] Yorke to Weymouth, October 8 and 12, 1779; Yorke's memorial of the same date (Sparks MSS., LXXII; Bancroft MSS., America, Holland and England).

[2] Extract, Resolution of the States General, October 15, 1779 (Sparks Dutch Papers). Yorke reported to his government that the wounded in Jones' fleet had been cared for, and paid this tribute to the American: "Jones has so far acted humanely" (Yorke to Weymouth, October 22, 1779, in Sparks MSS., LXXII).

that the "intrigue of the Court of Versailles," as he termed it, would advance the English cause in the United Provinces.[1] The British ambassador does not seem to have been well informed in this case, because, according to other records, Jones was received enthusiastically by the Dutch people. In the city theater at Amsterdam a public ovation was given him and songs in his praise were sung in the streets.[2] That the French had their hands in the affair was soon obvious when two French cutters entered the Texel and anchored near Jones' ships.[3] Even a fortnight after Yorke submitted his memorial, the States General had not yet passed a resolution upon the matter. The province of Holland declared that the United Provinces had for more than a century followed the principle, laid down in several regulations, of not deciding whether those who had taken vessels at sea were entitled to do so or not. Such an action must be left to the proper judges. Still the Republic would not give shelter to captors, other than Dutch, and their prizes, except in cases of emergency, as during bad weather, etc. Jones and his vessels must therefore leave Dutch waters as soon as they were able to sail. No ammunition or ship materials were to be delivered to him, except what he needed for reaching the open sea and the next foreign harbor.[4]

This decision was, in general, adopted by the States General, but did not meet with the approval of Sir Joseph Yorke. He addressed a still more urgent note to the States General. The ambassador based his demand for the restitution of the "Serapis" and "Scarborough" and the release of their crews on the treaty of Breda in 1667, confirmed by that of 1716 and also by those concluded later. According to the regulations the captains of foreign war

---

[1] Yorke to Weymouth, October 15, 1779 (Sparks MSS., LXXII).
[2] Colenbrander, Patriottentijd, I, 165; Griffis, Brave Little Holland, 231.
[3] Yorke to Weymouth, October 19, 1779 (Sparks MSS., LXXII).
[4] Extract, Resolutions, Holland and Westfriesland, October 21, 1779 (Sparks Dutch Papers).

vessels, when entering Dutch waters, had to show their commissions. If these were found illegal—that is, if they were not issued by a sovereign power—the captains were to be regarded as pirates.[1] To his government Yorke reported the following:—

"As well to the Prince as to the Ministers of the Republic, I proved the very great moderation and forbearance on the part of His Majesty who had given more than time sufficient to force this little squadron to sea, or to the Court of Versailles to produce a legal authority on the part of His Most Christian Majesty for their acts of hostility against Great Britain; that as neither of these events had come into our aid, it was not possible with honor, or with regard to other friendly powers, to abstain any longer from demanding what we were entitled to by the Law of Nations and by Treaty."

The ambassador added that he was displeased with the evasive answer of the States General to his previous memorial, and that he had therefore delivered a new note to the president of the States General, after showing it to the Grand Pensionary.[2] The resolution of the States General concerning Yorke's new memorial resulted in a refusal to restore the vessels. The United Provinces, they declared, would adhere to their old principle not to decide whether the prizes were taken legally or not, but Jones would be told that he must leave Dutch waters.[3] The latter measure was contradicted by Amsterdam. Her deputies to the Assembly of the States of Holland and Westfriesland asserted that Jones could not be compelled to sail, since such a step would

---

[1] Extract, Resolutions of States General, October 29, 1779 (Sparks Dutch Papers; Bancroft MSS., America, Holland, and England).

[2] Yorke to Weymouth, October 29, 1779 (Sparks MSS., LXXII).

[3] Resolution of the States General, November 19, 1779 (Bancroft MSS., America, Holland, and England; Sparks MSS., CIII).

At this time ugly attacks—probably instigated by the English party—were made against Jones in Dutch newspapers. He was described as a "rough, unpolished sailor" and a "man of little understanding and no morals or sensibility." Friends of the American cause (de Neufville, Dumas, van der Capellen) intended to defend Jones by publishing certain papers of the latter concerning the restoring of the Selkirk plate (Wharton, II, 599) in which his noble character was revealed, but the captain refused his permission (Neufville to van der Capellen, November 9, 1779; van der Capellen to Jones, without date; Jones to van der Capellen, November 29, 1779, in Beaufort, Brieven van der Capellen, 150–153).

be contrary to the resolution of the States General of November 3, 1756, which provided that "Commissie vaarders"
—vessels possessing proper commissions—would be admitted to Dutch waters.[1] The English ambassador reported
indignantly to his government that his memorial was not
complied with. The States General, he said, passed over
treaties and had recourse to interior regulations, no matter
when taken and under what circumstances.[2]

The matter took now a sudden turn in another direction,
foreseen, however, by many. The States General received
a letter from the Prince of Orange, stating that he had, in
conformity with their resolution of November 19, given
orders to Vice-Admiral Reynst to urge Jones politely, but
firmly, to depart from the Texel. Reynst had sent Captain
van Overmeer on board the "Serapis" to execute the order.
Overmeer found, however, that the "Serapis" was not
commanded by Jones any longer, but by a French captain,
Cotineau de Corgelin, who held possession of it in the name
of the King of France. The same was the case with the
other English vessel, and Reynst had therefore found himself unable to carry out his order, since the vessels were
not commanded by Jones.[3] The French ambassador at the
Hague subsequently pretended that Jones had a French commission.[4] Yorke was quite pleased with this development
of the Jones incident, considering it a victory over the
French party in the United Provinces. He wrote to the
Foreign Office in London:—

"I cannot help observing upon the turn this affair has taken, that
it has not ended so disagreeably for us as it appeared likely to do at
first. The arrival of the squadron under an American flag was
meant to procure some kind of avowal of American Independence,
whereas the Court of Versailles has at least been obliged to cover it

[1] Extract, Resolutions of Holland and Westfriesland, November
13 and 17, 1779 (Sparks Dutch Papers; Nieuwe Nederlandsche
Jaerboeken, 1779, p. 1365).
[2] Yorke to Stormont, November 23, 1779 (Sparks MSS., LXXII).
[3] Extract, Resolution of States General, November 26, 1779
(Sparks Dutch Papers).
[4] Yorke to Stormont, December 14, 1779 (Sparks MSS., LXXII).

with a French mask.[1] The change in its appearance will probably too, enable me to effectuate an exchange of prisoners, which was impracticable in its former shape; and, lastly, the best part of the nation is at the bottom highly offended at the contempt it is treated with, when it was so easy to have prevented it at the beginning."[2]

An interesting light is thrown upon the affair by a conversation between Captain Cotineau and Reynst which was submitted in writing to the States General by the stadtholder. Cotineau had said that he was to be regarded as a French officer though Jones had chosen to show an American flag. The ships had been armed in France and Louis XVI had sent on board one lieutenant-colonel with 150 men. The "Comtesse de Scarborough" had been taken by Cotineau himself, and he had declared to the prisoners from the beginning that they were French prisoners of war. When Reynst showed surprise that the vessels had been flying two flags, using sometimes one and sometimes the other, Cotineau answered that Dr. Franklin in Paris had given permission to use the North American flag. The French flag had been shown only from December 7. Reynst had tried in vain to obtain a copy of the French commission to John Paul Jones, and it was suspected that it had not yet arrived.[3] In fact, however, Jones refused emphatically to

---

[1] Yorke was right. Jones had no French commission. He wrote to van der Capellen, " I never bore nor acted under any other commission than that I have received from the Congress of the United States of America" (November 29, 1779, in Beaufort, Brieven van der Capellen, 153).

[2] Yorke to Stormont, December 14, 1779 (Sparks MSS., LXXII).

[3] Extract, Resolution of States General, December 22, 1779 (Sparks Dutch Papers).

In conformity with an advice from the Duc de la Vauguyon, Jones had told the Dutch commandant at the Texel that his French commission had not been found among his papers since the loss of the " Bon Homme Richard," and he feared that it had gone to the bottom in that ship; but, if it was really lost, it would be an easy matter to procure a duplicate of it from France (Jones to Vauguyon, November 4, 1779, in Wharton, III, 398).

Of the different stages of the Jones incident the Prussian envoy at the Hague, Thulemeier, sent detailed accounts to Frederick the Great (Bancroft MSS., Prussia and Holland, under dates 1779, October 8, 12, 15, 19, 26, 29; November 2, 16, 19, 23, 30; December 14, 17, 28, 31).

accept the French commission. The French naval agent at
Amsterdam, de Livoncourt, wrote to him :—

"Meanwhile I can make no more entreaty, if you persist in not
using the commission which I was charged to send you. Reflect
that all the French here in the service of the king have strongly at
heart to maintain the republic in sentiments favorable to the allies
of his majesty. It is in conformity with these views, and for the
good of the common cause, and only for this transient object, that
the commission, for the origin of which you imagine a thousand ill-
natured motives and which finally you refuse to accept, has been
addressed to you.

"You know all that I have had the honor to say to you on this
subject has been as well for your personal quiet as for the honor
and satisfaction of the common allies."[1]

Jones, flying only the American colors, and not showing
the French flag on the "Alliance," which he now commanded, nor producing any French commission, was requested by Vice-Admiral Reynst to inform him whether
the "Alliance" was to be considered a French or an American vessel. In the first case Jones would be expected to
show the French commission, to hoist the French flag and
pendant, and to confirm it with a salute from his guns. In
the second case Jones was asked not to neglect any opportunity to depart according to the orders of the States General.[2] The American answered that he had no orders to
hoist the flag of France. He could not display any other
than the American colors, unless he received orders for that
purpose from Dr. Franklin. Besides, he was ready to sail
whenever the pilot was ready to conduct the "Alliance" to
sea.[3] On December 27 Jones put to sea,[4] having stayed at
the Texel almost three months. This long delay, in spite
of the many entreaties of the Dutch government to depart,
was necessitated partly by indispensable repairs of the vessels under his command, and partly by the vigilance of
a superior number of English war vessels at the exits of
the roads at the Texel. For Great Britain the stay of John

---

[1] December 17, 1779 (Wharton, III, 431).
[2] Reynst to Jones, December 17, 1779 (ibid., III, 430).
[3] Jones to Reynst, same date (ibid., III, 430).
[4] Jones to Dumas, December 27, 1779 (ibid., III, 450).

Paul Jones in Dutch waters furnished subsequently a welcome pretext for the reproach to the United Provinces that they protected American pirates in their ports.[1]

---

[1] This discussion is somewhat ahead of the chronological order. Chapter III is devoted to the British accusations that the Dutch, directly or indirectly, supported the cause of America. Since the Jones episode formed one of the chief complaints of England in this respect, it seemed best to mention it here. Below, p. 129.

CHAPTER IV.

Early Relations Between the Two Republics.

The attempts of American representatives to raise a loan in the Netherlands formed part of the general financial policy of the Americans. The latter expected to borrow from Europe funds with which to meet the momentary exigencies of their newly created commonwealth. Therefore the Dutch loan must be considered in connection with other foreign loans. The majority in Congress, led by Richard Henry Lee and Samuel Adams, arranged a series of missions to European courts for the purpose of borrowing money, though those courts had given no intimation that they would receive American envoys. In several cases it was even more or less evident in advance that the reception would be refused. Only in one instance was it known beforehand that American representatives were welcome. France, contemplating joining the war against England, had intimated that envoys from North America would be received, at least in a private capacity. First Silas Deane, then Benjamin Franklin, and finally Arthur Lee was sent to France,[1] and all were well received by the French court.[2]

Fearing that premature complications with England would result from assisting the American colonies openly, France decided to do so clandestinely. The famous dramatist and secret agent of the French court, Beaumarchais, established a mercantile house in Paris under the fictitious name of Roderique Hortalez and Company for the special purpose of buying military stores and selling them to the Americans. As headquarters of the firm the "Hotel de Holland" was selected, a building erected under the reign

---

[1] Above, p. 123.
[2] Wharton, I, 291.

70

of Louis XIV by the Dutch Republic as the residence of its
minister at the French court, but vacant now for many
years.[1] Both Deane and Arthur Lee negotiated successfully
with Beaumarchais, with whom they made an agreement
for furnishing munitions of war to the American colonies.
The French government supported Beaumarchais by paying to him one million livres for the use of the Americans
and providing him secretly with ammunition from the royal
arsenals. France urged the court of Spain, with which she
was allied by the so-called family compact, also to assist
Beaumarchais with one million livres for the same purpose.
This sum was paid to him through the Comte de Vergennes.
The Americans were to pay to Hortalez and Company
American produce in return, but the consignments of the
colonies to France consisting of tobacco, indigo, etc., soon
almost ceased, after such shipments had been repeatedly
intercepted by the English, and after the rumor had spread
in America that the whole transaction was a mere pretext
of France for the maintenance of nominal neutrality.[2]
Beaumarchais then received another million from the King
of France.[3] The subsidies, thus furnished by France to
the American colonies through Beaumarchais, became later
the subject of controversies between the latter and the
United States, the question being whether the Americans
ought to pay in full for the goods which they received from
him, or whether the money given to the French agent by
his government was intended as gratuitous assistance to
the United States.[4]

Already at this early stage of the Revolution Americans
contemplated a loan in the United Provinces. On November 2, 1776, Carmichael wrote from Amsterdam[5] to the com-

---

[1] Wharton, I, 370.
[2] Ibid., I, 374.
[3] Bayley, National Loans of the United States, 6.
[4] Wharton, I, 381 ff.; Bayley, National Loans of the United States,
5 ff.; Dewey, Financial History of the United States, 47.
[5] William Carmichael of Maryland happened to be in Europe at
the beginning of the American Revolution. He was in Paris when
Silas Deane arrived there as commercial and political agent from

mittee of secret correspondence that he had endeavored to induce Dutch merchants to invest in direct commerce with America. He had also tried to find out the sentiments of the people of the United Provinces in general respecting the Americans, and to learn whether, in case of necessity, the United States would be able to negotiate a loan, and, on the other hand, whether England would be able to obtain further credit. Arriving but two days after the accounts had reached Amsterdam of the misfortune of Long Island, William Carmichael found many even of the sanguine friends of America dejected and the partisans of England almost in a frenzy of joy. In this disposition, he said, it was easy to see that no hopes could be entertained of engaging merchants in direct trade. He found that they had the greatest inclination to serve the Americans, and at the same time to help themselves, for no people saw their interest clearer; but their fears that America might be subdued, the confident assertions of the friends of England confirming these apprehensions, the prodigious sums they had in the English funds, with this unlucky business at New York, all conspired to prevent direct speculations.[1] An American loan was, therefore, in Carmichael's opinion, not yet practicable in the Provinces, but he was confident that, in case the final success of the American colonies should become evident, or either France or Spain should recognize American independence, funds might be had from the Dutch. As soon as the lenders should see that the first payments of interest were made punctually, plenty of money would be offered by Dutch houses. As security for such loans he proposed the issue of bonds similar to those current in the

---

the United States, and lived with him for some time, aiding him in his official business. When the Prussian minister in Paris suggested that Frederick the Great would like to be informed on American commerce by a competent American citizen, Deane proposed to Carmichael the undertaking of that mission. Carmichael accepted and went to Berlin by way of Amsterdam (Wharton, I, 577). It was then that he studied the political situation in the Netherlands and tried to further the American cause there.

[1] Wharton, II, 185.

Netherlands, and suggested that they should be lodged in a public bank in Europe.

Such sounding of Dutch financial circles could not long remain unknown to the British ambassador at the Hague. He reported to his government that, according to rumors, his "bastard brother ambassador" Deane was at Amsterdam, endeavoring to borrow money for Congress, and that the American commissioner even had proposals drawn up for that purpose. Yorke added that he could not conceive of the Dutch lending a stiver to the Americans, because the colonies were not in a position to give any security. "This," he concluded, "is but a poor bait to take in old sharpers."[1]

While there was no prospect yet of raising a loan in the United Provinces, the American commissioners were more successful in France. The French government, not yet ready to join the war, when asked by the commissioners[2] to provide the Americans with ships, men, and warlike stores, declined, since such aid could not be rendered without becoming known to the English. A loan, however, was less dangerous in this respect, there being little difficulty in keeping monetary transactions a secret. In the beginning of the year 1777 Louis XVI granted, therefore, two million livres[3] to the Americans, demanding no promise of repayment but requiring absolute silence.[4] This made the com-

---

[1] Yorke to W. Eden, November 15, 1776 (Sparks MSS., LXXII).
[2] Bolles, Financial History of the United States, 227.
[3] Five French livres equal about one American dollar.
[4] According to Bayley (National Loans, 10, 11), this loan was not obtained from the French government directly, but from the Farmers General, to whom Franklin and Deane were referred, because that private corporation, "engaged in the collection of the national revenue of France, might loan public moneys, if encouraged to do so by the government, without causing any diplomatic complications." (The Farmers General leased the public revenues, paying to the government a certain fixed sum.) The contract dated March 24, 1777, was signed by Franklin, Deane, and a representative of the Farmers General. In contradiction to this, Bolles (Financial History, 228) states that it was proposed to obtain money from the Farmers General, but as it was difficult to settle all the terms, the Crown granted the money. De Knight-Tillman, History of the Currency of the Country and of the Loans of the United States, 17.

missioners hopeful of raising enough money for paying the interest upon $20,000,000 of paper money issued by Congress. They advised Congress to draw on them for sums equal to the interest of what they had borrowed, when such interest should become due. Before the end of the year the commissioners obtained another loan from France, amounting this time to three million livres.[1]

Meanwhile the relations between the American agents in Paris and the Netherlands were kept up. Dumas furnished addresses of Dutch firms, with whom the Americans could deal, and promised to send more in future,[2] though there was no better prospect yet for a loan. It is interesting to observe that England's credit also was low at this period. Thulemeier, the Prussian envoy at the Hague, who had instructions to inform his master, Frederick the Great, about everything noteworthy, reported in January, 1778, that the credit of Great Britain was very precarious. This was due partly to the enormous number of business failures in London, but largely to the court of Versailles. The French government, he said, aimed at the ruin of the English credit by secretly buying British funds and selling them at a considerable loss.[3]

In the United Provinces there was especially one friend and admirer of the United States who made an ardent attempt to obtain a loan in his country for the Americans. This was Joan Derk van der Capellen.[4] He explained to the Dutch capitalists that the credit of America, based upon a country rich in products, was supported by a really republican government. This credit, he argued, was infinitely more secure than that of England, which suffered from an enormous national debt and depended only on a commerce which had become very uncertain, while its sole guarantee was a despotic and awkward government. Van

---

[1] Bolles, Financial History, 228–229.
[2] Dumas to A. Lee, September 23, 1777 (Lee MSS., Library of Harvard University, III).
[3] Thulemeier to Frederick II, January 23, 1778 (Bancroft MSS., Prussia and Holland).
[4] Above, pp. 23, 31.

der Capellen was, however, not yet able to collect a sum large enough to be offered to the Americans. He suggested, therefore, to Franklin a method by which the Dutch might be induced to invest their money in American securities. Congress, he said, should offer propositions which would be advantageous enough to enable the Dutch to withdraw their money from England without loss in spite of the low rates of the British funds. For this purpose he recommended a fundamental law, to be passed by Congress, to the effect that the interest of the loan should not be reduced unless a restitution of the capital was offered. The interest must be high and be offered for a number of years. This, the Dutch statesman thought, would be the most efficient and most humane way of bringing the war to a speedy end in favor of the Americans. It would, at the same time, serve to separate his country gradually from Great Britain, and to attach it more and more to the interests of the United States.[1] The American commissioners in Paris conceived now the plan of opening a loan officially in the United Provinces. In May they wrote, " We mean to apply for the loan desired to the moneyed men of Holland."[2] Still, though the disposition in Holland seemed to be favorable to the American cause, they apprehended that it was not yet warm enough to produce any decided success. This would only be possible when Great Britain appeared more enfeebled. Dumas published in the United Provinces an essay by Arthur Lee, which he hoped would have some effect.[3] It explained that the success of the American arms would reestablish American commerce upon its ancient free footing. Since the Netherlands were thus to profit by the victory of the United States, the Americans looked chiefly to the United Provinces for support. The memorial then continued :—

---

[1] Van der Capellen to Franklin, April 28, 1778 (Beaufort, Brieven van der Capellen, 64–65).

[2] A. Lee to the Committee of Foreign Affairs, May 23, 1778 (Wharton, II, 609).

[3] A. Lee to the Committee of Foreign Affairs, June 1, 1778 (ibid., II, 603).

" The extraordinary remittances which the people of America have made to the merchants of Great Britain since the commencement of this dispute is a proof of their honor and good faith; so much more safe and advantageous is it to trust money with a young, industrious, thriving people, than with an old nation overwhelmed with debt, abandoned to extravagance, and immersed in luxury. By maintaining the independence of America a new avenue will be opened for the employment of money, where landed property, as yet untouched by mortgage or other incumbrances, will answer for the principal, and the industry of a young and uninvolved people would insure the regular payment of interest. The money-holder would in that case be relieved from the continual fears and apprehensions which every agitation of the English stocks perpetually excites. He might count his profits without anxiety, and plan his moneyed transactions with certainty."[1]

The commissioners shortly afterwards informed their government that they were going to send to the United Provinces the proposals for a loan as soon as Franklin, who was entrusted with forming the plan, should have the proposed bills printed and the business prepared for execution.[2] More than a month and a half later these preparations were not yet finished. " We are signing the notes for the loan in Holland, which is a work of time," Arthur Lee wrote to his superiors.[3]

While the American commissioners were thus working for a loan in the Netherlands, they continued to ask for further assistance from France. Their application to the French government for the privilege of borrowing two million sterling from private sources, in order to redeem so many of the bills of credit in the United States as would be sufficient to restore the remainder to their original value, was not complied with.[4] A further request was made by Franklin to the court at Versailles for a quarterly payment of three quarters of a million livres, whereupon the king consented to advance 750,000 livres more.[5]

The main reason why it was so difficult for the United

---

[1] A. Lee's Memorial for Holland (Wharton, II, 545).
[2] A. Lee to the Committee of Foreign Affairs, June 9, 1778 (ibid., II, 609).
[3] A. Lee to the Committee of Correspondence, July 28, 1778 (ibid., II, 671).
[4] Bolles, Financial History, 230.
[5] Ibid., 234; Gerard to the President of Congress, February 9, 1779 (Wharton, III, 41).

States to obtain assistance in Europe was that their credit was poor. Another was that the principal European nations were arming for war, and all had to borrow money, some offering rates of interest considerably higher than those proposed by the Americans. There remained, therefore, only two motives for lending money to the United States: either benevolence or the desire to humiliate Great Britain. Since this condition of the European money-market continued for rather a long period, there was not much hope left of obtaining loans from individuals. It could only be expected from governments.[1] The American commissioners in France were almost in despair. "Our currency," wrote John Adams in the fall of 1778, "can not engage our attention too much. And the more we think of it, the more we shall be convinced that taxation, deep and broad taxation, is the only sure and lasting remedy. Loans in Europe will be very difficult to obtain. The powers at war, or at the eve of war, have such vast demands, and offer terms so much better than ours, that nothing but sheer benevolence to our cause can induce any person to lend us. Besides, a large foreign debt would be a greater evil, for what I know, than a paper currency."[2] Arthur Lee expressed himself similarly:—

"Congress must not trust to the success of a loan, which, for the following reasons, I apprehend will be found impracticable.

"The war in Germany supervening on that between us and Great Britain, and the preparations for it by France and Spain, have raised and multiplied the demand for money, so as to give the holders of it their choice and their price. The empress queen has engrossed every shilling in the Netherlands. England has drawn large sums from the Hollanders, who can not easily quit their former market. France is negotiating a loan of one hundred million livres, which will exhaust Geneva and Switzerland. The money-holders regard the lending their money at such a distance as Jacob did the sending Benjamin into Egypt, and it is time only will make them endure the thought of such a separation.

"These are the difficulties which the circumstances of things oppose to our scheme of a loan, and render the aid of some other operation necessary for sinking the superabundant paper."[3]

---

[1] Bolles, Financial History, 231.
[2] Adams to R. H. Lee, August 5, 1778 (Wharton, II, 677).
[3] A. Lee to the Committee of Foreign Affairs, August 21, 1778 (ibid., II, 691, 692).

The experience with their first loan in the United Provinces was not such as to make the commissioners hopeful. In a joint letter they informed Congress in September, 1778, that they had taken measures in Amsterdam for borrowing money of the Dutch.[1] These steps consisted in negotiating American obligations signed by the commissioners in Paris, their value being one thousand guilders each, bearing five per cent. interest and to be redeemed ten years after issue.[2] A certain number (about two hundred and eight) were lodged in the French house of Horneca, Fizeaux, and Company at Amsterdam.[3] These papers were not taken up at all. Van der Capellen suggested that the negotiations would be more successful if, instead of the obligations being signed by Franklin, Lee, and Adams, Congress, represented by its president and secretary, would do so under the official seal. The Dutch were accustomed to similar contracts with their states. Besides, Congress must promise expressly not to reduce the interest during the terms of the bonds. In his opinion ten years was too short a period, and he recommended extending it to twenty. Van der Capellen considered also very injurious to the American credit the false reports which were spread in the Netherlands by the English, and which could not be corrected by the friends of the American cause since the latter were not kept informed of the facts. He deemed it of the utmost importance that measures should be taken to furnish reports to the Dutch that were absolutely true, even in regard to the misfortunes of the Americans. The Dutch statesman then offered his services to make such news public. A description of the existing condition of the United States, the form of government in the separate states, the facility with which foreigners might settle there, the prices of the various qualities of land, together with a concise history of the war, and the cruelties committed by the English would, in his opinion, work

---

[1] Franklin, Lee, and Adams to the President of Congress, September 17, 1778 (Wharton, II, 722).
[2] Thulemeier to Frederick the Great, November 24, 1778 (Bancroft MSS., Prussia and Holland).
[3] Yorke to Suffolk, October 16, 1778 (Sparks MSS., LXXII).

wonders in a country where America was known only from the gazettes. Van der Capellen stated also that he had invested 20,000 French livres with the firm of Horneca and Fizeaux for American securities. He was convinced that it would be more advantageous to the American cause to procure one hundred thousand livres from fifty persons and from different parts of the country than to receive even a million from a single capitalist. He had interested a number of compatriots in the Dutch loan, when letters from London arrived, stating that the American people were dissatisfied with Congress and there were grave dissensions between the French and the Americans and also among the Americans themselves. The consequence was a general distrust in the success of the Revolution. Van der Capellen expressed his desire that Congress would find means to assure the Dutch that, whatever turn the war might take and of whatever nature the final peace with Great Britain might be, the capital and interest of the debts contracted during the struggle would be secure. Unless these apprehensions of the Dutch should be relieved, support for the American cause could not be expected in the United Provinces.[1]

At the beginning of 1779 there was yet no hope for a loan. "The prospect of a loan in Europe," wrote John Adams to Congress, "after every measure that has been or could be taken, I think it my duty to say frankly to Congress, is very unpromising. The causes of this are very obvious, and can not be removed; the state of our country itself and the course of exchange would be sufficient to discourage such a loan if there were no other obstruction, but there are many others. There are more borrowers in Europe than lenders; and the British loan itself will not be made this year at a less interest than seven and a half per cent." He saw no hope of relief but in taxation and economy. The people of the United States, in his opinion, must be destitute of sense as well as of virtue, if they would not be willing to

---

[1] Van der Capellen to Trumbull, December 7, 1778 (Beaufort, Brieven van der Capellen, 89–93).

pay the cost of their defence, since they had one powerful ally (France) and could expect others, while England was exhausted and had no ally at all.[1]

The loan in the United Provinces was a failure. Louis XVI, in order to encourage it, had consented to guarantee the interest of three million livres. Toward the end of May, 1779, however, the loan amounted scarcely to 80,000 florins. The work of the commissioners was greatly hampered by the efforts of the separate states of the United States to obtain loans in Europe, especially when their agents offered higher rates of interest than the representatives of Congress were able to propose.[2] " Running all over Europe, asking to borrow money," the states created such a belief in the distress and poverty of the country as to make it undesirable for foreigners to enter into close relations with the United States.[3]

In connection with the American attempts to effect a loan in the Netherlands, Stephen Sayre[4] (Arthur Lee's secretary) must be mentioned. According to Sir Joseph Yorke this " noted American agent " arrived at Amsterdam, but was received openly nowhere except at the house of Jean de Neufville. The ambassador stated that the purpose of Sayre's visit was " to find any enthusiasts dupes enough to advance money upon the security of lands in America."[5] These land schemes are of sufficient interest to be mentioned, as Sayre discussed them while at Amsterdam. Having travelled through a great part of Germany and the northern states of Europe, he was of opinion that many persons were waiting impatiently for the moment of safety, that is, the certainty of the independence of the United States, to embark for America in order to settle there. Others were anxious to make investments in America, like

---

[1] John Adams to Jay, President of Congress, February 27, 1779 (Wharton, III, 70).
[2] Franklin to the Committee of Foreign Affairs, May 26, 1779 (ibid., III, 188–192).
[3] Bolles, Financial History, 236.
[4] Above, p. 61.
[5] Yorke to Lord Weymouth, May 21, 1779 (Sparks MSS., LXXII).

de Gorne, the minister of state of Frederick the Great. Congress should therefore appropriate a district of land near some of the middle states in America, containing three or more degrees of latitude and longitude, to be set apart as security for the subscribers to American loans. This district should be divided into square lots of one hundred acres each of cultivable land, numbered and registered in the public offices of the states. Each subscriber, according to this scheme, would be entitled to the first number unoccupied, as he applied for location. The inhabitants of the district were to enjoy the privileges constitutionally belonging to the people of the other states. An interest of a certain per cent. would be paid to the subscribers until they had located their lands. The land certificates should be transferable, so that those who did not settle in America might be able to sell their shares. Sayre was of opinion that upon such a plan the agents of Congress would have no difficulty in borrowing large sums of money in the United Provinces, and at low interest, too, because America was offering such advantages as no other country could boast of, viz., that of giving landed security and unembarrassed choice of immediate possession. Besides, he thought, America would secure the sympathy and friendship of the United Provinces by such a loan.[1] Mr. Sayre's scheme seems to have been too fantastic ever to have been taken into serious consideration.

In July, 1779, van der Capellen noticed that the people of the Netherlands were beginning to see the dangerous position of England and to think more favorably of the American cause and the credit of the United States. He informed his friends in America accordingly and suggested that something should be done to profit by this change of public opinion.[2] He impressed on the Americans again that in order to strengthen the credit of the United States it would be necessary to make the Dutch better acquainted with American affairs and for that purpose to have a system of

---

[1] Sayre to van der Capellen, June 23, 1779 (Beaufort, Brieven van der Capellen, 154–156).
[2] Van der Capellen to Trumbull, July 6, 1779 (ibid., 109).

6

continuous and trustworthy intelligence established regarding the vicissitudes of the war. Van der Capellen expressed strong hopes that his efforts concerning the American loan might succeed. In the Netherlands there were many Roman Catholics and these were much in favor of the United States. A great number of them were residing in his province, of whom he knew many, and through them he expected to be able to influence others of their faith. It was now the right moment to act.[1]

These communications were received with much enthusiasm in the United States, and probably formed the principal cause for the subsequent appointment of Laurens, President of Congress, as special agent to the United Provinces.[2] The Dutch statesman worked indefatigably for the American cause, even publishing extracts from his correspondence with leading Americans (Trumbull and Livingston), and inducing friends and relatives, like his cousin, Baron van der Capellen tot de Marsch, to contribute to the American loan.[3] But this experiment, also, was a failure.

For a moment, a brighter prospect was opened when Mr. Neufville, a Dutch banker (not the same with whom John Adams negotiated later), offered to Franklin in the spring of 1779 large sums, provided the business should be taken from the house then employed for placing the American bonds with the United Provinces. Unfortunately he proved to be an adventurer. At first he asked that "all the estates, real and personal" in the thirteen United States should be mortgaged to him, also that a fifth of the capital sum borrowed should every year for five years be laid out in commodities and sent to Holland, consigned to him, to remain in his hands as security for punctual payments, till the time stipulated for final payment should be completed. As another condition he proposed that all vessels of merchandise coming from America to Europe should be consigned

---

[1] Van der Capellen to Livingston, July 16, 1779 (Beaufort, Brieven van der Capellen, 113–115).
[2] Livingston to van der Capellen, March 15, 1780 (ibid., 214).
[3] Van der Capellen to Livingston (ibid., 112).

to him or his correspondents. Franklin rejected these conditions with indignation, and Neufville then came down to the terms employed by the other house. No complaints having been preferred against the latter, Franklin was not in favor of a change, especially as he had commenced to doubt Neufville's reliability. Franklin therefore answered evasively that if the banker could procure a list of subscribers amounting to about the promised sum, Neufville's proposition would be considered. Neufville, in contradiction to his pretensions, was not able to furnish such a list, but, instead, sent Franklin a new set of extravagant propositions. The American commissioner then dropped all correspondence with him. After this experience, Franklin wrote in the fall of 1779: " The truth is, I have no expectations from Holland while interest received there from other nations is so high and our credit there so low; while particular American States offer higher interest than the Congress, and even our offering to raise our interest tends to sink our credit. My sole dependence is now upon this court [France]."[1] But the year 1779 was almost ended, and no funds had been secured from France for more than a year. No wonder that the American commissioners seemed to have no hope at all in a foreign loan at this time. One of them wrote:—

"I perceive by the journals that a committee is appointed for framing a plan of a foreign loan. It is my duty to say that there is not the least probability, in the present situation of things, of obtaining any adequate loan in Europe, and to beseech Congress not to let the vain expectation of that divert their attention from trying every resource at home. It is necessary that the impressions to our discredit which have arisen from the unsuccessful attempts that have been already made should be allowed to wear off and some favorable event occur, such as the enemy being obliged to draw off their troops, before it will be possible to succeed in such a plan. In the mean time the repetition of ineffectual attempts will only debase your credit more, and especially if they are accompanied with the offer of more than ordinary interest, which ever augments the suspicion of the insecurity of the principal and that the borrowers are themselves conscious of their insufficiency."[2]

---

[1] Franklin to Jay, October 4, 1779 (Wharton, III, 361, 362) ; Bolles, Financial History, 236–238.
[2] Arthur Lee to the Committee of Foreign Affairs, November 6, 1779 (Wharton, III, 401–402) ; Bolles, Financial History, 239–240.

Another effort of the American commissioners to draw the two republics nearer together should not be overlooked, namely, the proposal of a treaty of amity and commerce. Already in the spring of 1777 Vauguyon had informed his government of a suggestion that had been made to Mr. van Berkenrode, the Dutch envoy to the court of Versailles, by Franklin and Deane. These gentlemen had solicited the States General to favor the commerce of the United States, which would give them great advantages. The commissioners, according to Vauguyon, had offered to go to the Netherlands in order to negotiate, or, in case this should not be considered convenient, they were willing to treat with a deputy of the United Provinces in Paris. The French ambassador had also learned that the Dutch, after many deliberations, had decided to authorize Berkenrode to make an answer which, without rejecting the offer of the Americans, would not betray any eagerness to accept it.[1] About a year later, rumors were spread that Franklin was expected in Holland to negotiate a treaty of commerce. These reports, Sir Joseph Yorke observed, made only little impression in the Netherlands, but served to show the temper of the times.[2]

On February 6, 1778, France openly espoused the part of the United States, in concluding a treaty with them. It was stipulated that, in case Great Britain should declare war upon France, neither of the contracting parties should make peace separately, and that England must recognize the independence of her former American colonies before a general peace might be thought of. The treaty was ostensibly commercial. On March 18, Béranger, the French chargé d'affaires at the Hague, informed the ministers of Holland and the president of the States General, on behalf of his government, of the conclusion of the convention, causing thereby a great sensation.[3] The exact terms of the treaty, however, were not yet made known to the Republic, no copy

---

[1] Vauguyon to Vergennes, May 30, 1777 (Sparks MSS., LXXXIII).
[2] Yorke to Suffolk, April 3, 1778 (Sparks MSS., LXXII).
[3] Thulemeier to Frederick II, March 20, 1778 (Bancroft MSS., Prussia and Holland).

of it being transmitted. Dumas, after a conference with the Grand Pensionary of Holland, asked the American commissioners in Paris to send one for the Grand Pensionary, from which another might be drawn for the regency of Amsterdam.[1] Franklin thereupon sent a copy of the treaty to the American agent, but Vauguyon was instructed by the French minister of foreign affairs, who had conferred with the American commissioners on the subject, to prevent a formal communication until express orders were sent to that effect. The ambassador was, however, authorized to allow the Grand Pensionary of Holland and the regency of Amsterdam to read the treaty, and to assure them, as he had done before,[2] that no exclusive commercial advantages had been stipulated for France. Vauguyon was also charged to inform the Dutch that no free ports had been accorded to the Americans in France except for commodities of their own growth, such as tobacco, which were not introduced into France from the Netherlands. For everything else the former English colonies would be subjected to the same rules and rights as other privileged nations, and these provisions could therefore in no way be offensive to the United Provinces.[3] Sir Joseph Yorke, who appears not to have known of the confidential proceedings just mentioned, was at a loss to know why the treaty had not been communicated to the Republic, and suspected the reason to be that the French had granted favors to the Americans which they withheld from the Dutch, especially regarding free ports.[4] In the autumn of 1778, when the treaty between France and America was no longer a secret, Vauguyon received two copies of it from his government for communication to whomever he thought proper, but he was forbidden even then to deliver them to the Dutch ministers officially.[5] On October 22, a printed copy was handed to the Grand Pen-

---

[1] Dumas to the Commissioners in Paris, May 29, 1778 (Arthur Lee MSS., Harvard University).
[2] Yorke to Suffolk, March 27, 1778 (Sparks MSS., LXXII).
[3] Vergennes to Vauguyon, June 21, 1778 (ibid., LXXXIII).
[4] Yorke to Suffolk, July 20, 1778 (ibid., LXXII).
[5] Vergennes to Vauguyon, October 15, 1778 (ibid., LXXXIII).

sionary, who brought it to the knowledge of the States General. The latter discussed the matter secretly, but no official action was taken.[1]

Vauguyon secretly sounded Dutch politicians to see if they favored a convention between France, Spain and the Republic for the mutual protection of their commerce. The Netherlands were not yet ready to take such a step. The Grand Pensionary, van Bleiswijck, was much pleased with the proposition, but declared that he would not be able to win the Prince of Orange for it. France did not insist, and the Republic considered it now almost a favor to be left undisturbed in the enjoyment of neutrality. In truth, France had become aware of the fact that the United Provinces were more advantageous to her as a neutral power than as an ally. The Dutch navy was too weak to be of any real service, in case the Netherlands should join the war. On the other hand, their large commercial fleet would be of the greatest importance for France, as long as Dutch navigation remained undisturbed by the belligerents.[2] France therefore now left it entirely to the Americans to further their own cause in the United Provinces. On April 28, Franklin, Arthur Lee, and Deane addressed to the Grand Pensionary a letter, already known to and approved by the city of Amsterdam, in which they expressed the desire of Congress to enter into closer relations of friendship and commerce with the United Provinces. The commissioners requested that their letter be submitted to the States General.[3] The Grand Pensionary, however, did not comply with this wish. He knew that this proposition of the United

---

[1] Secret Resolution of the States General, October 28, 1778 (Bancroft MSS., America, Holland and England).

[2] Colenbrander, Patriottentijd, I, 127–130.

[3] Franklin, Lee, and Adams to Dumas, April 10, 1778 (Wharton, II, 546, 547).
Thulemeier reported to his royal master on May 26, 1778, that Franklin's letter proposing to the Grand Pensionary in the name of Congress " the conclusion of a treaty of commerce " had been accompanied with menaces in case of a refusal to recognize American independence. Three days later, however, he corrected this statement, asserting that no such menaces had been made (Bancroft MSS., Prussia and Holland).

States would not be accepted by the Dutch sovereign body, and, with the consent of the Prince of Orange, communicated it, confidentially, to the members of the States of Holland only. Each city, which had a vote in that province, was secretly provided with a copy.[1] It was thought that in this way every offence to the English government would be avoided.[2] So many persons knowing of the letter, it proved, however, impossible to conceal it long from the English ambassador. Yorke said that the very fact of the Dutch attempt to keep the communication of the American commissioners a secret showed the prevailing sentiments. Sir Joseph soon took occasion to confer with the Prince of Orange. " I was really sorry," the ambassador wrote of this conference, " for the Prince of Orange, who not being prepared by the Pensionary before I saw him, shewed more concern and embarrassment than I ever saw in him before, and convinced me that he had been led into it without feeling the consequence, and overpersuaded by others. I flatter myself not to have omitted anything which was proper to be said to him, which he received very kindly, and with strong assurances of attachment to the King, and personal regard to me: I left him with a strong and friendly recommendation not to suffer himself to be so trapped again."[3] Yorke had also a conversation on the subject with the Grand Pensionary, who was rather embarrassed with the ambassador's manner of " opening the business," the latter affecting " not to give credit to it." Van Bleiswijck admitted the fact of the American proposal and that he had communicated it to some members of Holland, not thinking it proper to keep such a letter entirely to himself. Yorke's question why he had not seen fit to inform the English government of this step, either through him or the Dutch envoy in London, was answered evasively. The Grand Pensionary said that he had not looked upon it as a matter of sufficient im-

---

[1] Colenbrander, Patriottentijd, I, 130; Blok, Geschiedenis van het Nederlandsche Volk, VI, 326.
[2] Young, History of the Netherlands, 627.
[3] Yorke to Suffolk, private, May 29, 1778 (Sparks MSS., LXXII).

portance, and that, besides, he was not properly authorized
to communicate it officially to the English government.
However, he did not hesitate then to send a copy of the letter
to Yorke.[1]

While the government of the United Provinces was still
too much in awe of Great Britain to enter into closer relations with the United States, the principal city, Amsterdam,
engaged in negotiations with the Americans, thereby finally
causing a breach with England and involving the Dutch
Republic in a disastrous war, as will be seen in a later chapter.[2] In July, 1778, van Berckel, pensionary of Amsterdam,
requested Dumas, the American agent, to express to the
plenipotentiaries of the United States at Paris the gratitude
and appreciation of the regency of Amsterdam for having
been furnished with a copy of the French-American treaty.
"May we hope that circumstances will permit us soon to
give evidence of the high esteem we have for the new republic, clearly raised up by the help of Providence, while the
spirit of despotism is subdued; and let us desire to make
leagues of amity and commerce between the respective subjects which shall last even to the end of time. What troubles
me is that it is not in our power to make the other members
of the government do as we could wish; in which case the
republic would be at once disposed to another course."[3]
Dumas forwarded a copy of this letter to the commissioners
in Paris and another one to Congress. He informed van
Berckel soon afterwards of a letter which he had received
from William Lee, then in Frankfort. The latter wrote
that he was not disposed to make haste, especially in important affairs, but he could not help saying that there might
be danger of the good people in Holland losing some advantages in commerce with America by their too great caution.
He had reason to believe that the British ministry had

---

[1] Yorke to Suffolk, official, May 29, 1778 (Sparks MSS., LXXII);
Thulemeier to Frederick II, July 7, 1778 (Bancroft MSS., Prussia
and Holland).
[2] Below, pp. 152 ff.
[3] Van Berckel to Dumas, July 31, 1778 (Wharton, II, 674).

already sent orders to their commissioners to yield the point of independence, provided they should obtain some exclusive benefit in America.[1]

Afraid that the British commissioners, in their negotiations with the United States, might arrange some measures excluding the Dutch from American commerce, the burgomasters of Amsterdam sent a "Declaration" to Dumas. They expressed a desire to conclude a treaty of commerce and amity with the republic, provided Congress should not enter into engagements with the English which might prove "hurtful or prejudicial" to Dutch commerce, "directly or indirectly." Amsterdam not being able to negotiate a treaty independently of the States General, her ministers could think only of preparing such a convention. "It is plain," wrote van Berckel in his letter to Dumas on September 23, 1778, "that a treaty of commerce can not be concluded unless the principal commercial city of the republic gives its consent thereto, and that it can not give its consent without having examined the terms. This examination may as well precede as follow the acknowledgment of the independence of America by the English, in which case we should gain much time."[2] Already on the fourth of the

---

[1] Dumas to van Berckel, August 17, 1778 (Wharton, II, 687, 688).
[2] Wharton, II, 738, 739.

Since these negotiations of the city of Amsterdam with Congress caused much heated controversy afterwards (below, pp. 152 ff.) the wording of the " Declaration," which showed that the conclusion of a draft treaty with Congress originated principally in self-defence, will be of interest:—

"AMSTERDAM, September 23, 1778.

" The undersigned pensionary of the city of Amsterdam, has the honor to make known to those who are duly authorized by the Congress of the United States of America that he is empowered by the burgomasters of the aforementioned city to declare in their names that provided the said Congress do not enter into any engagement with the English commissioners which may be hurtful or prejudicial to the commerce of the republic of the United Provinces, directly or indirectly, the aforesaid burgomasters on their side will be entirely disposed, as far as depends on them, so to direct the course of affairs, that whenever the independence of the said United States of America shall be recognized by the English, a perpetual treaty of amity shall be concluded between this republic and the aforesaid United States, containing the most extensive reciprocal advantages in relation to the commerce of the subjects of the two powers.

same month a prominent merchant of Amsterdam, Jean de Neufville, who was much interested in American commerce had with the authorization of van Berckel formulated with William Lee at Aix-la-Chapelle a draft treaty which was to be considered only after the recognition of American independence by Great Britain.[1]

Lee, who had entered upon these negotiations without special authority from Congress, reported them in detail. After his arrival at Frankfort[2] he found an opportunity of negotiating a treaty of commerce with the province of Holland and West Friesland. He proceeded so far as to agree on the draft of a treaty with Mr. de Neufville and felt sure Congress would approve of it, as it contained all the substantially advantageous articles of the commercial treaty with France and some beneficial and agreeable additions. The negotiations had been conducted on both sides with great secrecy, which was absolutely necessary in order to procure final success with the United Provinces; for though the city of Amsterdam and the States of Holland paid about five sixths of the whole taxes for the support of the government, which consequently gave them very powerful weight and influence, yet they had no power by their constitution of entering into such a treaty without the concurrence of the other provinces. In some of the latter the Prince of Orange, who greatly favored England, had an overdue influence. This, Lee said, rendered secrecy of the

---

" The undersigned has the honor further to declare, that it is the will of said burgomasters that this declaration may be employed as shall be thought expedient, with the necessary precaution that it shall not come to the knowledge of those interested, to prevent, if possible, or at least to obstruct, the execution of a plan which has no other object than to promote the mutual happiness and the true interests of the two republics.

" E. T. Van Berckel."

[1] Blok, Geschiedenis, VI, 326.

[2] William Lee was charged to work for the American cause in Germany and Austria. It was while in the former country that he negotiated with de Neufville, who had been commissioned there by van Berckel. Probably the negotiation was held there in order to avoid suspicion, which could not have been prevented if the meeting had taken place in the United Provinces.

last importance, until the Patriots in Holland had secured success. Only then the business could be agitated in the States General, where it must be passed to have full authority.[1]

To Lee it appeared to be of no inconsiderable importance that he had obtained from the pensionary an engagement by which the States General would be prevented from taking any measures that might be injurious to the United States, provided America should not take any measures injurious to Holland. This engagement the pensionary alone was capable of complying with, because his single negative would be sufficient to prevent the States General from entering into any such measures, and consequently the states would be prevented from giving any aid to Great Britain against France.[2] The American commissioners in Paris, informed of Lee's transactions at Aix-la-Chapelle, did not approve of the provision that the treaty should be considered only after the recognition of American independence by Great Britain. "We would only remark that the mentioning it in the declaration as a thing necessary to precede the conclusion of such a treaty '*that the American independence should be acknowledged by the English*' is not understood by us, who conceive there is no more occasion for such an acknowledgment before a treaty with Holland than there was before our treaty with France. And we apprehend that if that acknowledgment were really necessary *or waited for,* England *might* endeavor to make an advantage of it in the future treaty of pacification to obtain for it some privileges in commerce perhaps exclusive of Holland. We wish, therefore, that idea to be laid aside, and that no further mention may be made to us of England in this business."[3]

France was aware of the fact that the principal men of

---

[1] W. Lee to Committee of Foreign Affairs, September 12, 1778 (Wharton, II, 715, 716).
[2] Same to same, October 15, 1778 (ibid., II, 787, 788).
[3] Franklin, Lee, and Adams to Dumas, October 16, 1778 (ibid., II, 799).

Amsterdam desired closer relations with the Americans, but she knew equally well that the States General would not join in these efforts before all fear of England's resentment had gone.[1] Yorke also was suspicious of secret negotiations between Amsterdam and the United States, though he did not know their nature and had in particular no knowledge of the draft treaty.[2] The American commissioners, however, did not overestimate the value of this secret agreement with the city of Amsterdam, and when Dumas hinted that some of the friends of the American cause in the Netherlands wished the commissioners to propose a treaty to the Dutch government, they answered that it would really be a great pleasure to them to be instrumental in cementing a union between the two republics of Holland and the United States by a treaty of amity and commerce similar to that lately concluded with France, or varying when circumstances might require it. But, having received no answer from the Grand Pensionary to a letter which they had written to him some months before, expressing their disposition toward such a good work, they apprehended that any further action of that kind on their part would not, at present, be agreeable; though they still would hold themselves ready to enter upon such a treaty when it should seem good to the States General.[3]

At first, the efforts of the Americans to have the States General accredit an American minister were also unsuccessful. As early as July 2 and 3, 1777, Congress, according to the minutes in the Secret Journal of Congress, had deliberated on the question of sending a representative to the States General at the Hague.[4] Almost a year later (April

---

[1] Vergennes to Vauguyon, September 13, 1778 (Sparks MSS., LXXXIII).

[2] Blok, Geschiedenis, VI, 326.

Yorke was satisfied to report to Lord Suffolk about a year later (July 10, 1779) that the States of Holland had taken no notice of the letter from the American agents in Paris to the Grand Pensionary (Sparks MSS., LXXII).

[3] Franklin, Lee, and Adams to Dumas, September 27, 1778 (Wharton, II, 747, 748).

[4] Wharton, II, 362, 363.

10, 1778), Franklin and Arthur Lee informed Dumas that John Adams, having shortly before arrived at Paris as the successor of Silas Deane, then recalled to the United States, had told them of the resolution of Congress to send a minister to the Netherlands. Though there was the best disposition toward the United Provinces in America, the measure, according to Adams' report, had been postponed for fear that the reception of an American envoy might inconvenience the States General at present, on account of the still existing connections with Great Britain.[1] That the apprehensions of Congress in this respect were well founded is evident from a letter of van der Capellen toward the close of the year in which he stated that the time seemed distant when the States General would receive an American minister. Except in Amsterdam the English party was still too strong in the United Provinces.[2]

It is interesting to note what John Adams said in this connection of the United Provinces and their relations to the United States. He held that the similitude of manners, of religion, and in some respects of constitution; the analogy between the means by which the United Provinces and the United States arrived at independence; but above all the attractions of commercial interest would infallibly draw them together. This connection would probably not show itself in a public manner before peace or a near prospect of peace, because too many motives of fear or interest placed the Hollanders in a dependence on England. Nevertheless, if the King of Prussia could be induced to take the Americans by the hand, his great influence in the United Provinces might contribute greatly to conciliate the friendship of the latter for the United States. Loans of money and the operations of commercial agents or societies would be the first threads of connection.

From the inquiries of the commissioners at Paris, Adams said further, it appeared that some money might be

---

[1] Wharton, II, 545, 546.
[2] Van der Capellen to Erkelens, December 7, 1778 (Beaufort, *Brieven van der Capellen*, 82).

borrowed in the United Provinces, and from the success of several enterprises by way of St. Eustatia it seemed that the trade between the two countries was likely to increase, and Congress might think it expedient to send a minister to the Hague. If they should, it would be proper to give him a discretionary power to produce his commission, or not to show it, as he should find his mission likely to succeed, and to give him full powers and clear instructions concerning the borrowing of money. As to the man himself, he should have consummate prudence with caution and discretion that would be proof against every trial.[1]

As late as February, 1780, Adams had to inform Congress that an American minister was much wished for in the United Provinces but that he might not yet be received publicly.[2] All efforts to bring about closer financial, commercial, or diplomatic relations between the two republics had up to this point completely failed.

---

[1] John Adams to the President of Congress, August 4, 1779 (Wharton, III, 281, 282).

[2] Same to same, February 27, 1780 (ibid., III, 526).

CHAPTER V.

ENGLISH AGGRESSIONS AND, DUTCH DEFIANCE.

Since the last war between Great Britain and France[1] the United Provinces had gained a considerable part of that trade with France which was formerly in the hands of England. An extended commercial intercourse had been going on, ever since, between the Republic and French ports. Dutch vessels carried to France, together with many other goods, large cargoes of ship-building materials and naval munitions, which were purchased by the Dutch mostly from the northern countries. Corresponding quantities of merchandise were taken back in return, so that in fact this trade had become one of the principal branches of Dutch commerce.[2] While the carrying trade of the United Provinces had thus been steadily increasing, their naval strength as a belligerent power had since the great wars of the seventeenth century declined to the same degree.[3] How weak their position in this respect was may be judged from the number and state of their war vessels. In the sea battles of the eighteenth century ships of sixty and more cannon were considered most effective. Of such vessels England had 122, France 63, and Spain 62. The United Provinces possessed only 11, which, besides, were older than those of the other nations mentioned.[4] It was evident that after such neglect of her navy, the Republic in times of war would be at the mercy of her seafaring neighbors.

By a treaty concluded between England and the United Provinces in 1674 a novel principle had been introduced in the naval intercourse of the two countries, namely, that in

---

[1] 1756–1763.
[2] Cérisier, Observations Impartiales d'un Vrai Hollandois, p. 1.
[3] Fitzmaurice, Shelburne, 112.
[4] Colenbrander, Patriottentijd, I, 153.

case of war free ships made free goods. According to this stipulation either country was allowed to carry in its vessels —with exception of contraband of war—goods of a nation with which the other was at war. Naval provisions and materials for the construction of ships were not to be considered contraband by the contracting parties and were therefore exempt from seizure. All effects, however, found on an enemy's vessel, even if belonging to one of the two contracting countries, might be confiscated.[1]

While this treaty had rendered large profits to Great Britain whenever the Netherlands were at war, she was opposed to its stipulations in her own wars and especially since the beginning of her troubles with the American colonies. " I took care," said Yorke after an interview with the ministers of Holland in 1776, " to be very particular about the inadmissibility of any claim to the abused stipulation of *free ships, free goods* in the Treaty of 1674," and he added with satisfaction that both the Grand Pensionary and the griffier had admitted that the treaty could not with justice be pleaded in cases of rebellion.[2]

These remarks regarding the commercial and naval relations of the United Provinces with France on the one hand and with England on the other will show the great influence which the events described in this chapter had on the American Revolution. France, after her alliance with the United States, could give effective assistance to the latter only by having at her disposal a powerful fleet of war vessels. A ready and large supply of ship materials and naval munitions was required to strengthen her naval power. It was only natural that the United Provinces should continue to furnish these supplies, since England, still bound by the treaty of 1674, was not expected to be able to object to it. Great Britain, however, confident in her naval superiority, set aside

---

[1] Cérisier, Observations Impartiales, 33; Fitzmaurice, Shelburne, 112.

[2] Yorke to Suffolk, August 6, 1776 (Sparks MSS., LXXII).
This report was made on the occasion of the restoration of the Dutch ship " Judith Aletta " by a sentence of the English Court of Admiralty.

her treaty obligations and used every means to intervene in the commercial relations between France and the Netherlands.

Already in the beginning of the American Revolution frequent searches by the English of vessels coming from Dutch ports aroused deep indignation and apprehension among the merchants of Amsterdam and Rotterdam. In the spring of 1777, the rumor prevailed that the British authorities had issued orders to search all vessels leaving the ports of the United Provinces.[1] Later in the year the English began to take Dutch vessels not only in Europe, but also in the West Indies,[2] which measure brought forth a clamor from the merchants of Amsterdam for the protection of their commerce and an official complaint from the Republic presented by Count Welderen to the court of St. James.[3] A convoy to the West Indies was granted by the States General in November, much to the disappointment and dissatisfaction of Yorke,[4] who must have seen in this step, proposed by the States of Holland and sanctioned by the States General, an alarming proof of the weakening of the English party in the United Provinces. The citizens of Amsterdam had gained a decided victory in this matter, and, anxious to increase their influence still more, desired to be represented at the court of St. James by a diplomat of their own choice. Count Welderen, they said, did not show enough fervor in supporting their interests, and they suggested to the States General the sending of an ambassador chosen from among the magistrates of Amsterdam. The petition, however, was not considered, and Welderen remained in his official posi-

---

[1] Vauguyon to Vergennes, April 19, 1777 (Sparks MSS., LXXXII).
[2] Dumas to the Committee on Foreign Affairs, August 22, 1777 (Wharton, II, 378).
[3] Yorke to Suffolk, private, September 24, 1777 (Sparks MSS., LXXII) ; Dumas to the Committee on Foreign Affairs, October 14, 1777 (Wharton, II, 408).
[4] Resolutions of the States General, November 3, 1777 (Sparks MSS., CIII) ; Yorke to Suffolk, November 7 and 19, 1777 (Sparks MSS., LXXII).
The convoy sailed in December (above, p. 58).

tion in London.[1]   Dumas, in discussing the political situation in the Republic, said he had been told by the pensionary
that the United Provinces owed the conservation of their
liberty to the noble resistance of the United States, because the English were trying to establish despotism in the
Republic.   Their faction, he proceeded, was defeated now
together with its principal supporter, Sir Joseph Yorke,
whose influence, he thought, was much reduced.[2]   It is not
surprising that under these circumstances the English party,
and especially the British ambassador, were constantly ap-
prehending that the Dutch might not remain neutral.
Yorke pretended to have news from Paris to that effect.[3]
The Prussian envoy at the Hague also informed his king
that after the rupture between France and England, the
United Provinces, it was generally feared, would only
with difficulty be able to remain neutral.[4]   England would
probably claim the help stipulated by treaties, but the party
of neutrality would be victorious, since the actions of Great
Britain had not been such as to make new friends in the
United Provinces or to strengthen their old ones there.[5]

When matters between Great Britain and France grew
more and more serious, the former began to look for aid
to the United Provinces.   The state of the Dutch military
as well as naval forces was, however, so deplorably bad that
direct assistance could hardly be expected.   Yorke did his
best to induce the Prince of Orange to have effective
measures taken for the augmentation of the Dutch army.
William V, a willing tool in the hands of the English, was
found, also on this occasion, sincerely attached to George
III and the cause of Great Britain.   The prince's efforts,

---

[1] Thulemeier to Frederick II, January 23, 1778 (Bancroft MSS.,
Prussia and Holland).
[2] Dumas to the American Commissioners, January 23, 1778 (Arthur
Lee MSS., Harvard University).
[3] Yorke to Suffolk, February 10, 1778 (Sparks MSS., LXXII).
[4] Thulemeier to Frederick II, March 27, 1778 (Bancroft MSS.,
Prussia and Holland).
[5] Same to same, March 31, 1778 (ibid.).

however, threatened to be nullified by the stubborn resistance of Amsterdam.[1]

Yorke received stricter instructions for his conduct in this case. The king, he was told, had seen with great concern how little prospect there was for the adoption of the Prince of Orange's proposals regarding the augmentation of the Dutch forces. Since the independence of the Republic depended on such a measure, the ambassador would be sensible of the necessity of putting her forces on a respectable footing at the present moment. He was asked to consider that the propriety and utility of enforcing every argument possible to encourage the stadtholder and the Dutch ministers for this object must be obvious. The States General could not consider their own defenceless state as consistent with those maxims of prudence and sound policy which brought the Republic to the degree of prosperity and wealth which it enjoyed. The letter then came more to the point, suggesting that in the war between Great Britain and France, Great Britain would have a right to call for those succors to which she was entitled by treaty. In this case the Republic would make " but an indifferent figure in the eyes of Europe " if she should not only be incapable of fulfilling her engagements, but even be unable to defend herself. The instructions, in conclusion, said that Great Britain would never permit the subjects of the Republic to become the carriers for England's enemies, and that the old claim of free ships, free goods would never be admitted.[2]

The ambassador, conscious of the weakness of his position, did not hesitate to call the attention of his superiors to it. His antagonists in the United Provinces, he said, had a great advantage over him, for while he recommended vigorous measures and showed the danger to which the Republic was exposed, the French ambassador recommended quiet and ease without expense except for the protection of commerce. As soon as the Prince of Orange had recommended

---

[1] Yorke to Suffolk, March 31, April 3 and 7, 1778 (Sparks MSS., LXXII).
[2] Suffolk to Yorke, April 14, 1778 (Sparks MSS., LXXII).

the augmentation of troops, Vauguyon had told some principal members of the government that the United Provinces had nothing to fear from France, either in the Netherlands or upon the lower Rhine, since His Most Christian
Majesty wished for peace, but that the dignity as well as the
interests of the Republic required a strong navy. On account of these conditions, Yorke had to arm himself with
patience in the prosecution of the business, and he implored
his superiors to do likewise. He suggested that he might be
obliged to request orders for formally demanding military
aid, for if the Dutch violated one treaty, because they would
or could not give assistance, they had no right to claim the
privileges of 1674 which were so notoriously detrimental to
Great Britain because of free ships and free goods.[1] The
military proposition of the stadtholder had been defeated,
principally by the resistance of Amsterdam, which city gave
as reason for her attitude that by the increase of the Dutch
army the jealousy of some neighboring power might be
excited while, on the other hand, no real protection was offered to the Republic. Thulemeier no doubt was right when
he suspected that France had had a hand in the game.[2]

To what degree the decline of England's reputation had
progressed at this period is shown in a confidential letter
written by Yorke. It had become a fashion, he said, to
look upon Great Britain as unable to maintain the contest
with her former colonies in America. He attributed this to
the many libels published in England. Some fortunate
event was absolutely necessary, either in America or at sea,
to restore in the political world the appearance which Great
Britain had "such a right to assume." Then her neighbors
would soon speak again "the language of respect and
friendship."[3] The ambassador, of course, judged chiefly
from the conduct of the Dutch and perhaps from the attitude of Vauguyon and his followers in the United Prov-

---

[1] Yorke to Suffolk, April 21, 1778 (Sparks MSS., LXXII).
[2] Thulemeier to Frederick II, April 21, 1778 (Bancroft MSS.,
Prussia and Holland).
[3] Yorke to Suffolk, private, May 29, 1778 (Sparks MSS., LXXII).

inces. He was highly indignant at the French ambassador's achievements and blamed him almost solely for the discontent which was spreading more and more in the Republic at the English aggressions at sea. France was taking advantage of every trifling event, in order to incite the Dutch merchants to complain.[1] The smallest outrage of a privateer at sea was swelled into an article for the Dutch gazettes to represent England as bent upon ill treating the trade and subjects of the Republic.[2] Of course, the French party used to the best possible advantage the weapons which England herself furnished them so abundantly.

Sir Joseph was, at this time, almost in despair and highly discontented with everything and everybody in the United Provinces, but especially with the Prince of Orange. "His Majesty's ambassador," he wrote, "is very singularly circumstanced in such a Situation. His Instructions, the Interest of his Country, his own Wishes, all unite to bind him to the Stadtholderian Party, and yet the little Union which is permitted in that Party, and the total want of Concert, leave him almost without assistance to counteract the Ambassador of France. The great difficulty of all proceeds from the want of firmness in the Prince of Orange, who with the best Intentions, a thorough knowledge of his Country's and his own Interest, and convinced of the existence of the Intrigue and its consequences, takes no step whatever to stem the Torrent, but contents himself with thinking and saying, that tho' he has not the force to carry what he wishes, he has however a *Liberum Veto* to reject whatever may be improperly proposed by others."

To bring about a change and to rouse the Prince of Orange "at least to a sense of his own Danger, and of his Duty to himself, his Family and his Country," Yorke proposed a curious method which clearly shows his misconception of the political situation. He suggested that Frederick the Great should be induced to influence the stadtholder,

[1] Yorke to Suffolk, July 28, 1778 (Sparks MSS., LXXII).
[2] Same to same, private, August 28, 1778 (ibid.).

basing this odd recommendation on the supposition that the King of Prussia owed gratitude to England, because George III had, in Frederick's existing contest with Austria over the Bavarian succession, "openly and generously espoused the Prussian Cause." This proposal, however, was not acted upon by the English government.[1]

The hostilities between England and France began in June, 1778,[2] and with them serious troubles for the United Provinces. The aggressions of the English became more and more open and also more frequent. In July they began to stop Dutch vessels in the English Channel. In the precarious position of the English this action was surprising. In the midst of the dangers, Thulemeier wrote, which menaced Great Britain from all sides, the English continued to heap impositions on the Dutch. Recently five large merchant vessels of the latter had been taken as prizes.[3] Nothing could be more welcome to France than these actions of the enemy. Her consuls and agents at foreign ports were charged to make public Great Britain's treatment of the United Provinces and to announce that it was very unsafe for Dutch ships to sail without convoy. Amsterdam urged that the Dutch navy be increased in order to free the Republic from this tyranny. Yorke remarked thereupon, "This country is running headlong into a dependence on the Court of Versailles."[4] On September 14,

---

[1] Yorke to Suffolk, August 25, 1778, most private (Colenbrander, Patriottentijd, I, 134, 374-376).

The answer which Yorke received left no doubt concerning the relations between the courts of St. James and Berlin: "His Prussian Majesty confines his Expressions of Cordiality to H. M. in his quality of Elector only; all his Communications in the Dispute with the Court of Vienna have been limited to H. M.'s Electoral Minister; the Servants of the Crown have been strictly excluded, and His Language with regard to this Country is very little changed. Many things therefore must happen (to speak openly to Your Excellency) before He can be enough considered as a Friend to be applied to in the Manner you suggest" (Suffolk to Yorke, September 1, 1778, most private, in Colenbrander, Patriottentijd, I, 134, 376).

[2] Colenbrander, Patriottentijd, I, 129.

[3] Thulemeier to Frederick II, September 1, 1778 (Bancroft MSS., Prussia and Holland).

[4] Yorke to Suffolk, September 8, 1778 (Sparks MSS., LXXII).

the States General received a lengthy petition from the merchants of Amsterdam and Rotterdam, asking for protection against the excesses of English war vessels and privateers.[1] The seizing of Dutch vessels by the English, however, continued. Before the end of September twenty-nine had been taken.[2]

In consequence of a complaint transmitted to the court of St. James by Count Welderen, some Dutch vessels had been released and Yorke reported from the Hague that this measure had a good effect in the United Provinces for the moment.[3] He was, however, very much mistaken, since Welderen, by direction of the States General, handed another memorandum in much stronger terms to the English cabinet transmitting the grievances of the Dutch merchants. The States General, he wrote, had seen with satisfaction that the vessels "Martina" and "Hendrik en Alida" (taken when sailing from Curaçao and St. Eustatia directly toward the Republic), the "Debora en Maria," "de Hoop," and "Adriana" (when bound from the United Provinces to France) had been released, since it removed the fear that England intended to ruin the commerce of the United Provinces. On the other hand, Great Britain, so far, had not offered any indemnity for the cost and damages occasioned by the seizure, and the captors, it seemed, had not received any mark of displeasure from His Majesty the King. The States General had learned with the greatest surprise that English vessels possessing commissions from the king had repeatedly violated Dutch territory in America, and especially had almost blockaded the rivers of Essequibo and Demerari. There were also other complaints of the capture and other molestations of Dutch vessels by British men-of-war and privateers, in violation of the treaty of 1674. The United Provinces had no other resources than

---

[1] Sparks Dutch Papers; Thulemeier to Frederick II, September 18, 1778 (Bancroft MSS., Prussia and Holland).

[2] Thulemeier to Frederick II, September 25, 1778 (Bancroft MSS., Prussia and Holland).

[3] Yorke to Suffolk, September 15, 1778 (Sparks MSS., LXXII).

commerce and navigation, and the welfare of the Republic therefore depended wholly upon the freedom of her ships. The Dutch trusted that His Majesty would disapprove of the action of his subjects, contrary to the express provisions of the treaties, and that all Dutch vessels seized would be released and an appropriate indemnity paid which should cover the real cost and damages caused by their capture and delay. In conclusion Welderen said that the States General were confident His Majesty would find means for rendering impossible the recurrence of such violations of Dutch territory and Dutch navigation.[1]

The Dutch feared that by the interruption of their navigation their credit, the basis of every commercial country, might be undermined. Freight and commission trade, the most important contributors to the revenues of the United Provinces, were suffering most, and the merchants of the United Provinces became alarmed lest those branches of their commerce might wholly pass to rival countries which were able to defend their interests effectively against England. It was dangerous to suffer the molestation of commerce for another reason. There was a possibility, or rather a probability, that France might take countermeasures.[2] In fact, the French ambassador was working in this direction. Louis XVI, he declared to the Dutch ministers, was pleased with the recent action of the United Provinces regarding the defence of their navigation and promised the assistance of France. Vauguyon, however, stated that the regulations which France had published regarding the navigation of neutral powers would be revoked if England did not adopt similar measures within six months. The Dutch flag could not be respected by France if this was not done by Great Britain.[3]

The English, realizing that they were rapidly losing ground in the United Provinces, released some Dutch ships, and

---

[1] Welderen's memorial of September 27/28, 1778 (Bancroft MSS., America, Holland, and England).
[2] Cérisier, Observations Impartiales, 39 ff.
[3] Yorke to Suffolk, September 25, 1778 (Sparks MSS., LXXII).

orders were given for the dismissal of the rest except those which had naval or warlike stores on board. The British government contemplated also the issue of positive directions which would effectually prevent the taking of the Dutch vessels destined for French ports or the United States, but not carrying contraband. Naval munitions of every description were still to be seized, together with the vessels on which they were found. Whatever might be the consequences, every means would be exerted to prevent His Majesty's enemies from being supplied with such stores. Yorke was directed to call the attention of the Dutch government to the treaty of alliance with the States General of the year 1668. According to its stipulations any hostile act against the King of Great Britain and his subjects would form a casus foederis, entitling England to call upon the United Provinces for assistance. Yorke was to explain to the Dutch that this treaty was not less binding for them than the commercial treaty of 1674 for the English. The inference from this could be easily drawn. The United Provinces, upon requisition, would not be in a position to render the stipulated assistance, and Great Britain, consequently, would not be obliged to keep the treaty of 1674. The ambassador was directed to express these views of the English cabinet very cautiously and without taking any public step, in order to avoid altercation or disagreeable discussions.[1]

In the meantime, the complaints of Dutch merchants to the States General regarding English outrages at sea continued. Yorke reported that during the two days preceding the date of his letter no less than thirteen such complaints had been presented. He asserted that the French were intriguing in Amsterdam with the object of exciting public opinion to a point where the magistrates would have to yield. The latter would thus be compelled to ask the States General for protection against England and satisfaction for the losses sustained. The French were not scru-

---

[1] Suffolk to Yorke, September 29, 1778 (Sparks MSS., LXXII, CIII).

pulous in their means for attaining this end, declaring that
Great Britain had no other view than to annihilate Dutch
trade and navigation, and representing acts of violence committed by English adventurers as acts of the British government.[1]

That the complaints of the United Provinces, however,
were not wholly unjustified, as Yorke tried to represent
them, is seen from the fact that in October forty-two vessels
had been taken by the English.[2]   Moreover, the States General were rather reluctant in voicing the public opinion in
this matter.   When the merchants of Friesland sent up a
petition similar to those of the citizens of the province of
Holland and demanded by their deputies new instructions
to Count Welderen, the States General refused, on the
ground that this request contained no other matter than
what had already been brought to the knowledge of the
English government.[3]

France now took a step further in her policy regarding
the United Provinces.   Vauguyon, according to instructions
from Paris, called upon the Prince of Orange and the Dutch
ministers, representing to them the necessity " of supporting
their trade to the Baltic and insisting upon the stipulations
of the Treaty of 1674, respecting naval stores."   That those
articles should be safe under the flag of the Republic, he said,
was of the greatest importance, and if England pursued her
present course, France would certainly alter her conduct and
visit Dutch vessels with the same vigor.   He inquired
whether or not the Dutch would protect, by convoys, their
vessels carrying naval stores, adding that France would
efficiently support such defensive measures.   The ambassador was answered that representations had already been
made to Great Britain.[4]

---

[1] Yorke to Suffolk, October 2, 1778 (Sparks MSS., LXXII).
    Regarding the Dutch grievances see also Thulemeier's report of
the same date to Frederick II (Bancroft MSS., Prussia and Holland) ; Cérisier, Observations Impartiales, 39 ff.
[2] Thulemeier to Frederick II, October 6, 1778 (Bancroft MSS.,
Prussia and Holland) ; Colenbrander, Patriottentijd, I, 133.
[3] Yorke to Suffolk, October 10, 1778 (Sparks MSS., LXXII).
[4] Yorke to Suffolk, October 16, 1778 (Sparks MSS., LXXII).

The official English answer to the Dutch representations arrived at the Hague, but brought no change in the existing conditions. Count Welderen had been informed by Lord Suffolk that the English admiralty was directed to allow free transit to all Dutch merchant vessels, except those carrying contraband goods, and especially ship-building timber. It cannot be surprising that this answer did not satisfy the Dutch. It was rumored, according to an announcement of the admiralty at Amsterdam, after the beginning of November, that vessels bound for France or England would be granted such convoys as they required.[1] Great Britain was now ready to buy at an appraised value the naval munitions seized on Dutch vessels and brought to her ports. Besides she would pay the freight on the cargoes and compensate the proprietors for all expenses and losses occasioned by the detention of their vessels. Investigation regarding the actions of British captains in the territories of the United Provinces in America, especially on the rivers of Essequibo and Demerari, was also promised, and any culpables would be punished.[2]

The public mind in the United Provinces, however, was aroused too much to be appeased by Great Britain's weak attempts at reconciliation. Amsterdam continued her clamoring for protection,[3] and anonymous pamphlets were widely circulated, irritating the people still more. The reason, said an anonymous author, why England persecuted the Dutch was innate hatred and her jealousy of Dutch commerce and navigation. Even some of his countrymen tried to justify the hostile attitude of the English. The

---

[1] Thulemeier to Frederick II, October 16, 1778 (Bancroft MSS., Prussia and Holland).

[2] Suffolk to Welderen, October 19, 1778 (Bancroft MSS., America, Holland, and England); see also Davies, History of Holland, III, 445–446, concerning England's attitude with regard to the Dutch timber trade.

The promise regarding Essequibo and Demerari was repeated in December, 1778 (Suffolk to Welderen, December 11, 1778, in Bancroft MSS., America, Holland, and England).

[3] Thulemeier to Frederick II, October 20, 1778 (Bancroft MSS., Prussia and Holland).

pretext was often heard that the Dutch ships seized by the English had been carrying forbidden goods, but this could not be maintained as long as it was not shown that all of them had contraband on board. England, of course, did not like to have the United Provinces provide France with material for ship building. Had it not been equally hard for the Dutch to see Great Britain furnish the same materials to France from the treaty of 1674 to the peace of Nymwegen? The question was not what was liked, but what was permitted by the treaties.

It was furthermore said, continued this writer, that Dutch navigation from harbor to harbor in France strengthened England's foe, but he did not see how a reproach could be constructed from this, since the Republic was living in peace with France, and an order from the Dutch authorities forbidding this trade would be a breach of neutrality. He would also not let pass the argument pronounced by friends of England in the United Provinces that a number of French ports were blockaded by British vessels and therefore Dutch vessels must not enter them, especially when loaded with ship timber, because in this case proof would be required that the ports were really and efficiently blockaded. It was further said that England's attitude was justified by the failure of the United Provinces to furnish assistance in the war of 1756 to 1763. This was contrary to facts, for the Dutch had assisted Great Britain both by troops and ships during the last war. In return the English had seized so many Dutch ships that the United Provinces suffered more from England than from France, then their enemy. In conclusion he recommended as means for bringing about a change: frequent use of convoys; joining other nations, especially the United States of America, in the protection of commerce; pleading freedom of navigation, within the spirit of the treaties; and finally the strengthening of the forces of the Republic by all means.[1]

---

[1] Onderzoek van Groot-Brittanjes Gedrag, 140–147.

Such clever work on the part of the Patriots[1] did not remain without results. The appeals to the Dutch authorities for protection against England became more and more urgent. On October 23, 1778, the merchants of Amsterdam, Dordrecht, and Rotterdam addressed another petition to the States General expressing their dissatisfaction with the answer of the English ministry, and, pointing out once more the immense damage done to the United Provinces by Great Britain's proceedings regarding the timber trade with France, demanded redress of their grievances.[2]

In order to come to a friendly understanding with the United Provinces, if possible, Yorke was charged by the Foreign Office in London to negotiate with the Dutch.[3] In execution of this instruction he handed, on November 2, 1778, a memorial to the States General. Though, he said, the French threatened to invade Great Britain and her territories, the king, his master, still refrained from calling upon the United Provinces for the assistance stipulated by the most solemn treaties, and especially that of 1678, and the separate article of the treaty of 1716. All that was requested at present was a conference for discussing various articles in question in the treaties. It was not at all the intention of the king to disturb the customary commerce of the United Provinces with France, except in military and naval munitions. It was to be hoped that the sense of justice of the United Provinces and their friendship for Great Britain would prevent them from having naval munitions carried into France under the cover of convoys.[4]

The American agent at the Hague, learning of Yorke's

---

[1] In this connection van der Kemp, one of the foremost Patriots in the United Provinces, must be mentioned. Concerning the question of unlimited convoys he published anonymously a Collection of State Papers, with a preface by " Junius Brutus Secundus Frisco." Of him van der Capellen wrote on May 12, 1780, " The unlimited convoy and the whole Patriot party owe more than is known to this clergyman " (Fairchild, van der Kemp, 45).

[2] Sparks Dutch Papers, I, 88.

[3] Thulemeier to Frederick II, October 27, 1778 (Bancroft MSS., Prussia and Holland).

[4] Secret Resolution of the States General, November 2, 1778 (Bancroft MSS., America, Holland, and England; Sparks MSS., CIII).

step, predicted that the latter would find in Amsterdam formidable adversaries who were firmly resolved on an absolute refusal of the English requests. Dumas found also that the irritation against England was even growing, especially among the nobility.[1] The States General did not hasten their reply to Yorke. The Grand Pensionary, however, told him that convoys might perhaps be refused, but that the value of a conference must be regarded as very doubtful, since the stipulations of the treaty of 1674 were distinct, and as to the other treaties, the Republic was not at all obliged to furnish assistance.[2]

This friction between Great Britain and her ally naturally tended to further the cause of the United States. "In short," wrote the American commissioners at this time, "we see no probability of England's forming any alliance against America in all Europe, or, indeed, against France; whereas, on the other side, from the astonishing preparations of Spain, the family compact, and other circumstances, and from the insolent tyranny of the English over the Dutch and their consequent resentment, which has shown itself in formidable remonstrances as well as advances towards a treaty with us, there is reason to believe that if Great Britain perseveres in the war, both of these powers will at length be involved in it."[3]

Correct as this view proved to be in the end, there was no prospect yet of the United Provinces joining the war. England knew the feebleness of the Republic too well to be afraid of this. As to a treaty with the United States, even France was convinced that the Dutch would take such a step

---

[1] Dumas to the Commissioners in Paris, November 4, 1778 (Wharton, II, 829).

[2] Colenbrander, Patriottentijd, I, 135, 136.

Colenbrander remarks to this: "We see how small the board was on which the government was stepping now, and how no balustrade was there to hold on. A nice conduct, to insist upon a treaty which guaranteed very extended and advantageous privileges to the merchants, and then to refuse all protection . . . The denial of convoy would have had reason only if England had demanded it as a temporary measure pending the negotiations regarding the treaty . . . ."

[3] Franklin, Lee, and Adams to the President of Congress, Passy, November 7, 1778 (Wharton, II, 831, 832).

only if they could do it without running any risk.[1] Yorke's memorial of November 2 had been referred to the committee of naval affairs for examination and report. This committee was now of the opinion that the conference asked for by the British ambassador concerning the meaning of the treaties relative to naval stores should be refused, but that the admiralty should not grant convoys for the protection of these materials. It was thought by many that Amsterdam might be able to thwart these plans by insisting upon the strict observance of the treaties. "Otherwise," the American agent at the Hague remarked, "the servile submission of the nation to the lash of the English will expose it to that of the French also, who will deprive it of the privileges it has heretofore enjoyed in their country, and will seize its vessels, after the example of the English."[2]

Both parties in the United Provinces now worked in every way possible to have the decision of the States General favorable to their respective views. Amsterdam, without doubt, was most deeply interested in the question of convoys. Large speculations had been made there in the business of furnishing naval stores to France, and during the preceding summer such large quantities of munitions had been purchased by the merchants that money became scarce in that city. One of the means by which the French party at Amsterdam expected to influence the government of the United Provinces was by causing the insurance firms henceforth not to insure Dutch vessels destined for France or the French colonies. This trick, which was expected to create a general cry for convoys, failed because of a counterstroke of the British party. The rich banker Hope, an English partisan, temporarily established himself as insurer, which brought the regular insurance firms quickly back to their business. The partisans of Great Britain on their part did not disdain to put into circulation anonymous incendiary pamphlets. In

---

[1] French Minister of Foreign Affairs to Vauguyon, November 9, 1778 (Sparks MSS., LXXXIII).
[2] Dumas to the Commissioners at Paris, November 10, 1778 (Wharton, II, 834, 835).

one of them it was said that Dutch merchants could lose three vessels out of four destined to carry naval munitions to France, and still make a profit.[1]

The merchants of Amsterdam began to call upon the stadtholder, making him personally responsible for the consequences of a refusal to grant unlimited convoy. Jean de Neufville, their speaker, requested efficient measures for the protection of the commercial interests of the country, referring to the prince as the admiral-general of the United Provinces and emphasizing the fact that a number of war vessels were already lying in the harbors, ready for action. The Prince of Orange answered evasively, that, for the year 1779, the construction and fitting out of thirty-two vessels had already been requested, and that every attention would be paid to the protection of commerce and navigation.[2] The States of Holland, deliberating on Yorke's memorial of November 2, did not at first reach a conclusion, but decided to determine by the majority of voices whether or not convoys should be granted for naval stores. A protest against such a measure was filed by the members from Amsterdam, led by Pensionary van Berckel, on the ground that the constitution required unanimity in this case, but they were overruled. At the same time Vauguyon informed the principal officers of the government, and through them the pensionaries of the cities, that Louis XVI expected the Republic to cause her flag to be respected by protecting her commerce according to the English-Dutch treaty of 1674. Other-

---

[1] Colenbrander, Patriottentijd, I, 136.

In footnote 3, ibid., Colenbrander says, " Thulemeier deelt het pamfletje mee bij zijn dépêche van 24 November 1778." Undoubtedly this pamphlet is identical with the one which G. Bancroft found with Thulemeier's report of November 10, 1778. In Bancroft's MSS., Prussia and Holland, these remarks appear at the end of that letter: " Accompanying this dispatch is an interesting paper ' Examen des plaintes des négocians d'Amsterdam au sujet de la saisie des vaisseaux Hollandais chargés de bois de construction pour la France.' . . . It has no date and no signature, but from its contents one would conclude it was written by Yorke. . . . It is an argument in favor of Great Britain upon the construction of the treaty of 1674."

[2] Blok, Geschiedenis, VI, 327.

wise, the ambassador declared, "the king is immovably fixed in his determination to deprive the [Dutch] nation of those advantages which his majesty, out of pure kindness, and without any obligation by treaty, has hitherto permitted it to enjoy in the ports of France."[1] The fear of England, however, was still too great; the assembly of the province of Holland refused the employment of convoys by merely a majority of voices.[2] Amsterdam protested, declaring the resolution void, since, according to the constitution, it could be passed only by a unanimous vote.

The English party triumphed, and Sir Joseph Yorke hastened to send a special messenger to London to transmit the news. Dumas expected that the English government would boast of this victory in Parliament and in the press, while the protest of the city of Amsterdam would probably not be mentioned. He gives an interesting description of the sentiment prevailing among the deputies after this curious session. "I will only add," he said, "that to-morrow morning the members from the great city [Amsterdam] will depart, and with them all the glory of Belgium [sic]. The others are ashamed of their own work, dare not boast of it, and hang down their heads. It has even been attempted to circulate the report that the famous resolution was adopted unanimously and in conformity with the wishes of the great city."[3]

Deputations were again sent to the States General, the Prince of Orange, and the ministers of the Republic,[4] but not from Amsterdam only. The States of Zealand entered officially with the States General a request for convoys to France.[5] Still the resolution which excluded from convoys

---

[1] Dumas to the Commissioners at Paris, November 13, 1778 (Wharton, II, 837).
[2] Thulemeier to Frederick II, November 13, 1778 (Bancroft MSS., Prussia and Holland).
[3] Dumas to the Commissioners at Paris, November 20, 1778 (Wharton, II, 843).
[4] Thulemeier to Frederick II, November 20, 1778 (Bancroft MSS., Prussia and Holland).
[5] Secret Resolution of the States General, November 13, 1778 (Sparks MSS., CIII).

8

only masts and ship timber, but no other naval munitions,
was passed by the States General.[1] Serious consequences
were feared. The Patriots like van der Capellen were
shocked and indignant. Amsterdam protested[2] and was
expected to refuse payment of her contributions to the expenses of the Republic, amounting to about one quarter of
the whole, and even to ask assistance of France, which
would certainly be granted. The latter power was likely to
execute her threats of seizing, in her turn, English property
on board Dutch ships, and of depriving them of the privileges they enjoyed in French ports.[3] These considerations
probably caused the Dutch government to withdraw everything that looked like submission to the English demands. Count Welderen, therefore, had to hand to the
British government a declaration which contained only the
refusal of the conference asked for. The resolution concerning convoys was not mentioned at all.[4]

The old question, whether the army or navy was to be
increased, was soon taken up again in the United Provinces.
"The friends to themselves and to us," wrote Arthur Lee
from Paris, "are for augmenting their marine; the purchased advocates of England and the dependents of the
Stadtholder are for increasing their army." The French
party, of course, was eager to strengthen the Dutch navy
in order to be able to fight England at sea. The English
party, on the other hand, was anxious to increase the army
of the United Provinces so as to meet any attack from
France on land. The latter seemed to be determined to
carry out her threats regarding the seizure of English goods
on board neutral vessels,[5] but, in reality, she was much more

---

[1] Colenbrander, Patriottentijd, I, 137; Doniol, Histoire, III, 718.
[2] Van der Capellen to Erkelens; same to Governor Trumbull, December 7, 1778 (Beaufort, Brieven van der Capellen, 82 ff.).
[3] Dumas to the Committee on Foreign Affairs, December 3, 1778
(Wharton, II, 847).
[4] Colenbrander, Patriottentijd, I, 137.
[5] Arthur Lee to the Committee of Foreign Affairs, December 5,
1778 (Wharton, II, 850).
The provinces of Holland and Friesland, which depended chiefly
on commerce and ship-building, urged the increase of the navy;
Utrecht, Overyssel, Guelderland, and Zealand, under the influence

anxious to have the sending of Dutch cargoes of naval munitions to her ports continued.

Vauguyon obtained from his government the approval of a plan, conceived in connection with Amsterdam, for thwarting the consequences of the resolution. The preparations for carrying out the scheme were completed when the ambassador visited the city on December 2.[1] Five days later he presented a memorial to the States General in which a clear and precise explanation was requested whether or not the United Provinces were determined to maintain a perfect neutrality. The King of France would decide according to the answer of Their High Mightinesses whether to maintain or to annul the orders already given. Partiality would be manifested by the States General if they did not make the most strenuous exertions to procure for the Dutch flag all the freedom belonging to an independent state, and for their commerce all the respect which the law of nations and treaties secured to it. In the case of such a breach of neutrality His Majesty would be compelled to suspend not only the advantages which the United Provinces enjoyed as neutrals, but also the material and gratuitous favor which their commerce enjoyed in French ports.[2]

---

of the stadtholder, that of the army. A proposition brought forth by the Prince of Orange as a compromise, namely, to increase army and navy simultaneously, the former by fifty or sixty thousand men, the latter by fifty or sixty sails, was rejected by the States of Holland (Davies, History of Holland, III, 450; Resolutions of Holland and Westfriesland, March 10, 1779, in Sparks Dutch Papers; David Hartley, March 12, 1779, in Hansard, Parliamentary History, XX, 277).

Finally, the demand regarding the land forces was entirely refused, while the building of only thirty-two vessels was granted; but this number was soon augmented to fifty-two (Kampen, Verkorte Geschiedenis, II, 293).

[1] Colenbrander, Patriottentijd, I, 137.

[2] Wharton, II, 854, 855; Bancroft MSS., America, Holland, and England; Nieuwe Nederlandsche Jaerboeken, 1779, p. 164; Sparks Dutch Papers; Blok, Geschiedenis, VI, 329; Colenbrander, Patriottentijd, I, 137; Kampen, Verkorte Geschiedenis, II, 292 ff.

On July 26, 1778, France had issued liberal regulations regarding the shipping of all those countries which, within six months, would give proofs of their neutrality (Colenbrander, Patriottentijd, I, 137, note). The United Provinces, of course, enjoyed the advantages from these regulations besides the special privileges that had been conceded to them.

Besides taking this official step, Vauguyon accentuated in private conversations the determination of his royal master to take away from the Dutch trade all the privileges granted, in case the answer of the States General should not be satisfactory. He told the stadtholder very plainly that the latter's personal welfare, together with that of his family, might depend on the resolution of the States General and endeavored to get the Princess of Orange to influence her husband in favor of the French cause. He reached Princess Wilhelmine through her lady-in-waiting, Fräulein von Danckelmann, but was unsuccessful, since Wilhelmine answered that she did not intend to interfere in matters of state.[1] The prospect of the compliance of the States General with the French king's demand was not bright. The committee which was appointed to deliberate on the answer to Vauguyon's memorial decided that no change should be made in the resolution concerning convoys. When the ambassador learned this he immediately sent a note to the Grand Pensionary demanding a precise answer, yes or no.[2] The English party, however, was again victorious. In the assembly of the province of Holland on December 19, an evasive answer had already been formulated, which merely expressed the desire of the United Provinces to maintain strict neutrality. The deputies of the city of Amsterdam protested[3] as on November 18; nevertheless the resolution

---

[1] Nijhoff, Brunswijk, 171, 308; Colenbrander, Patriottentijd, I, 137, 138.

[2] Secret Resolution of the States General, December 29, 1778 (Sparks MSS., CIII).

[3] The deputies of Amsterdam contended that even if the refusal of convoys for vessels carrying ship timber could be supported on any principle of law or justice, England would not be benefited by it, because those goods could be supplied to France equally well by Sweden, Denmark, and the other nations of the North. The measure would result only in a transfer of this valuable trade from the United Provinces to other nations.

The merchants of Friesland urged that they had hitherto employed above two thousand ships, chiefly in the timber trade which was now virtually annihilated (Davies, History of Holland, III, 449).

Cérisier in a pamphlet dated December 6, 1778, and entitled " Observations d'un Vrai Hollandois " defended the American cause, but at the same time admonished the Dutch to remain neutral.

was adopted by the States General. On December 30, the agent of the latter handed it to Vauguyon, who refused to accept it, "as not being such as the king demanded." It was then resolved to send the answer to Berkenrode, the Dutch envoy at Paris, with instructions to hand it to Louis XVI.[1]

The Prince of Orange, exasperated, now sought protection from Frederick the Great, King of Prussia. It appears that Vauguyon's intimation that the safety of the stadtholder and his family was in danger had greatly alarmed William. He described to the king the critical situation in which the United Provinces were placed, and tried to convince him that the resolution regarding convoys was not the outcome of partiality for England. Frederick was entreated to protect the stadtholder and his family, for fear that France would cause a revolution in the United Provinces in order to upset the present government and constitution, and to do away with the stadtholder's office. William requested also Prussia's assistance in case France should invade the Republic.[2]

Frederick, who was still involved in the Bavarian succession controversy, showed no inclination to become entangled in the contest between England and France. He answered evasively that William knew best the real interests of the Republic, which alone should be decisive in her present delicate position. He recommended that the stadtholder should consult the constitution of the United Provinces for guidance in this dilemma. The Princess of

---

[1] Dumas to the Commissioners at Paris, December 18, 1778 (Wharton, II, 860, 861); same to the Committee of Foreign Affairs, January 1, 1779 (ibid., II, 872–875); Vaterlandsche Historie, XXV, 264; Thulemeier to Frederick II, December 22, 1778 (Bancroft MSS., Prussia and Holland); Secret Resolution of the States General, December 30, 1778 (Bancroft MSS., America, Holland, and England); ibid., December 31, 1778 (Sparks MSS., CIII).

[2] Nijhoff, Brunswijk, 172, 312.

This correspondence was begun with the approval of the Duke of Brunswick. It was thought necessary to inform Frederick differently from Thulemeier, who was suspected to have " sterke liaisons " with Vauguyon (Nijhoff, Brunswijk, 172).

Orange, notwithstanding her assertion to the French ambassador that she would never interfere in affairs of state, began at this juncture a lively political correspondence with her uncle, and the latter abandoned his reserve in communicating his opinion to her. "You have done too much for the English," he wrote to her on January 13, 1779, "you permit them to pillage your vessels at their pleasure. The French thought they might make use of the same imperious tone as the English, and you feel now the inconvenience." As a remedy he recommended that they should think more of the Republic than of her neighbors, and show preference for neither the British nor the French. The Republic must not become the slave of either, but remain the friend of both, and by means of her navy make herself respected at sea.

Frederick modified this advice in a letter of March 7, 1779, in which he stated why, in his opinion, the United Provinces ought to keep both powers in good humor. His reasons were, that the Republic had neither a formidable fleet, nor an army large enough to withstand a great power, and, furthermore, that she had no allies and consequently could not expect assistance from other powers. He did not consider the present troubles of the Dutch serious, but hoped, as he wrote to the princess on March 14, that they might prove small clouds which would soon pass. A few days later, on March 22, Frederick recommended closer relations with France. The question, he said, at present was to secure by convoys the merchant marine of the Republic against the English, in order to prevent the latter from enslaving her. If the French, he added, intended to attack the United Provinces, it would be too late to augment the army, since all the world was at war, and especially a great number of Germans were serving in America. In a letter, dated April 14, he became even more explicit regarding the course to be taken. The large Dutch cities, he said, did not want to lose their commerce, and since their vessels carried more goods to French than to English ports, they did not like their stadtholder to be ruled by the arrogant haughtiness of the British ambassador at the Hague, but he continued to recommend the utmost caution in order not to make matters worse. On May 31, he suggested ample supplies for the island of St. Eustatia, a measure which would reconcile the French, since they would need those provisions in America. In short, the best course would be to bring about closer connections with France. Whatever might be the outcome of the present war, it would leave England utterly exhausted for many years and unable to mix in the affairs of the continent of Europe. Thus, whatever services the United Provinces might render, Great Britain would be unable to repay them, and would always remain the rival of the Dutch in commerce and navigation. On the other hand by pleasing France the United Provinces would retain their important trade with that country and, above all, preserve the Republic in her present state. The French had no reason to undermine the prerogatives of the stadtholder, which the English would be unable to restore if they should be lost through French attacks or intrigues.[1]

It is thus clearly shown that Frederick the Great sought to influence the United Provinces against England, and there is no doubt that, to some extent at least, he was responsible for their final attitude toward their former ally, especially concerning the question of convoys. The Prussian king, therefore, indirectly, sided with the Americans in this case as he did in others.[2]

---

[1] Colenbrander, Patriottentijd, I, 142–145, 380–384; Blok, Geschiedenis, VI, 329, 330.

[2] Regarding Frederick the Great's attitude toward the United States and the assistance which he rendered them, see of more recent authors, pro and contra: Pfister, Amerikanische Revolution, II, 160–168; H. Schoenfeld, Die deutschen, insbesonders preussischen Beziehungen zu den Vereinigten Staaten vor und während des Revolutionskrieges (Belletristisches Journal, Jahrgang 40, no. 25, 17. Juni, 1891, pp. 10–11; no. 26, 24. Juni, 1891, pp. 3–4); H. Schoenfeld. Anfänge deutschen Lebens und deutscher Politik in Amerika (Allgemeine Zeitung, München, Beilagen nos. 168 & 169, 30. & 31. Juli, 1897); Paul Leland Haworth, " Frederick the Great and the American Revolution " (American Historical Review, April, 1904).

On January 5, 1779, Berkenrode, the Dutch envoy in
Paris, reported to the States General that Vergennes also
had refused to accept their answer to Vauguyon's memorial.
The French minister had requested him to withdraw the
reply in friendship, otherwise the king would issue edicts
which would be very disadvantageous for the United Provinces. Vergennes added the advice that the States General
should thereafter negotiate with Vauguyon.[1] The subsequent proceedings in the Netherlands, however, proved
again the supremacy of the English party.[2] On January 16,
while the States General were still deliberating on the question, the French ambassador again presented a memorial.
It contained the projected edict of Louis XVI excluding the
United Provinces from the favors which France granted
to neutrals on the sea and in her ports. An exception was
made concerning the city of Amsterdam only, which was
allowed to enjoy all former privileges. This step of the
French government caused great emotion in the United
Provinces. Vauguyon was told that it was against the
Dutch constitution to treat with one city only, but he replied that this was neither a treaty nor a convention between
France and Amsterdam, but that the city merely continued
to enjoy what she had enjoyed before. The Republic ought
to be well satisfied that, by means of Amsterdam, she would
not lose all trade with France. The ambassador notified the
Grand Pensionary that his royal master had fixed January
26 for publishing the new order, in case he should, in the
meantime, not have received the answer which he demanded.
A few days before that date, a decision not having been
reached, a courier was dispatched from the United Provinces to Paris in order to obtain, if possible, a further delay of a week. In the beginning of February, however, the
States General had not yet informed Vauguyon of their
answer.[3]

---

[1] Sparks MSS., CIII, Ingekomen Brieven, IV.
[2] Arthur Lee to the Committee of Foreign Affairs, January 5,
1779 (Wharton, III, 13).
[3] Dumas to the Commissioners at Paris, January 12 to February

The French edict of December 25, 1778, not taking immediate effect, the United Provinces adopted expedients for carrying on their usual trade with France in a way which should not aggravate the situation. At the Texel were fifteen vessels ready to sail with naval munitions destined for France, and along with them about three hundred others with ordinary cargoes, also bound for France or her colonies. Nine war vessels were detailed to accompany this latter mercantile fleet to its destination, but it was suspected that the fifteen vessels for which no convoy was permitted had mingled among them. All passed the English Channel without accident. Thulemeier and Frederick the Great thought that this might be a good way to satisfy France, and, at the same time, not irritate Great Britain too much.[1]

Count Welderen, on the other hand, was again directed to make representations to the English court regarding the capture of Dutch vessels, emphasizing the fact that, according to the treaty of 1674, naval supplies were not considered contraband of war. He was to insist that all Dutch ships still held in British ports should be released immediately and direct orders given that the navigation from and to the colonies, from and to France, and from one French port to the other—contraband always excluded—was not to be disturbed in future.[2] The delay which the States General had requested regarding the execution of the French edict was granted by Louis XVI, and Vauguyon consequently was directed to notify them that, on February 8, the new rules would be published and executed, un-

---

16, 1779 (Wharton, III, 18-22); Secret Resolution of the States General, January 18, 1779 (Bancroft MSS., Holland, America, and England); same of February 5, 1779 (Sparks MSS., CIII); Thulemeier to Frederick II, January 22, 1779 (Bancroft MSS., Prussia and Holland).

[1] Thulemeier to Frederick II, January 12, 1779 (Bancroft MSS., Prussia and Holland); Colenbrander, Patriottentijd, I, 138, 139.

[2] Resolutions of Holland and Westfriesland, January 21, 1779 (Sparks Dutch Papers); Secret Resolution of the States General, January 26, 1779 (Sparks MSS., CIII); W. Lee to the Committee on Foreign Affairs, February 25, 1779 (Wharton, III, 65, 66).

less convoy should be granted to all Dutch vessels carrying naval munitions and especially timber.[1]

Amsterdam did not remain isolated in her opposition to the resolution of the States General of November 19, 1778. She was soon joined by the city of Haarlem, whose regents were Anti-Orangists. From this city there was a considerable export of fine linen to France, and the merchants who were interested in this trade feared harm if the edict should be executed. Moreover, the pensionary of the city, Zeeberg, shared van Berckel's views, and from now on the two cities cooperated regarding this question. Zealand promised William V full support in his attitude concerning convoys. Friesland, on the other hand, was less willing to follow the stadtholder's policy, owing to the fact that her regents were rather aristocrats than Orangists. The other provinces were less interested in the matter and would follow the least expensive policy, namely, that which rendered costly armaments at sea unnecessary. The English party, therefore, still prevailed, and when on February 18, 1779, the States General reached a resolution in answer to the French ambassador's note of January 16, there was no change of front. Vauguyon was requested to procure a revocation of the ordinance of December 25, 1778. He again refused to accept the resolution, since he was permitted to transmit to his royal master only the clear and precise answer that Dutch vessels carrying naval munitions would be protected. Every other reply, he said, was to be regarded as negative, and the French edict would immediately become valid.[2]

The ordinance was now published, but its execution was suspended by the French king until March 1.[3] All the privileges which Dutch vessels had enjoyed in French ports

---

[1] Secret Resolution of the States General, February 1, 1779 (Sparks MSS., CIII) ; Thulemeier to Frederick II, February 5, 1779 (Bancroft MSS., Prussia and Holland).

[2] Colenbrander, Patriottentijd, I, 145, 146; Blok, Geschiedenis, VI, 330; Secret Resolution of the States General, February 19, 1779 (Sparks MSS., CIII) ; Thulemeier to Frederick II, March 5, 1779 (Bancroft MSS., Prussia and Holland).

[3] Thulemeier to Frederick II, March 5, 1779 (Bancroft MSS., Prussia and Holland) ; Vaterlandsche Historie, XXVI, 28.

were revoked; orders were given to all French war vessels and privateers to search Dutch vessels destined for or coming from English ports in order to seize English goods; and, in addition, the import duty of fifty sous a ton, which was imposed in 1774 on Dutch ships trading to France, was renewed. Amsterdam and Haarlem, however, were not included in the provisions, on account of their animated appeals for unlimited convoys.[1] This was a clever stroke of French diplomacy calculated to defeat the English party in the United Provinces, because jealousy and financial losses must gradually draw the rest of Holland and the other provinces to Amsterdam and the French. At the same time France would continue to be supplied by the most powerful Dutch city, whose trade she could not afford to lose in this trying time of war. A few days later merchants of Rotterdam, and soon afterwards also of Dordrecht, sent strong petitions to the assembly of the province of Holland and the States General. It was requested that efficient means might be found to prevent the execution of the French edict, which must have the most disastrous consequences for their commerce.[2]

England by recklessly pursuing her policy made it easy for many of the Dutch to abandon the British party and to turn to the French. On March 26 the Prince of Orange, having finally fallen under the influence of the Grand Pensionary, van Bleiswijck, who inclined rather to France than to Great Britain, presented a note to Yorke, asking for an assurance that England would at least respect such convoys as did not protect vessels laden with ship timber. He received the answer that the king saw no reason for revoking the orders which had been given to the English admiralty in August, 1778, regarding the seizing of Dutch vessels carrying naval munitions. The resolution of the States General of November 19, 1778, which excluded ship timber but not

---

[1] Davies, History of Holland, III, 449; Kampen, Verkorte Geschiedenis, II, 292.

[2] Resolutions of Holland and Westfriesland, February 26 and March 5, 1779 (Sparks Dutch Papers).

other naval munitions from convoys had, therefore, not satisfied England and had not brought any change in the situation.   In consequence of this reply partisans of Great Britain in the United Provinces were completely discouraged,[1] so much the more as France now put her threat into execution by seizing a vessel from the city of Middleburg, and collecting a duty on freight and tonnage from Dutch vessels in French ports.[2]

Frederick the Great strongly condemned the attitude of Great Britain toward the Republic.   He thought their vigorous measures out of place and especially so the menaces of the English ambassador at the Hague, which did not produce the least effect, but tended only to agitate the minds of the people.[3]   The events showed that he was right.   Toward the end of March the assembly of the province of Holland passed a resolution that all ships except those carrying contraband of war should be protected by convoys.   No difference was to be made whether the vessels were transporting goods on their own account or for English, French, or neutral houses; nor was it to matter whence they came or whether they were destined for France, Great Britain, or neutral countries.[4]   The States General were asked to approve of this measure.   Merchants of the city of Rotterdam also repeated their former request for convoy.   They pleaded that their ships not only lay abandoned in their harbors, but for the few goods which were still allowed to be shipped foreign vessels had to be chartered in order to avoid the tonnage tax.   Their commerce with England, Scotland and Ireland was also ruined as a consequence of the French edict.   Worst of all, the new French tariff would deal the death

---

[1] Colenbrander, Patriottentijd, I, 150, 151 ; Thulemeier to Frederick II, March 19, 1779 (Bancroft MSS., Prussia and Holland).

[2] Thulemeier to Frederick II, March 16, 1779 (Bancroft MSS., Prussia and Holland).

[3] Frederick II to Thulemeier, March 24, 1779 (Bancroft MSS., Prussia and Holland).

[4] Resolutions of Holland and Westfriesland, March 30, 1779 (Sparks Dutch Papers) ; Thulemeier to Frederick II, April 6, 1779 (Bancroft MSS., Prussia and Holland) ; Colenbrander, Patriottentijd, I, 151.

stroke to the Dutch commerce. By this tariff, which had been in effect since May 1, a duty of fifteen per cent. had to be paid in France for all imports, besides the duties that had already been collected on the same goods. Some articles, as pitch, tar, masts, ship timber, ropes, etc., were left free, but these were dangerous to export because the English might seize the ships and cargoes.[1]

Since the beginning of April the aggressions of the British had even increased. Yorke in a memorial to the States General greatly resented the discrimination of the French regarding Amsterdam and Haarlem, which, he said, was only calculated to embroil the United Provinces in war with England.[2] Welderen reported about the same time that new orders had been sent to the commanders of English ships to arrest and bring to port all vessels, even if sailing under convoy, which were carrying naval munitions destined for France.[3] The States General resolved to ask Louis XVI not to discriminate among the provinces of the Republic,[4] but France continued the policy of strengthening the opposition in the United Provinces against the stadtholder and the English party. When, on March 30, the province of Holland had declared for unlimited convoy, the whole territory expected to be exempted from the oppressive French measure, and was greatly disappointed when this privilege remained confined to Amsterdam and Haarlem.

---

[1] Van der Capellen to Livingston, July, 1779 (Beaufort, Brieven van der Capellen, 116) ; Colenbrander, Patriottentijd, I, 160; Resolutions of Holland and Westfriesland, May 11, 1779, and of the States General, May 19, 1779 (Sparks Dutch Papers).

Regarding the secret resolution of the States General of April 26 to equip thirty-two vessels of war for the service of the year 1779 see Dumas' letter to the Committee of Foreign Affairs, May 15, 1779 (Wharton, III, 166–168).

[2] Yorke's Memorial, April 9, 1779, and Resolution of the States General of the same day (Bancroft MSS., America, Holland, and England; Sparks Dutch Papers; Vaterlandsche Historie, XXVI, 49).

Anonymous pamphlets supported Yorke, for example, " Avis à l'Auteur de la Lettre d'un Bon Patriote, sur le Mémoire, présenté aux Etats Généraux le 9 Avril, 1779, par M. l'Ambassadeur d'Angleterre."

[3] Secret Resolution of the States General, April 12 and 22, 1779 (Sparks MSS., CIII).

[4] Secret Resolution of the States General, April 18, 1779 (Sparks MSS., CIII).

The French government, aware that after Holland was satisfied the opposition in the rest of the provinces would lose its support and decrease, insisted upon the granting of unlimited convoy by the States General.[1] The assembly of the province of Holland was therefore repeatedly occupied with this question. In a resolution passed on June 11, it was said that speedy action had been expected from the States General on such an important matter, but two months had passed since March 30, when the resolution of the States of Holland and Westfriesland concerning unlimited convoy had been transmitted, and no answer had been received. The deputies of the province to the States General were then instructed to insist on the measure.[2]

When, toward the end of June, the States General had not yet passed a resolution, the province of Holland sent an ultimatum demanding a decision within four weeks. They resolved, furthermore, that in case unlimited convoys were not granted within that time, the States of Holland were to take matters up with the admiralties within the province. Since about nine tenths of the whole Dutch navy was under the administration of the admiralties, the province of Holland declared by her resolution that eventually she would alone decide the question of protection. At the same time circular letters were sent by Holland to the other provinces requesting them also to urge the measure of unlimited convoys.[3] In recognition of this step France immediately suspended both edict and tariff for the province of Holland, but only for the four weeks which had been allowed the States General.[4] The resolutions of the different provinces on the

---

[1] Colenbrander, Patriottentijd, I, 152.
[2] Resolutions of Holland and Westfriesland, June 4 and 11, 1779 (Sparks Dutch Papers).
[3] Resolutions of Holland and Westfriesland, June 24, 1779 (Sparks Dutch Papers); Colenbrander, Patriottentijd, I, 161; Van der Capellen to Dr. Richard Price, July 1, 1779, and to Livingston, July, 1779 (Beaufort, Brieven van der Capellen, 105, 106, 117); Blok, Geschiedenis, VI, 331; Doniol, Histoire, III, 782.
[4] Colenbrander, Patriottentijd, I, 161; Thulemeier to Frederick II, July 6, 1779 (Bancroft MSS., Prussia and Holland); Resolution of the States General, July 6, 1779 (Sparks MSS., CIII); Berkenrode's report, July 8, 1779 (Sparks Dutch Papers); Vaterlandsche Historie, XXVI, 84; Nieuwe Nederlandsche Jaerboeken, 1779, p. 169.

pending question were not favorable, most of them declaring
that the forces of the country were not in a state to successfully carry out the measure of unlimited convoys. The
province of Guelderland answered that she would vote for
unlimited convoy if the province of Holland, in return, would
vote for the augmentation of the Dutch army.[1]

This result was due to the activity of the stadtholder and
the English party. The Prince of Orange had summoned
the lieutenant-stadtholders of the provinces one by one to
his court and given them instructions for their attitude in
this contest.[2] Yorke proposed to his government as a last
resort to demand military aid from the United Provinces,
a step which would at least embarrass the enemies of Great
Britain. As an outward motive for such a measure, he
said, the fact might serve that France and Spain in June,
1779, had simultaneously declared war on England. This
had, in fact, happened one year after hostilities had begun.[3]
In accordance with this suggestion the ambassador was directed to deliver a memorial to the States General, in which
he asserted that France was threatening to invade Great
Britain, and his royal master was therefore obliged to claim
from the United Provinces without loss of time the succor
which was stipulated in the treaties of 1678 and after. It

---

[1] Resolutions of Holland and Westfriesland, July 21, 1779 (Guel-
derland) ; July 22, 1779 (Stad en Land) ; July 23, 1779 (Overyssel) ;
August 4, 1779 (Utrecht) ; September 1, 1779 (Friesland), in Sparks
Dutch Papers.

Amsterdam had pleaded for augmentation of the navy only, while
Guelderland wanted the army increased. There had been an alter-
cation in the States General on this question, especially between the
Grand Pensionary and the pensionary of Amsterdam (Yorke to
Suffolk, July 10, 1779, in Sparks MSS., LXXII).

[2] "The lieutenant-stadtholders were the persons by whom the
Prince governed the smaller provinces; except in Zealand it was an
official position for which one or the other prominent or influential
person with extended relations in his district was chosen" (Yorke,
July 9, 1779, in Colenbrander, Patriottentijd, I, 161, note 3).

The English party made strenuous efforts to convince the Dutch
that it would be more prudent and profitable for them to follow
England than France. An eloquent proof of these attempts forms
an anonymous pamphlet published in May, 1779, and entitled "Defense de Sir Joseph Yorke, Ambassadeur d'Angleterre, s'il en a
besoin."

[3] Colenbrander, Patriottentijd, I, 162.

was clear that a casus foederis existed according to the separate article of 1715.[1]

As the United Provinces were neither in a condition to furnish this aid, nor on account of the strength of the French party able even to grant it, the only course was to delay the reply. Consequently Yorke's memorial was taken over by the provinces for consideration, which meant that the matter would rest for any length of time. This delay, of course, would in itself have been an insult to Great Britain, if the measure had been put forward seriously. It had been intended to strengthen the English party and to embarrass the French partisans, but entirely missed its aim. Vauguyon remarked that the neglect of such an essential memorial in such grave circumstances meant a humiliating contempt of England. He thought it a good symptom for Great Britain's enemies, since it recalled the fable of the dying lion receiving a kick from the ass.[2]

The States General at the end of the stipulated four weeks had not reached a decision regarding convoys. The negotiations of the States of Holland with their provincial admiralty had also been unsuccessful. The latter, being controlled by the States General, showed no disposition to assist in so revolutionary a measure. In the meantime no convoys were granted at all, not even for vessels which were not carrying contraband or naval munitions. This inflicted an enormous loss upon Dutch commerce and navigation, but petitions to the States General were of no avail. This condition was due to a new proposal of the provinces to increase the Dutch army by 14,000 men, to which measure the cities of Amsterdam, Dort, Haarlem, Rotterdam, and Schiedam were opposed.[3] Yorke wrote that the probable outcome of it all

---

[1] Yorke's Memorial of July 22, 1779 (Bancroft MSS., America, Holland, and England; Sparks Dutch Papers; Blok, Geschiedenis, VI, 332).

[2] Vauguyon, August 24, 1779 (Colenbrander, Patriottentijd, I, 162, note 3); Franklin to Jay, October 4, 1779 (Wharton, III, 363).

[3] Resolutions of the States General, September 9, 1779; October 21, 1779 (Sparks Dutch Papers); Colenbrander, Patriottentijd, I, 163; Dumas to Franklin, September 14, 1779 (Wharton, III, 314, 315).

would be that a mercantile fleet would be sent out under convoy, pretending to protect only ships with non-forbidden cargoes, but that, as in the beginning of the year, a number of vessels laden with naval munitions would hide among the rest. The English government, therefore, warned the Dutch authorities that, this time, the vessels would not be permitted to pass without being searched.[1] The John Paul Jones incident, which occurred about this time, tended to strain the relations between England and the United Provinces still further.[2]

Toward the end of November Yorke addressed a new memorial to the States General. The king, he said, was surprised not to have received aid in answer to his request of four months before, and referred again to the separate article of 1716, which stipulated the casus foederis. French aggressions were to be seen in the declaration of war, the attack on the isle of Jersey, and the siege of Gibraltar. The combined forces of the House of Bourbon menaced the United Kingdom. A descent upon the British coast and a formidable invasion of England under the protection of all their naval forces was still their aim. The king therefore requested a speedy and precise answer to this important question. This memorandum was referred to the provinces also for deliberation[3] but the British demands did not impress the Dutch very deeply. Indifference was also shown by the French ambassador in the matter.[4]

On November 8, the Dutch provinces agreed that two merchant fleets, not carrying contraband of war or naval stores, should sail under the protection of several men of war. One was destined for the West Indies; the other, for France and Spain. With the vessels of the latter fleet were

---

[1] Yorke, September 7, 1779 (Colenbrander, Patriottentijd, I, 164, 165).

[2] Above, p. 62.

[3] Yorke's Memorial, November 26, 1779 (Bancroft MSS., America, Holland and England) ; Resolutions of the States General, November 26, 1779 (Sparks Dutch Papers) ; Trescot, Diplomacy of the Revolution, 84.

[4] Thulemeier to Frederick II, November 30, 1779 (Bancroft MSS., Prussia and Holland).

9

intermixed about 25 or 30 laden with hemp, iron, tar, pitch, etc., materials which by the resolution of the States General of November 19, 1778, were not excluded from convoy, and, at their own risk, also 18 or 20 ships whose cargoes consisted of ship timber.[1] The combined fleet left the Texel under the command of Vice-Admiral Bylandt, on December 27. On December 31 Count Welderen reported from London that, two days before, 30 to 40 merchant vessels under the convoy of some war vessels had been sighted in the Channel, and that, thereupon, Captain Fielding with six ships of the line and six frigates sailed from England.[2]

The Dutch and English vessels met off the Isle of Wight on December 31. Fielding asked permission of Bylandt to search the ships under the latter's convoy. The Dutch admiral declined, but showed papers signed by the skippers of all the vessels under his convoy stating that their ships were not carrying contraband of war. He added that no vessels with ship timber had been granted the privilege of convoy. Fielding, however, demanded also a declaration that the vessels had nothing on board of which ship material and especially cordage could be manufactured. Such a statement could not be made, since, as has been mentioned, some vessels laden with iron, hemp, etc., had been admitted to the convoy. The English commander declared that he would be compelled to use force for searching the ships. An encounter followed in which Bylandt, commanding only three ships of the line and three frigates, had to yield to the superior force of the English. Several vessels whose cargo consisted of ship material were taken by Fielding. A salute to the British flag was demanded and given. Bylandt was allowed to continue with the rest of his ships on his voyage, but refused to proceed and followed the captured ships to Spithead on the English coast.[3] When the news of

---

[1] Colenbrander, Patriottentijd, I, 166.
[2] Resolutions of the States General, January 4, 1780 (Sparks MSS., CIII).
[3] Davies, History of Holland, III, 451; Kampen, Verkorte Geschiedenis, II, 293; Welderen's report on the Bylandt-Fielding inci-

the incident became known at Amsterdam (on January 8), a great commotion occurred, especially on the stock exchange. It was thought impossible that England, still the friend and ally of the United Provinces, should have taken such a step.[1] The States General very soon instructed Welderen to make strong representations to the court of St. James concerning the capture and holding of the merchant vessels and to demand satisfaction for the insult done to the Dutch flag. At the same time Bylandt was ordered to sail back to the Texel with the war vessels under his command.[2]

The Bylandt-Fielding episode created a sensation all over Europe. Even in far-away St. Petersburg there was much talk about it, and the Dutch minister accredited to the Russian court reported that the English boasted greatly of this petty success.[3] When Count van Welderen handed an energetic memorial to Lord Stormont, the latter received it with indifference, remarking that an answer could be given only after the memorandum had been laid before the king; but that since the demand for aid had not been deliberated upon by the States General, England did not know whether to regard the United Provinces as friends and allies or only as friends and neutrals.[4] Great indignation was created at

dent, dated January 4, 1780, with enclosures; Missive van de Admiraliteit to Amsterdam (Sparks Dutch Papers); Vaterlandsche Historie, XXVI, 170 ff.

[1] Davies, History of Holland, III, 452; Nieuwe Nederlandsche Jaerboeken, February, 1780, p. 130; Thulemeier to Frederick II, January 14, 1780 (Bancroft MSS., Prussia and Holland). Thulemeier sent with this report a detailed description, dated January 4, 1780, of the encounter. Its author was a former Prussian officer, von Schöning, now "Lieutenant de marine à bord du vaisseau amiral du Comte de Biland." The title of the essay is "Relation des am 31. December 1779 der Flagge der Vereinigten Provintzen Zugefügten affronts durch eine Königliche Englische Escadre unter Commando des Commodore Charles Fielding."

[2] Resolution of the States General, February 17, 1780 (Sparks MSS., CIII; Sparks Dutch Papers); Thulemeier to Frederick II, January 21, 1780 (Bancroft MSS., Prussia and Holland).

[3] J. J. de Swart to the States General, February 1 and 4, 1780 (Bancroft MSS., America, Holland, and England); J. Adams to the President of Congress, April 7, 1780 (Wharton, III, 600).

[4] Welderen to Fagel, March 7, 1780, with enclosures; Welderen's Memorial to Stormont, March 6, 1780 (Bancroft MSS., America, Holland, and England); Resolution of the States General, March 13, 1780 (Sparks MSS., CIII).

Amsterdam by the decisions of the Court of Admiralty in
London of March 4 and 6, declaring those ships of Bylandt's
convoy confiscated which carried hemp, etc., while vessels
laden with ship timber and excluded from Bylandt's protection were released after their cargo had been purchased.[1]

About the middle of March the English government
answered Welderen's memorial by saying that Bylandt had
been the aggressor and that Fielding had acted in conformity
with his instructions, and that the search of suspicious merchant vessels was not only necessary but just.[2] This point
of view was rejected by the States General, who charged
Welderen to present another memorial to the English government insisting that Fielding was the aggressor,[3] because
he sent an armed sloop to search the merchant vessels under
Bylandt's command and consequently the latter's firing upon
the sloop was to be regarded as an act of self-defence. Welderen was to ask again for satisfaction and indemnification.[4]
The Dutch envoy in handing this memorandum to Lord
Stormont added verbally that the United Provinces had
never admitted the visitation of ships sailing under the convoy of Dutch war vessels, and that consequently, without the
least of doubt, Fielding had been the aggressor. Stormont

Stormont had already threatened in January that the Dutch would
be regarded as neutrals and the existing treaties annulled if they
did not furnish succors (Welderen to the States General, January
28, 1780, received February 7, 1780, in Sparks Dutch Papers).

[1] J. Texier and Company to the States of Holland and West
Friesland, March 16, 1780, and to the States General, March 17,
1780 (Sparks Dutch Papers).

[2] Welderen, on March 17, 1780, transmitted to the States General,
without comment, Stormont's answer of March 16 (Sparks Dutch
Papers; Bancroft MSS., America, Holland, and England).

[3] At the instigation of the Prince of Orange Count Bylandt was
placed before a Dutch court martial, but was acquitted on April 7,
1780 (Resolution of the States General, January 18, 1780, in Sparks
MSS., CIII); Thulemeier to Frederick II, January 25 and February
4, 1780 (Bancroft MSS., Prussia and Holland); Prince of Orange
to the States General, April 14, 1780 (Sparks Dutch Papers); De
Jonge, Geschiedenis, IV, 426.

[4] Resolution of the States of Holland and Westfriesland, April 8
and 18, 1780 (Sparks Dutch Papers); Resolution of the States
General, April 25, 1780 (Bancroft MSS., America, Holland, and
England); John Adams to the President of Congress, May 2, 1780
(Wharton, III, 646, 647).

answered that he would lay the memorial before the king, but that the latter was satisfied that the English commander had acted according to the treaties and to his instructions. Besides, it would not be in the power of the king to change the sentence of the Court of Admiralty.[1]

The United Provinces after the seizure of the ships under Bylandt's convoy naturally experienced great public excitement, but they were apparently not yet ready to side openly with the Americans. "The Dutch," wrote William Lee from Brussels in March, "are in a very disturbed state. As yet there does not seem to be a probability of their taking a decided and open part with us in the war. The influence and power of the Prince of Orange are unfortunately too great to permit them to adopt those measures which their honor and interest direct, and which I believe a great majority of the people wish. The prince is retained against us by the flattering prospect of marrying his daughter to the Prince of Wales."[2] In February, 1778, Thulemeier had predicted that in case of a search by the English of Dutch vessels sailing under convoy, and a subsequent hostile encounter, Amsterdam would be exasperated and would bring to pass an understanding between France and the United Provinces.[3] Grave were then the doubts which even the most ardent friends of England entertained in the United Provinces regarding the correctness of Great Britain's step. The Duke of Brunswick did not hesitate to tell Yorke that England's attitude seemed to be poor policy, since it only facilitated the growth of France's influence in the Republic, and sacrificed old friendship to the delusion that it would be possible to cut off from France the supply of naval muni-

[1] Welderen to the States General, May 2, 1780, with enclosure; Memorial to Stormont, April 25, 1780 (Bancroft MSS., America, Holland, and England); Resolution of the States General, May 8, 1780 (Sparks MSS., CIII); John Adams to the President of Congress, May 19, 1780 (Wharton, III, 689).

[2] W. Lee to John Adams, March 17, 1780 (Wharton, III, 556). Regarding the project of a marriage between the Prince of Wales and the stadtholder's daughter, see above, p. 22.

[3] Thulemeier to Frederick II, February 6, 1778 (Bancroft MSS., Prussia and Holland).

tions. The consequence would be that the whole Republic would be thrown into the arms of France.[1] The subsequent events show that he was justified in this prophecy.

The deliberations of the provinces on Yorke's memorials of July 22 and November 26, 1779, relative to the furnishing of aid had been continued without coming to any final conclusion.[2] The English ambassador, therefore, presented a third communication to the States General in March, demanding a satisfactory answer to his previous memorials within three weeks, or else Great Britain henceforth would regard the Dutch as neutrals and not as a "privileged" nation.[3] The States General instructed Welderen a few days afterwards to represent to the English government that the delay in answering Yorke's memorials regarding assistance was not a violation of the alliance between the two powers, since it was caused by the peculiar constitution of the United Provinces.[4] The Dutch envoy in carrying out these orders told Stormont that it would be impossible to receive the resolutions of all the provinces within three weeks and that the United Provinces therefore asked for a prolongation of the term. The English statesman answered that the time would not be extended, since Yorke in his last memorial had only repeated what had already been communicated to the States General on January 28.[5]   Yorke

[1] Nijhoff, Brunswijk, 182, 183.
[2] Resolutions of the States of Holland and Westfriesland, February 2 and March 15, 1780 (Sparks Dutch Papers); Resolutions of the States General, March 14, 1780 (Sparks MSS., CIII).
[3] Yorke's Memorial to the States General, March 21, 1780 (Sparks Dutch Papers; Bancroft MSS., America, Holland, and England); Colenbrander, Patriottentijd, I, 170; Davies, History of Holland, III, 452, 453.
John Adams seemed to be mistaken when he wrote to the President of Congress on March 29 that the treaties would be revoked by England after three months in case the answer of the States General to Yorke's memorial should be a refusal of the succors (Wharton, III, 579). See also John Adams' letter to the President of Congress of April 3, 1780 (ibid., III, 592).
[4] Resolution of the States General, March 24, 1780 (Sparks MSS., CIII); John Adams to the President of Congress, April 3, 1780 (Wharton, III, 592).
[5] Welderen to the States General, March 31, 1780 (Bancroft MSS., America, Holland, and England); John Adams to the President of Congress, April 14, 1780 (Wharton, III, 614).

was authorized to announce a delay only in case there should be a prospect that the States General would grant assistance.

Even the Prince of Orange gave up all hopes of changing the public sentiment of the Dutch, which was now becoming more and more anti-English. The resistance of the British party was broken, and most of the provinces (Holland, Groningen, Friesland, and Overyssel) voted against furnishing assistance to England, basing their refusal principally upon the non-existence of the case of invasion of British territory, which alone, they claimed, could have obliged them to comply with the demand of the English king.[1] When, after the expiration of the three weeks allowed for the answer of the States General, the latter had not passed a resolution on the subject, England carried out her menace. On April 17, Lord Stormont informed Count Welderen that the term had expired and transmitted an order of the king, which the latter had given in his council of the same day. It stated that the States General had deserted the alliance that so long subsisted between the crown of Great Britain and the Republic and had placed themselves in the condition of a neutral power, bound to England by no treaty. Therefore the Dutch would from this time be considered to be upon the same footing with all the other neutral states not privileged by treaty, and all particular stipulations respecting the freedom of navigation and commerce in time of war contained in the treaties between the two powers, especially in the marine treaty of 1674, were revoked.[2] At the same time the commanders of the English war vessels and privateers were ordered " to seize and detain all ships and

---

[1] John Adams to the President of Congress, April 10 and 14, 1780 (Wharton, III, 605, 613); Dumas to the President of Congress (ibid., III, 612); Vreede, Laurens Pieter van der Spiegel, II, 7.

[2] Welderen to the States General, April 18, 1780, with enclosures of April 17, 1780 (Bancroft MSS., America, Holland, and England); Blok, Geschiedenis, VI, 334; Colenbrander, Patriottentijd, I, 170; J. Adams to the President of Congress, April 28 and May 8, 1780 (Wharton, III, 635, 636, 664); Vaterlandsche Historie, XXVI, 303; Kampen, Verkorte Geschiedenis, II, 293; Davies, History of Holland, III, 453, 454.

John Andrews tried to justify the English step (Two Additional Letters, 106–109).

vessels belonging to the subjects of the States-General when they shall be found to have on board any effects belonging to the enemies of his majesty, or effects which are considered as contraband by the general law of nations."[1]

The question of assistance was thus settled before the States General had reached a final conclusion, but in respect to convoys the situation was different. The Bylandt-Fielding incident discouraged the friends of Great Britain in the United Provinces, while the partisans of France obtained supremacy in the assemblies of the several provinces. The result was that, on April 24, the States General almost unanimously[2] resolved to grant henceforth unlimited convoys. A few days later also a resolution was taken by them to fit out, for the protection of commerce and navigation, fifty-two ships of the line and frigates.[3] Vauguyon thereupon handed a memorandum to the States General in which he said that Louis XVI had applauded the efforts of the States General to have their flag again respected. The king had therefore ordered him to announce to the Dutch government that the recent French orders establishing a new tariff and otherwise encroaching upon the commerce of the United Provinces had been revoked. Furthermore the king would not confine himself to reestablishing the subjects of the States General in the enjoyment of former favors, but he would give the Dutch a signal proof of his benevolence, in

---

[1] John Adams to the President of Congress, May 13, 1780 (Wharton, III, 675, 676).

[2] The deputies of the province of Zealand alone opposed the measure (Blok, Geschiedenis, VI, 334); Vaterlandsche Historie, XXVI, 306.

[3] Colenbrander, Patriottentijd, I, 170; Thulemeier to Frederick II, April 28, 1780 (Bancroft MSS., Prussia and Holland).

Half a year later about two thirds of the fifty-two vessels were ready, though cannon and crews were partly wanting in numbers (Blok, Geschiedenis, VI, 334). This part of the Dutch armament was largely due to a number of petitions to the States General, and so forth, requesting protection of the navigation (J. Adams to the President of Congress, June 2, 4, 5, 10, and July 7, 1780, in Wharton, III, 758, 759, 762, 768, 769, 777, 839).

On May 31, 1780, Franklin reported to the President of Congress in regard to the vigorous arming of the Dutch (Wharton, III, 745).

returning to them all the sums which had been received by the French custom administration in virtue of the decree and tariff.[1]

The English policy of aggression was thus a complete failure. It did not result in the submission of the United Provinces to the English demands as had been desired and expected, but, on the contrary, in the refusal of all of them. Military assistance was denied, unlimited convoys granted, and the increase of the Dutch navy resolved upon. Great Britain's object had been to draw the United Provinces away from France, but instead, by what must be regarded as rather awkward diplomacy, she had only caused the relations between the two countries to become closer. The outlook for the Netherlands, however, was very gloomy. It was to be expected that English war vessels and privateers would try to do great damage to Dutch commerce and navigation, while the navy of the United Provinces was not in a state to render sufficient protection. Great depression, especially on the stock exchange at Amsterdam,[2] was the consequence.[3] There was, however, just at this period, a ray of hope that protection might be tendered to Dutch navigation by the powers of the North, a question which will be discussed in the next chapter.

---

[1] Vauguyon's memorial of April 26, 1780, with the decree of the French king's council of state of April 22, 1780 (Bancroft MSS., America, Holland, and England; Sparks Dutch Papers) ; J. Adams to the President of Congress, May 2, 1780 (Wharton, III, 644-646) ; Vaterlandsche Historie, XXVI, 307; Davies, History of Holland, III, 454.

[2] Colenbrander, Patriottentijd, I, 171.

[3] Regarding the question of convoys and succors see the speeches of the Earl of Shelburne and Lord Stormont in Parliament on June 1, 1780 (Hansard, Parliamentary History, XXI, 633-635, 637, 642-644).

CHAPTER VI.

The United Provinces drawn into War with England.

The position of England was becoming extremely critical. She had to depend entirely upon herself in her struggle not only with her former American colonies, but also with France and Spain, while the United Provinces were commercially supporting her enemies. In the desire to be backed by one of the great European powers in the pursuance of the war, Great Britain approached Russia.

Sir James Harris (later given the title of Lord Malmesbury), a very clever diplomat, was sent to the Russian court in order to arrange, if possible, an alliance. He found two diverging political influences at work in the Russian capital, one emanating from Potemkin, who was rising in favor with Empress Catherine II, the other from Panin, the secretary of the Russian Foreign Office and also a favorite, but whose star was fading. Harris resolved to use the former statesman for his purposes, neglecting and thereby provoking against himself the other. The ambassador was soon to see his mistake in undervaluing Panin's influence.

Potemkin was able to arrange for Harris two secret interviews with the empress, during which she consented to an alliance with England. Upon his report to the British government, the ambassador received full powers to negotiate the treaty. In the meantime Panin, from whom the preliminary proceedings had been concealed, became aware of what was going on and succeeded in convincing his imperial mistress of the impracticability of the proposed coalition. Consequently negotiations were formally refused to Harris. For a moment, however, it seemed that in spite of Panin's counteractions he would be able to bring the two powers nearer together, or, at least, to inflame the empress against England's foes.

Two Russian vessels carrying corn were seized in the Mediterranean by the Spaniards, who were desirous of keeping all provisions from Gibraltar, which stronghold they still hoped to recover from the English rule. Catherine was very indignant when she heard of the fate of these ships, and Harris with Potemkin's assistance cleverly took advantage of the empress' ill humor in order to incite her more against Spain. Satisfaction was to be imperatively demanded while a fleet of war vessels was to sail from Cronstadt as quickly as it could be fitted out. Panin, however, soon discovered this scheme, also, and thwarted it in a most ingenious way. He told Catherine that the incident was deplorable and condemnable, but that it was the outcome of a false principle of public law rather than a proof of the ill-will of the Spaniards. This, he declared, was the proper moment to protest against such proceedings, and, since England agreed with Russia in the condemnation of the seizure, she would likewise concur with Catherine in condemning the system. The empress thereupon accepted his plan of sending to the belligerents a declaration that in future such violations of neutral rights would not be endured. The northern and central powers were to be invited to join in this action. Catherine was thus made to believe that her step would not only conform to the desire of Harris, but make her the head of a large confederation united in the pursuance of a noble aim.[1]

Her ultimate purpose was to establish the principle (which, however, had already been pronounced in the English-Dutch treaty of 1674) " that the navigation of neutral powers should remain as free and unobstructed in time of war, as in that of peace; and that provided their ships were not laden with contraband goods, they should enjoy the liberty of conveying, free of seizure and restraint, all other articles whatever, though belonging to the subjects of the powers at war."[2] What appealed to the empress

---

[1] Trescot, Diplomacy of the Revolution, 73–76.
[2] J. Andrews, History of the War with America, France, Spain, and Holland, IV, 4.

above all was the prospect which opened itself for enlarging Russian commerce and navigation. American, British, French, and Spanish merchant vessels were liable to capture by the belligerents, and, consequently, appeared only in reduced numbers on the seas. Russia now had an opportunity to start an enormous carrying trade. She possessed a sufficient number of ports and had at her disposal an energetic and bold population which could be used to advantage in the merchant service.[1] Under present conditions, however, commerce and navigation were not secure even for neutrals. "From every shore of Europe, from almost every quarter of the globe, in fact," complaints resounded of English aggression and piracy. Russia herself had experienced heavy losses. A large number of Dutch vessels were employed by Russian merchants, and many of those ships had been captured by the English. On the other hand, no country owned a navy sufficiently large and effective to cope with the English.[2] The only way to render the seas again free and secure seemed to be a combination of the naval forces of the various countries interested. To create such a coalition was now planned by Catherine. Her message to the different courts was written and sent secretly.

The declaration dated February 26, 1780, stipulated in detail :—

1. That all neutral vessels should be able to navigate freely from one port to another, even upon the coasts of the powers at war.

2. That the effects belonging to the subjects of the belligerents should be free in neutral ships, excepting always contraband goods.

3. That naval stores and provisions should not be considered contraband unless belonging to the government of a belligerent.[3]

---

[1] Wharton, I, 447.
[2] Davies, History of Holland, III, 455.
[3] As was expressed in the treaty of 1734 between Russia and England and in that of 1674 between the United Provinces and

4. That a port should be considered blockaded only if it was guarded so well that no attempt could be made to enter into it without evident danger.

5. That these principles should serve as a rule when there was a question regarding the legality of prizes.[1]

Ambassador Harris was absolutely ignorant of the nature of the Russian missive sent abroad. The empress herself told him that a communication would shortly be made to the English court which would completely meet the wishes expressed to her, and the English diplomat eagerly reported this answer to his authorities. The disappointment and indignation following the receipt of the Russian note by the British cabinet were therefore great. Instead of being a blow at England's enemies, the declaration presented a new maritime law which was directly opposed to the whole maritime policy of Great Britain and to a practice which she could least afford to dispense with in her present critical condition.[2]

Bitter were the criticisms of Russia's attitude made by contemporaneous English writers. " It was," wrote one of them, " a matter of peculiar astonishment that Russia should be at the head of a combination so injurious to Great Britain. The favors she had received from the British ministry, in her late war with the Turks, and still more the commercial benefits resulting from a connection with this country, seemed to secure the good will of Russia, and even its assistance, in case of necessity. Little, therefore, was it expected that it should prove the first of all European potentates in that inimical declaration, the intent of which was to deprive Great Britain of the principal resources that enabled her to stand her ground in the midst of so many difficulties."[3] Concerning the reception which the

England, only arms, ammunition, and military accoutrements should be considered as contraband (Davies, History of Holland, III, 455, 456).

[1] John Adams to the President of Congress, April 10, 1780 (Wharton, III, 608); Mahan, Influence of Sea Power upon History, 1660–1783, p. 405.

[2] Trescot, Diplomacy of the Revolution, 76, 77.

[3] J. Andrews, History of the War, IV, 3, 4.

English government gave Catherine's declaration, the same author said that Great Britain, contrary to her custom and character, was compelled to "temporise" on this trying occasion. "Her answer to this mortifying declaration, though guardedly expressed, was not wanting in terms sufficiently clear to remind Russia how different a part Great Britain had acted to her in the day of need."[1] Even much later, English critics expressed themselves scarcely less severely, numbering Catherine among the concealed, if not the open, enemies of Great Britain.[2]

The northern powers, Sweden and Denmark, considered Russia's offer favorably, their main products, naval stores and grain, being those of which England was chiefly interested in depriving her enemies. The coalition to which Catherine's plan finally led was called the Armed Neutrality, because the contracting parties, neutrals in the present war, bound themselves, if need be, to defend their principles by a combined armed fleet of a fixed minimum number.[3] It formed an important factor in the American Revolution. England had not only lost her last hope of a continental alliance, but saw herself seriously hampered in her naval actions even by inferior European sea powers. Moreover, the Armed Neutrality added a new enemy to her foes, the United Provinces of the Netherlands.

The belligerents, against whom Sir James Harris had advised Catherine, cleverly seized the opportunity to turn the affair to their own account. Spain made restitution and recognized the new maritime code, thereby reconciling the empress. France praised the wisdom of Catherine and con-

---

[1] J. Andrews, History of the War, IV, 4.
See the answer which the English court made to the declaration of the Empress of Russia in J. Adams' letter to the President of Congress, May 8, 1780 (Wharton, III, 661, 662).
[2] See Fitzmaurice, Shelburne, III, 83.
[3] Mahan, Influence of Sea Power, 405; Pfister, Amerikanische Revolution, II, 181.
Portugal, influenced by England, did not accede to the treaty, much to the disgust of France and Spain, who were indignant at her partiality for Great Britain (Carmichael to the Committee of Foreign Affairs, August 22, 1780, in Wharton, IV, 39).

sented to the principles of the Armed Neutrality, which the former claimed had already been .expressed, in general, by her ordinance of 1778.[1] For the protection of the commercial interests of Russia it seemed at least desirable, if not necessary, that the United Provinces also should accede to the Armed Neutrality. Catherine therefore instructed Prince Gallitzin, her envoy extraordinary at the Hague, to negotiate with the States General to this effect.[2]

Already in March, 1780, John Adams had written from Paris that there were rumors of the conclusion of a quintuple alliance between Russia, Sweden, Denmark, Prussia, and the United Provinces for the maintenance of the honor of the flags of these powers. Yet he thought that such a combination would be more advantageous to France and Spain than to Holland, because it would facilitate the providing of their marine arsenals with ship timber, hemp, etc. This would greatly embarrass Great Britain, since her policy had always been to prevent the growth of the navies of her enemies by intercepting their supplies.[3] Adams' announcement, however, was premature.

Prince Gallitzin entered upon his new duties about this time. Couriers from St. Petersburg arrived with despatches and he immediately conferred with the president of the States General,[4] presenting also a memorial to that assembly.

---

[1] Trescot, Diplomacy of the Revolution, 77.

Franklin advised Congress also to conform to the principle of the Armed Neutrality, that free ships made free goods, by giving orders to American cruisers not to molest foreign ships (Franklin to the President of Congress, August 9, 1780, in Wharton, IV, 24). Congress, acting upon a motion of Mr. Adams, resolved: "That the board of admiralty prepare and report instructions for the commanders of armed vessels commanded by the United States conformable to the principles contained in the declaration of the Empress of all the Russias on the rights of neutral vessels.

"That the ministers plenipotentiary from the United States, if invited thereto, be and hereby are respectively empowered to accede to such regulations, conformable to the spirit of the said declaration, as may be agreed, upon by the Congress expected to assemble in pursuance of the invitation of her Imperial majesty" (Wharton, IV, 81).

[2] Davies, History of Holland, III, 456.

[3] J. Adams to the President of Congress, March 18, 1780 (Wharton, III, 558).

[4] Same to same, April 7, 1780 (ibid., III, 599).

It contained a copy of the declaration of the empress to the belligerent powers, and invited the United Provinces to make common cause with her. Gallitzin, according to his memorandum, did not doubt that the States General would consider this invitation and make, without delay, a declaration to the powers actually at war, founded upon the same principles as those of the empress. Negotiations with the other neutral powers on this subject were suggested.[1]

The States General informed the several provinces of the Russian proposal and asked for quick action.[2] Deliberations were eagerly taken up by Holland and there was a prospect that a decision would speedily be reached. The American agent at the Hague felt sure that this resolution would settle the matter "agreeably to the views of the empress and to the general wishes of all good men." The other provinces would soon follow suit, and their action must accelerate the general pacification. "This intelligence," he remarked, "is thought, not only by myself but by many others, very important to the United States."[3]

England dreaded most the accession of the United Provinces to the Armed Neutrality. The Dutch navy, it is true, was utterly ineffective, yet under the protection of that coalition, Dutch commerce and navigation would not only do immeasurable damage to England's commercial interests,[4] but by the undisturbed furnishing of naval munitions to France and Spain considerably strengthen the position of the foes of Great Britain. What sentiments prevailed in English official circles regarding this question is shown by a report of Thulemeier to the effect that, according to a com-

---

[1] Memorial of Dimitri Prince de Gallitzin to the States General, April 3, 1780, with enclosure "Declaration aux cours de Londres, Versailles et Madrid" (Bancroft MSS., America, Holland, and England; Sparks Dutch Papers); Thulemeier to Frederick II, April 4, 1780 (Bancroft MSS., Prussia and Holland); J. Adams to the President of Congress, April 10, 1780 (Wharton, III, 606–608).

[2] J. Adams to the President of Congress, April 14, 1780 (Wharton, III, 613, 614).

[3] Dumas to the President of Congress, April 13, 1780 (ibid., III, 611, 612).

[4] Pfister, Amerikanische Revolution, II, 181.

munication made to him by Gallitzin, Count Welderen had secretly informed his superiors of imminent danger threatening from England. The Dutch envoy had learned that in a council held at St. James, most of the English cabinet officers had recommended a declaration of war against the States General in case the latter should accept the invitation extended to them by Russia. Prince Gallitzin observed to the Prussian envoy that he deemed this a trick of the ministry in London, because he could never believe that the British government would use the invitation of the empress as a pretext for a war with the United Provinces.[1]

On April 13 the province of Holland resolved to accept Catherine's invitation to conferences. A copy of the resolution was to be transmitted to Prince Gallitzin, de Swart, the Dutch resident at St. Petersburg, and the ministers of the United Provinces at the courts of Copenhagen, Stockholm, and Lisbon.[2] Other provinces soon followed,[3] as had been predicted by Dumas. The empress, through de Swart,[4] expressed her gratitude to the Dutch that her proposition had been received so favorably by the States General and the provinces.[5] Panin hoped that the United Provinces would

---

[1] Thulemeier to Frederick II, April 28, 1780 (Bancroft MSS., Prussia and Holland).

[2] J. Adams to the President of Congress, April 28, 1780 (Wharton, III, 638, 639); Thulemeier to Frederick II, April 18, 1780 (Bancroft MSS., Prussia and Holland).

[3] Guelderland and Zealand. J. Adams to the President of Congress, May 8, 1780 (Wharton, III, 655).

[4] De Swart was apparently not a very capable diplomat. "The Dutch Resident, Swart," said Harris of him, "is a man neither of birth nor character, totally improper for the post he fills. . . . One of the most despised and unnoticed of my colleagues" (September 20, 1779, and April 28, 1780, in Harris, Diaries and Correspondence of James Harris, First Earl of Malmesbury, I, 225, 257). The Grand Pensionary called him "un être trop peu considérable pour être chargé d'une commission importante" (Vauguyon, June 23, 1780, in Colenbrander, Patriottentijd, I, 179). Still Amsterdam declared to the stadtholder that it wanted no other minister at St. Petersburg than de Swart. Yorke concluded that the resident was sold to Amsterdam and that he was the only one who served the city well (Yorke to Stormont, June 20, 1780, in Sparks MSS., LXXII).

[5] J. J. de Swart to the States General, June 6, 1780 (Bancroft MSS., America, Holland, and England).

endeavor to arm vessels and to take their share in the protection of commerce and navigation. He thought it necessary, above all, that the States General should send a declaration like that of Russia to the belligerent powers.[1]

The dread of England, however, still prevailed in the Netherlands and it was feared that she might take revenge by seizing the East and West Indian possessions of the United Provinces. On June 29, 1780, the city of Amsterdam passed a resolution in which it was declared that the accession to the league of the Armed Neutrality should be based on the condition that Russia and the other neutral powers guarantee to the United Provinces all the "possessions fixed and immovable" of the latter, both in and out of Europe.[2] This decision was inserted in the acts of the provincial assembly of Holland, at the Hague, July 1, 1780. Here it was thought necessary that a defensive treaty of alliance and also the guarantee of the Dutch possessions in both Indies should form the basis of negotiations with Russia. Many of the deputies disapproved of this proposition. The Russian ambassador, on the other hand, was much dissatisfied with the turn affairs had taken and attributed it to the Prince of Orange and the English partisans.[3]

A few days later the American commissioners at Paris

---

[1] Secret Resolution of the States General, June 13, 1780 (Sparks MSS., CIII).

[2] Wharton, III, 831.

[3] Thulemeier to Frederick II, July 7, 1780 (Bancroft MSS., Prussia and Holland).

It seems that, in this question, the Duke of Brunswick rather than the Prince of Orange was opposed to the accession of the United Provinces to the Armed Neutrality. The duke repeatedly called the stadtholder's attention to the danger which such a step would involve, but in vain. Brunswick therefore supposed that the prince's attitude was due to Frederick the Great's influence. On February 28, 1780, the latter had written that the Republic should try to render her position at sea formidable and to conclude for the protection of commerce a defensive alliance with Sweden and Denmark. This, he thought, was the best means for bringing England back to a reasonable behavior (Nijhoff, Brunswijk, 186).

Brunswick's reason for distrusting the Russian policy was that after all Catherine (and her favorite Potemkin) inclined rather to England, and that therefore the league of neutrals would do no harm to that power.

were advised from the Hague that "the talk had been of a congress to be held in that residence." The Empress of Russia was said to have expressed her desire of having all the conferences take place at St. Petersburg, and the Prince of Orange, thereupon, had proposed and the States General agreed to the sending of Baron van Wassenaer-Starrenberg and Baron van Heeckeren van Brandsenburg as ministers plenipotentiary to Russia in order to take part in conferences to be held there for the protection of neutral commerce.[1] In fact, however, the provinces were as indecisive on this question as on all others, the negotiations with Russia dragging slowly.

The American agent at the Hague thought the English party responsible for this procrastination, as they continued to perplex, delay, and cross everything. In his opinion the English intrigued in the United Provinces more than in all Europe besides.[2] They tried apparently every possible means to keep the Netherlands from taking part in the league of the Armed Neutrality. According to Prince Gallitzin the English court informed Count Welderen that the king would not hesitate to declare war upon the United Provinces in case the latter should formally accede to the maritime association. At the same time Ambassador Yorke was said to have insinuated at the Hague that if the Netherlands should abstain from entering into close relations with the northern powers, the king would unofficially issue orders by which the molestation of Dutch commerce would be discontinued.[3] At the beginning of August Lord Stormont asked the Dutch envoy if he had news from his government. The English cabinet, he stated, had been informed that the Republic intended to send a declaration to the British court,

---

[1] J. Adams to the President of Congress, July 14, 1780 (Wharton, III, 857).

Adams spelled the names of the two plenipotentiaries Baron de Waassenaar Starrenburg and Baron van Heckeren de Brantrenburg.

[2] Dumas to the President of Congress, July 15, 1780 (Wharton, III, 861); Carmichael to the Committee of Foreign Affairs, September 9, 1780 (ibid., IV, 53).

[3] Thulemeier to Frederick II, August 1, 1780 (Bancroft MSS., Prussia and Holland).

similar to that of Russia. He had, therefore, instructed Yorke to make known to the States General how offensive such a step must be to England, because the Republic was bound by engagements rather to assist Great Britain than to oppose her. If she should follow Russia's example, this would necessarily create the impression that she was inclined to be unfriendly toward England. The latter, Stormont concluded, earnestly wished to continue the old friendship with the United Provinces.[1]

Regarding the instructions given to the plenipotentiaries, Starrenberg and Brandsenburg, we learn from Thulemeier that the two Dutch noblemen, after their arrival at St. Petersburg, were to ask first for the guarantee, not as an essential condition, but as a favor, and then to inform the empress that the States General were very willing to make the required declaration to the belligerent powers. To render this step more effective, the United Provinces, however, wished to enter into closer relations with Russia. The plenipotentiaries were also to announce that the States General proposed to Catherine to unite the naval forces of the neutral powers and to put them into service for the protection of their subjects by forming several squadrons according to the pleasure of the empress.[2]

The Republic began now to put her navy on a better footing by manning her war vessels. According to John Adams, who had arrived at Amsterdam in a private capacity, she had great success in this because large premiums were paid for seamen, as much as sixty ducats a man. As an outward sign of the friendly relations existing between the United Provinces and Empress Catherine, Russian men-of-war arrived in Dutch waters and anchored off the Texel, their officers going ashore and visiting Amsterdam.[3] The English ambassador at the Hague now became more in-

---

[1] Welderen to the States General, August 4, 1780 (Bancroft MSS., America, Holland, and England).

[2] Thulemeier to Frederick II, August 11, 1780 (Bancroft MSS., Prussia and Holland).

[3] J. Adams to the President of Congress, August 14, 1780 (Wharton, IV, 29).

sistent. He continued to disapprove strongly of sending plenipotentiaries to St. Petersburg, suggesting that the differences between Great Britain and the United Provinces could easily be adjusted by nominating one or two plenipotentiaries for direct negotiations with the English ministry at London.

In the meantime the Dutch ambassadors had arrived at the Russian capital and were received by the empress. They thanked her on account of their masters and said that the Republic was not only willing to accede to the concert proposed for the protection of navigation, but to leave entirely to her discretion by what means it was to be effected. During the first interview the guarantee regarding the Dutch possessions in the East and West Indies was not mentioned.[1] Soon despatches arrived at the Hague from the plenipotentiaries stating that a convention was being negotiated upon the basis of that concluded by the northern courts with two additional articles. One was concerning the restitution of the ships which Great Britain had taken from the Republic, the other provided that in case the United Provinces should be attacked or molested because of their accession to the Armed Neutrality, the other parties to it would be bound to defend them. In a separate article it was to be stated that the aim of the maritime league was to bring about peace between the belligerents.

When John Adams heard of this, he said that he would dread any interposition of the assembly at St. Petersburg, since it was impossible for them to understand the subject, and America was not represented. "If they should take into consideration the affair of peace," he continued, "I should be apprehensive of some recommendations to save the pride, or what they would call the dignity, of England, which would be more dangerous and pernicious to America than a continuance of the war."

The reports from St. Petersburg showed also that Eng-

---

[1] Thulemeier to Frederick II, September 26, 1780 (Bancroft MSS., Prussia and Holland); J. Adams to the President of Congress, September 28, 1780 (Wharton, IV, 72).

land was still very active in her efforts to prevent the accession of the United Provinces to the northern league. The ministers plenipotentiary learned from the Russian minister that Ambassador Harris had taken steps in this direction. He was said to have informed Catherine that his court would respect the Armed Neutrality of the northern powers, provided that the United Provinces should not be admitted to it.[1] In fact, Sir James had received instructions from Lord Stormont, dated September 19, to use his influence with the empress in order to prevent the accession of the Dutch. Harris pointed out to Prince Potemkin that the empress should see while it was yet time "the dangers to which she exposed England, the difficulties in which she would involve herself, and the ruin to which she devoted Holland, if she joined with the Dutch in support of their unjust claims and ungrateful conduct."[2]

The Dutch plenipotentiaries consequently advised their government not to expect that, by delaying a final resolution or by further representations, anything could be gained. The only possibility of admission to the Armed Neutrality, they declared, lay in a quick decision.[3] No further mention was made of the guarantee. It had become known toward the end of September that Catherine had not only refused to grant it, but had demanded, as condition of the admittance of the Dutch, that the Republic should first make the declaration to the belligerents which Russia had presented to them in March. This attitude of the empress caused great disappointment and discouragement in the United Provinces. Amsterdam, however, supported by Vauguyon, adhered to the plan of becoming a member of the northern alliance.[4]

---

[1] Dumas to Franklin, October 3, 1780, and J. Adams to Dumas, October 4, 1780 (Wharton, IV, 76–78).
[2] Harris to Stormont, October 6/17, 1780 (Malmesbury, Correspondence, I, 337).
[3] Secret Resolutions of the States of Holland, October 13, 1780 (Sparks Dutch Papers) ; Carmichael to the Committee of Foreign Affairs, October 15, 1780 (Wharton, IV, 99, 100).
[4] Colenbrander, Patriottentijd, I. 181.

It was most important for England to prevent the accession of the Dutch to the Armed Neutrality, otherwise it would be difficult to cut off the providing of France and Spain with naval stores and ship timber, which were not considered contraband by the neutral league. For this reason war had to be declared upon the Republic before she presented to the British government the declaration demanded by Russia. Now was the time for England to act, because it became evident that having grown desperate the Dutch would join the league without their East and West Indian possessions being guaranteed to them by Russia and the alliance. It would have been foolish for the English to state the actual reason which led them to this step, because Russia and the northern powers might have sided with the Republic. Most welcome to them, therefore, was an occurrence which furnished a pretext for hostilities. This was the capture of the person and papers of Laurens, the former president of the Congress of the United States.

Henry Laurens was appointed to "negotiate a foreign loan" and at the same time as "a commissioner to negotiate a treaty of amity and commerce with the United Provinces of the Low Countries," his instructions being dated October 26, 1779.[1] His commission was resolved upon November 1, 1779, but adverse conditions had kept him from sailing until early in the fall of 1780.[2] On September 3, while the packet on which he was a passenger was off the coast of Newfoundland, she was captured by the British boat "Vestal." Laurens threw the bag containing his papers overboard, but the weight affixed to it proved insufficient, and bag and papers fell into the hands of the British.[3] Laurens

---

[1] Secret Journals of Congress, II, 283, 285, 290, 314, 320 (Wharton, III, 394).

[2] Laurens to the Committee of Foreign Affairs, January 24, February 14 and 24 (Wharton, III, 468, 494, 516; ibid., IV, 56, footnote).

At what time and from what place Laurens sailed does not appear from his correspondence.

[3] Laurens to the Committee of Foreign Affairs, September 14, 1780 (Wharton, IV, 56); J. Adams to the President of Congress, October 31, 1780 (ibid., IV, 109, 110).

was taken to England in the sloop of war "Fairy" and imprisoned in the Tower of London.[1] Among the papers were letters from J. D. van der Capellen and others, pointing out the friends of the American cause in the United Provinces, and above all the draft treaty arranged by William Lee and Neufville in 1778.[2] This draft treaty was deemed sufficient to furnish a pretext for war, if need be, and England determined to use it to the best advantage. There was no reason to suppose that "the Northern Powers would espouse a quarrel founded on an intrigue unknown to them."[3]

The English government sent the papers to Yorke, who said that he was not surprised at the facts they revealed, since he always suspected intrigues between France, Amsterdam, and the rebels in America. He consulted Griffier Fagel, who agreed that the ambassador should communicate the documents to Prince Louis of Brunswick. With the latter Yorke was especially satisfied, because Brunswick promised to cooperate with him, not only in encouraging the stadtholder, but also in drawing every advantage from the discovery in the interest of England. Acting upon the duke's advice, Yorke, on October 16, informed the Prince of Orange of what had happened, finding him, however, already prepared by Brunswick. The stadtholder was of Yorke's opinion that, if the draft treaty had been an act of the States General, it should be considered as an aggression and a declaration of war. But even as it was, William agreed that the discovery would justify every measure England might take against the United Provinces "without any

---

[1] Extract of letters from Louden to Dumas, October 6, 10, and 17, 1780 (Wharton, IV, 84, 85).
[2] Above, pp. 89 ff.
[3] Yorke to Stormont, October 17, 1780 (Sparks MSS., LXXII). Van der Capellen in a letter to John Adams, dated November 28, 1780, judged the conduct of the English rightly when he stated that the object of the English was " de nous [the Dutch] entrainer en guerre *avant* d'être admis à la Neutralité armée, afin de donner occasion aux Puissances confederées de pouvoir nous refuser comme n'aiant pas la qualification requise, savoir d'être *une puissance neutre* " (Beaufort, Brieven van der Capellen, 206).

other neutral power being concerned in it." The prince did
not doubt that this "lucky" discovery would greatly assist
the cause of Great Britain. Yorke thought that the affair
could not fail "to occasion a wonderful alarm" in the
United Provinces, and that the enthusiasm existing there
for the alliance of the Armed Neutrality would be greatly
reduced, which would in itself be a great point, "if nothing
else happens." It would, he said, also thoroughly open the
eyes of the stadtholder.[1]

Brunswick advised the Prince of Orange not only to communicate the discovery to the burgomasters of Amsterdam,
but to make it as widely known as possible. A good way
to proceed would be to inform the burgomasters first only
of the draft treaty and a letter of Mr. de Neufville upon
the subject. The other papers should be kept in reserve in
order to frighten those concerned with the fear of additional knowledge which the prince might have of their plot.
The stadtholder should then ask categorically whether the
city of Amsterdam had authorized Pensionary van Berckel
to negotiate such a treaty with the English colonies in
America as an independent state, although they were not
recognized by the United Provinces nor by most of the other
nations. He could not believe, the prince was to declare,
that they would have done this without the knowledge of
the other members of the state and of the stadtholder. In
order to draw the most advantage from the discovery,
Brunswick told Prince William that other provinces ought
to be speedily informed of it, which would be easy since all
were assembled together. This might perhaps be the best
means of preventing the Dutch declaration regarding the
Armed Neutrality from being submitted to the belligerent
powers. The discovery might serve as an argument to save
the United Provinces from the embarrassing position in
which France had placed them. He did not doubt that
the English government had notified Ambassador Harris
at St. Petersburg, who would make good use of it with

---

[1] Yorke to Stormont, October 17, 1780 (Sparks MSS., LXXII).

the empress. As a measure of precaution Duke Louis recommended that the originals of the papers should not be intrusted to Temminck or the other magistrates of Amsterdam, but that only copies be transmitted.[1]

The stadtholder, acting upon this advice, summoned Temminck for an explanation of the matter. The burgomaster replied that Berckel had only carried out the instructions of the regency of Amsterdam.[2] A direct trade with the United States must be of the greatest advantage to the United Provinces; besides, the negotiations had only been casu quo. It was an obsolete transaction which was without effect. It had been occasioned by intelligence received at Amsterdam that the English commissioners sent to America had been directed to exclude the United Provinces from trading with America in case a reconciliation should be effected. Other countries would have been admitted to such commerce.[3] William V told Temminck then that the matter would be laid before the States of Holland on the same day, and demanded that the pensionary should not be present during that meeting of the provincial assembly.[4] Before proceeding to the latter the stadtholder handed the papers to the secret committee of the States General, where they were taken ad referendum to be communicated to the provinces.[5]

The States of Holland declared that they had no knowledge of the matter and demanded an explanation from the city of Amsterdam.[6] On October 25 the answer from Am-

---

[1] Brunswick to the Prince of Orange, October 17, 1780 (Nijhoff, Brunswijk, 320, 321).

[2] Above, p. 89.

[3] Thulemeier to Frederick II, October 24, 1780 (Bancroft MSS., Prussia and Holland); Yorke to Stormont, October 24, 1780 (Sparks MSS., LXXII).

Yorke, in concluding his report, remarked, " From this narrative, which contains a full avowal and even a justification, it is evident to what a pitch the tyranny of Amsterdam has risen, and what may be expected from them if they continue to rule."

[4] Yorke to Stormont, October 20, 1780 (Sparks MSS., LXXII).

[5] Secret Resolution of the States General, October 20, 1780 (Sparks Dutch Papers).

[6] Secret Resolutions of the States of Holland and Westfriesland, October 20, 1780 (Sparks Dutch Papers).

sterdam, dated October 24, practically repeated the statement made by Burgomaster Temminck to the Prince of Orange. The assembly of Holland transmitted the report to the States General, by whom it was referred to the provinces for deliberation.[1] Yorke presumed that the States General would finally disavow the conduct of the city of Amsterdam, but in his opinion this would not be giving the satisfaction to which England was entitled. He proposed, therefore, that satisfaction should be formally demanded, blaming only Amsterdam for this incident. In case of a refusal, or if an answer should be withheld, Amsterdam might be separated from the rest of the Republic in every respect, just as should seem best to England. Ships belonging to Amsterdam might be brought up and retained until satisfaction was given, or the Texel and Vlie, forming the gates to the Zuider Zee and consequently to Amsterdam, might be blockaded, while all the other ports of the United Provinces should remain open. An immediate demand for satisfaction, Yorke expected, would have a great influence on the northern powers, since he thought that they would not be inclined to quarrel with England for the sake of the Dutch.[2]

In execution of this scheme, the ambassador on November 10 presented a memorial to the States General, setting forth that the alliance of Great Britain and the United Provinces contributed to the happiness of the two nations, but the natural enemy of both wanted to destroy it and was supported in this effort by a faction in the Republic. On the other hand, the king's requisition of the stipulated assistance remained without effect, doubtless because of the influence of a dominant cabal. The king, however, hoped that the States General would return to the system which was founded by the wisdom of their ancestors, and had charged his ambassador to present the accompanying decla-

---

[1] Secret Resolutions of the States General, October 27, 1780 (Bancroft MSS., America, Holland, and England; Sparks MSS., CIII; Sparks Dutch Papers); J. Adams to the President of Congress, October 27, 1780 (Wharton, IV, 106, 107).
[2] Yorke to Stormont, October 31, 1780 (Sparks MSS., LXXII).

ration to Their High Mightinesses, the reply to which would be regarded as the touchstone of their intentions and their sentiments toward the English. The king asked of the States General a formal disavowal of the conduct of Amsterdam regarding the negotiations with America, and the exemplary punishment of the Pensionary van Berckel and his accomplices. In case the States General should refuse to comply with this request or remain silent, the king would be obliged to take such measures as the maintenance of his dignity required.[1]

John Adams, learning the contents of the English ambassador's memorial, observed, " Whether Sir Joseph Yorke, after 20 years residence in this Republic, is ignorant of its constitution, or whether, knowing it, he treats it in this manner on purpose the more palpably to insult it, I know not." To Adams, who seems not yet to have been aware of its purpose, this English measure must have been surprising. The sovereignty of the United Provinces resided in the States General, but Their High Mightinesses who assembled at the Hague were only the deputies. The real States General, in his opinion, were the regencies of the cities and the bodies of nobles in the several provinces. The burgomasters of the city of Amsterdam, called the regency, were therefore an integral part of the sovereignty. What would be said in England if the Dutch envoy at the court of London had handed a note to the king, in which any integral part of the sovereignty of Great Britain, as the whole House of Lords, or the whole House of Commons, was charged with conspiracy, factions, cabals, and sacrificing of general interests to private views, and had demanded exemplary punishment?[2]

---

[1] Sparks Dutch Papers; Bancroft MSS., America, Holland, and England.

[2] J. Adams to the President of Congress, November 16, 1780 (Wharton, IV, 153, 154).

On November 20, 1780, however, Adams wrote to van der Capellen that the King of England would commence hostilities against the United Provinces on pretense of an insult committed by the negotiation of Amsterdam with the United States (Wharton, IV, 157; Beaufort, Brieven van der Capellen, 201).

The memorial, made public in the Dutch gazettes by Yorke, was very much resented in the United Provinces, causing there considerable alarm.[1] Even the British partisans did not, in general, agree with it. The burgomasters of Amsterdam issued a detailed pamphlet in which they tried to justify their action,[2] being successful at least as far as the broad public was concerned. Yorke was not generally thought to be the author of the memorial, but Lord Stormont. It was believed that the former had in vain made representations in London predicting that such a step would cause too great dissatisfaction in the United Provinces. The fact was, however, that the ambassador, far from warning against strong measures, was the motive power behind the hostile attitude of the English government toward the Dutch Republic. Grand Pensionary van Bleiswijck rightly suspected that England was using this case as a means to prevent the accession of the United Provinces to the Armed Neutrality.[3]

Francis Dana, who, on a short visit to the United Provinces for the purpose of raising money, happened to be in Amsterdam with John Adams,[4] shared the same opinion. Holland and three other provinces had already declared for unconditional adhesion to the pact, while two more pleaded that the Dutch territories in both Indies should be previously guaranteed, without, however, making this an absolute condition. The only province which was against the measure was Zealand.[5] This Dana ascribed to the unlimited influ-

---

[1] Thulemeier to Frederick II, November 11, 1780 (Bancroft MSS., Prussia and Holland); Yorke to Stormont, November 14, 1780 (Sparks MSS., LXXII).

[2] Yorke to Stormont, November 3, 1780 (Sparks MSS., LXXII); Thulemeier to Frederick II, November 3, 1780 (Bancroft MSS., Prussia and Holland); Dana to Jonathan Jackson, November 11, 1780 (Wharton, IV, 151).

[3] Thulemeier to Frederick II, November 14, 1780 (Bancroft MSS., Prussia and Holland).

[4] Wharton, I, 574.

[5] When the wording of the declaration to the belligerent powers was deliberated upon by the States General, the deputies of Zealand protested (Secret Resolution of the States General, November 20, 1780, in Sparks MSS., CIII; Bancroft MSS., America, Holland, and England).

ence exercised there by the Prince of Orange, but possibly the other six states might accede without Zealand. The hesitation of the Republic was due to her not being prepared for war, since only twenty-six of the fifty-two war vessels voted for were ready for sea.[1]   At the beginning of November the report of the burgomasters of Amsterdam regarding the draft treaty had been examined by the states of the province of Holland in a secret session, and the action of Amsterdam disavowed, but a final resolution was postponed.[2]

In the meantime, the French party was not inactive, as may be seen from a letter of Sir Joseph Yorke to his government, in which, by the way, he accused Prussia of taking part in the intrigues.   "It is notorious," he said, "that the Cabal, supported by France and Prussia, is as inveterate as it is active, and that at the bottom all it does and all it means, is to gain time to be better prepared, and if possible, to draw the Northern League into the snare, by making their particular aggression a common cause with the pretended armed neutrality."[3]   Utmost vigilance was recommended to the ambassador by the authorities in London.   It would be essential, he was told, to watch John Adams as narrowly as possible, because it was suspected that he had at least some of the powers which were given to Mr. Laurens.[4]   On November 20, the States General resolved to accede to the Armed Neutrality without the stipulation of a guarantee regarding the East and West Indian possessions.   This decision was reached by a majority of votes, namely, those of Holland, Utrecht, Friesland, Overyssel, and Groningen against Guelderland and Zealand, the latter still insisting on the guarantee clause, though they agreed to the accession in principle.[5]

---

[1] Dana to Jonathan Jackson, November 11, 1780 (Wharton, IV, 152).

[2] Secret Resolutions of Holland and Westfriesland, November 3, 1780 (Sparks Dutch Papers).

[3] Yorke to Stormont, November 21, 1780 (Sparks MSS., LXXII).

[4] Stormont to Yorke, November 21, 1780 (Sparks MSS., LXXII).

[5] Gazette de Leyde, XCIV, November 24, 1780; J. Adams to the President of Congress, November 25, 1780 (Wharton, IV, 160).

John Adams considered it a mistake for the Prince of Orange to have produced Mr. Laurens' papers; and particularly was the way in which he did it unfortunate, since it was "justly offensive" to the United States. Yorke would have been the proper authority to submit the papers, for the prince in so doing appeared to be an instrument of the English ambassador, which did not at all recommend him to the Dutch nation.[1] Adams' remarks were made shortly after the States of Holland had passed a resolution which disapproved and disavowed the conduct of the magistrates of Amsterdam.[2] This resolution was passed by the States General without change and communicated to the English ambassador[3] by the Grand Pensionary in writing.[4]

Both resolutions failed to provide for the punishment of van Berckel, which the English memorial had demanded. Yorke answered, therefore, that the resolutions did not contain the satisfaction demanded, but that he imagined the king would look upon this decision of the States General as a first step toward a compliance with his demands. Regarding the accession of the Republic to the Armed Neutrality the ambassador reported that the messenger who was carrying the resolutions of the States General to St. Petersburg had been recalled by an express courier. Sir Joseph also learned that a letter from the Grand Pensionary had been handed to the messenger enclosing the resolution of the States of Holland upon the "American intrigue." The matter, he said, was represented in such a way that it must appear as if all the satisfaction necessary had been given to Great Britain. The courier was ordered to stop at the village of Voor-

---

[1] J. Adams to the President of Congress, November 25, 1780 (Wharton, IV, 161).

[2] Resolution of Holland and Westfriesland, November 23, 1780 (Groot Placaatboek, IX, 30; Sparks Dutch Papers; Sparks MSS., CIII; Bancroft MSS., America, Holland, and England); Thulemeier to Frederick II, November 24, 1780 (Bancroft MSS., Prussia and Holland); Yorke to Stormont, November 24, 1780 (Sparks MSS., LXXII).

[3] Secret Resolution of the States General, November 27, 1780 (Bancroft MSS., America, Holland, and England).

[4] Thulemeier to Frederick II, November 28, 1780 (Bancroft MSS, Prussia and Holland).

schooten and wait there, in order to receive the resolution of the States General upon the same subject for transmission to the Dutch plenipotentiaries at St. Petersburg.[1]

At the Rusian court the English intrigue was carried on with increasing zeal, but apparently without success. Count Panin, according to Sir James Harris, was "working every engine" to have the Dutch admitted to the Armed Neutrality. The British ambassador suspected that Panin was concealing the truth from Catherine, but hoped that the empress would not admit the United Provinces, unless all seven agreed in their opinion.[2] That the decision of the States General would not be unanimous Harris knew from Yorke, who kept him informed of the proceedings at the Hague. Sir James tried also to gain an ally in the Austrian envoy at St. Petersburg. In a letter addressed to the English ambassador at Vienna, Harris expressed his confidence that England's effort would succeed in cutting up by the roots the convention of the Armed Neutrality by taking from the United Provinces their title of neutrals, for the Dutch were an "ungrateful, dirty, senseless" people. He asked his colleague to prevail upon the court of Vienna to instruct Cobenzel, the Austrian representative at St. Petersburg, to assist Harris in influencing Catherine against the Netherlands.[3]

It remained no secret that Harris was instructed from London to declare to the empress that the Dutch by their negotiations with America had departed from neutral

---

[1] Yorke to Stormont, November 28, 1780 (Sparks MSS., LXXII).

John Adams, who in this instance was not so well informed as Yorke, thought that the recalling of the courier was intended for some change in the instructions sent to the Dutch plenipotentiaries in Russia, but, he said, it was unknown what alteration was to be made (J. Adams to the President of Congress, in Wharton, IV, 175).

[2] Harris to Stormont, November 18/28, 1780 (Malmesbury, Correspondence, I, 342).

The view that Catherine would not admit the United Provinces on the ground that the vote had not been unanimous was shared by Yorke (Yorke to Stormont, December 3, 1789, in Sparks MSS., LXXII).

[3] Harris to Sir Robert M. Keith, November 29, 1780 (Malmesbury, Correspondence, I, 345).

ground and should, therefore, not aspire to enjoy the same prerogatives as Russia, Sweden, and Denmark.[1] Yorke warned his government that too much care and pains could not be employed to keep the United Provinces from acceding to the Armed Neutrality.[2] All these efforts showed how great the apprehension of Great Britain was that the Dutch would escape her control.

At this time Sir Joseph Yorke presented a new memorial to the States General in which he insisted upon a satisfactory answer to his previous memorial regarding the draft treaty with the United States. The king, he said, put the punishment of the culprits in the hands of the States General, and only in the last extremity would charge himself with it. It was, however, pointed out to the ambassador that the States General had no jurisdiction over the individual provinces, and that they must leave the matter to the province of Holland.[3]

John Adams remarked regarding Yorke's action that a widening of the breach with the Republic by England did not seem probable, but if a rupture should occur, it would do no harm to the United States for Great Britain to have more enemies to contend with.[4] Even Yorke himself observed that the Dutch, in general, thought a serious quarrel with England impossible.[5] The Prince of Orange was in despair. At least so it seemed from a report of the English ambassador in which he stated that William V acted as if he had fallen into the hands of Great Britain's enemies.

---

[1] Thulemeier to Frederick II, December 1, 1780 (Bancroft MSS., Prussia and Holland).

[2] Yorke to Stormont, December 8, 1780 (Sparks MSS., LXXII).

[3] Gazette de Leyde, CI, December 19, 1780; Yorke to Stormont, December 12, 1780 (Sparks MSS., LXXII; Bancroft MSS., America, Holland, and England); Resolution of the States General, December 12, 1780 (Sparks Dutch Papers); Thulemeier to Frederick II, December 15, 1780 (Bancroft MSS., Prussia and Holland); J. Adams to the President of Congress, December 18, 1780 (Wharton, IV, 197).

[4] J. Adams to Cushing, December 15, 1780 (Wharton, IV, 193).

[5] Yorke to Stormont, December 3, 1780 (Sparks MSS., LXXII).

Yorke, as usual, talked very frankly to him about his conduct and that of the states toward England, avoiding, however, mentioning the negotiations with Russia and with the other powers of the Armed Neutrality.[1]

A few days after Sir Joseph had delivered his memorial, he was informed by the States General that it had been referred to the provinces and that a definite answer would be given as quickly as the constitution of the government would allow.[2] About the same time the British cabinet, learning on December 16 of the Dutch resolution to join the neutral league,[3] took final steps by directing Yorke to quit the United Provinces without taking leave.[4] This meant the severance of all diplomatic relations with the Republic, a measure almost equalling a declaration of war, and the friendship which had existed between the two countries for 106 years would cease.[5] However, the transmission of the orders to Yorke met with some delay, owing to rough sea, and in the meanwhile the Dutch envoy in London, informed by Stormont, reported to the States General the resolution taken by the English government, but his missive also was late in reaching the Hague. Welderen added that he was prepared to leave England as soon as he should receive orders to that effect from the States General, and that he would not go to court any more.[6]

This last English action was in keeping with the policy which the British government had followed ever since the American Revolution had begun. This was to render the Dutch as far as possible unable to assist England's enemies.

---

[1] Yorke to Stormont, December 12, 1780 (Sparks MSS., LXXII).
[2] Resolution of the States General, December 15, 1780 (Bancroft MSS., America, Holland, and England).
[3] Mahan, Influence of Sea Power, 406.
[4] Stormont to Yorke, December 16, 1780 (Sparks MSS., LXXII).
[5] Kampen, Verkorte Geschiedenis, II, 295; Doniol, Histoire, IV, 516; Davies, History of Holland, III, 463.
[6] Welderen to the States General, December 17 and 19; both letters were received at the Hague on December 25 (Bancroft MSS., America, Holland, and England); Resolution of the States General, December 25, 1780 (Sparks MSS., CIII).

Thus far England had been only partly successful, but now that all friendly relations between the two countries had ceased it would be easier to check the commerce and navigation of the United Provinces, which had proved so harmful to the English cause. There was, however, no time left for Great Britain to take this measure, since the accession of the Republic to the league of the Armed Neutrality was near at hand.[1]

The last Dutch courier had brought full powers to the commissioners of the United Provinces at St. Petersburg to accede on behalf of the States General to the league as proposed by the Russian court. The Russian envoy learned that as soon as everything was agreed upon the Dutch plenipotentiaries would produce credentials as ambassadors and sign the Convention under that title. They were also instructed to propose a treaty of commerce, on terms highly advantageous to Russia. Both of the commissioners had constantly been in conference with Panin, and, according to Harris, had found in him more facility and zeal than they could even have hoped for, since the Russian minister intended to urge the empress to lose no time in forming the connection which he represented to her as most salutary to her empire and most conducive to her glory.[2] Catherine agreed, and the plenipotentiaries signed on January 4, the acts then being dispatched to be ratified by the States Gen-

---

[1] E. Lusac, R. Vryaarts openhartige Brieven, I, 20.

For more than two years van der Capellen had asserted that England, in pursuance of her interests, needed a war with the United Provinces, and that she would have it (Van der Capellen to Vauguyon, in Beaufort, Brieven van der Capellen, 241).

[2] Harris to Stormont, December 8/19, 1780 (Malmesbury, Correspondence, I, 347, 348).

Harris' report of a conversation which he had with the empress is interesting. After he had explained to her why the Armed Neutrality was hurtful to England, Catherine asked him in return, "You molest my commerce; you hold up my vessels; I attach to that a particular interest; my commerce is my child, and you want me not to be angry?" (Harris to Stormont, December 13/24, 1780, in Malmesbury, Correspondence, I, 355). It was evident that Harris' mission had been a complete failure, at least as far as the formal conclusion of the Armed Neutrality was concerned. It was different regarding the execution of its principles.

eral.[1] That Russia, however, would give the Dutch no further support was the firm belief of Sir James Harris.[2]

On December 21, 1780, the States of Holland resolved that the provincial court of Holland should decide whether the papers taken from Laurens contained anything that, according to the constitution of the United Provinces, would justify criminal procedure against the burgomasters of Amsterdam and their pensionary.[3] On the following day the States General passed this resolution without change and Yorke was informed that only the States of Holland were competent in this matter.[4] Sir Joseph refused to accept this action, and suggested that the States General should transmit it to his court through Count van Welderen.[5]

Yorke received his letter of recall on December 24 and left the Hague on the following morning for Rotterdam and Antwerp to proceed from there to England.[6] The States

---

[1] J. Adams to the President of Congress, February 1, 1781 (Wharton, IV, 244–248) ; Dumas to the President of Congress, January 23, 1781 (ibid., IV, 200) ; Secret Resolution of the States General, January 22, 1781 (Sparks MSS., CIII).

Harris reported to his government that he was not able to prevent the admission of the Dutch to the neutral league, since Potemkin acted too late upon his advice (Harris to Stormont, December 29, 1780/January 9, 1781, in Malmesbury, Correspondence, I, 371).

[2] Harris to Stormont, December 13/24, 1780 (Malmesbury, Correspondence, I, 349).

John Adams' opinion was directly opposite. He thought the confederated powers would easily see that the real cause of offence was not the Dutch-American draft treaty but the accession of the Dutch to the Armed Neutrality, and that they would assist the Netherlands (J. Adams to the President of Congress, December 25, 1780, in Wharton, IV, 210).

[3] Resolutions of Holland and Westfriesland, December 21, 1780 (Sparks Dutch Papers).

[4] Resolutions of the States General, December 22, 1780 (Bancroft MSS., America, Holland, and England; Sparks Dutch Papers).

[5] Yorke to the States General, December 22, 1780 (Bancroft MSS., America, Holland, and England) ; Resolution of the States General, December 23, 1780 (Sparks Dutch Papers) ; Dumas to the President of Congress, December 19, 26, 27 (Wharton, IV, 199).

[6] Yorke to Stormont, December 29, 1780 (Sparks MSS., LXXII) ; J. Adams to the President of Congress, December 26, 1780 (Wharton, IV, 211) ; Gazette de Leyde, CIV, December 29, 1780, Supplement.

Regarding a pension of £2,000, granted to Yorke, and Pitt's com-

General, on their part, instructed Welderen to return to the United Provinces, but to transmit, before his departure, to the English government the declaration of the United Provinces regarding their accession to the Armed Neutrality.[1] It could afford only small consolation to the Dutch that the King of France assured them he would protect their legitimate and innocent commerce. He expected in return, he said, that they would take the most efficient measures in order to have their subjects fulfil scrupulously the conditions which guaranteed the liberty of their commerce.[2]

On December 20, George III issued a manifesto, which was communicated to van Welderen on the following day. It contained all the real and pretended grievances of England against the United Provinces and was intended to veil the actual reason for England's attitude.[3] The king attributed the conduct of the Republic to the prevalence in the United Provinces of a faction which was devoted to France and was following the dictates of that court. After the commencement of the war with France his ambassador had been instructed to offer friendly negotiations to the States General in order to obviate everything that might lead to disagreeable discussions, but no attention was paid to Yorke's proposition of November 2, 1778. After Spain joined the war, the States General were asked to carry out their obligations in accordance with Article 5 of the perpetual defensive alliance between England and the United Provinces of March 3, 1678, providing that the party of

pliment to his ability as an ambassador, see: William Pitt, Chancellor of the Exchequer, in debate of March 6, 1783 (Register, London, 1783, Vol. IX, p. 416).

[1] Thulemeier to Frederick II, December 25, 1780 (Bancroft MSS., Prussia and Holland).

The Dutch declaration was delivered to the French government on December 19 (Berkenrode to the States General, December 21, 1780, in Bancroft MSS., America, Holland, and England).

The Prussian foreign ministers, Finckenstein and Hertzberg, were informed of the declaration by the Dutch envoy at Berlin, Count van Heiden, on December 20 (Bancroft MSS., Prussia and Holland).

[2] Appendix to a letter of Berkenrode to the States General, December 28, 1780. The Appendix itself is dated December 23, 1780 (Bancroft MSS., America, Holland, and England).

[3] Le Politique Hollandais, No. 1, Chapter II, 7.

the allies not attacked should break with the aggressor within two months after the party attacked required it. The Republic had within two years not furnished any assistance, nor even answered England's repeated demands. On the other hand neutrality had been promised to Great Britain's enemies and secret aid given to them by facilitating the carriage of naval stores to France. Shelter had been granted to John Paul Jones in the Texel, protection and assistance had been rendered to the American rebels in St. Eustatia, and finally the Dutch had drafted a treaty with the American government. As no satisfaction had been given, the king must get for himself that justice which was not otherwise to be obtained.[1]

When Franklin saw a copy of the document, he remarked: " Surely there never was a more unjust war; it is manifestly such from their own manifesto. The spirit of rapine dictated it, and in my opinion every man in England who fits out a privateer to take advantage of it has the same spirit, and would rob on the highway in his own country if he was not restrained by fear of the gallows."[2]

Count Welderen in execution of his instructions tried in vain to hand the Dutch declaration to the British government. Lord Stormont refused to receive him on the ground that, as a consequence of the manifesto of the king, the Republic had to be regarded " as being in war with England."[3] Welderen was therefore compelled to leave England without fulfilling his instructions.[4]

---

[1] Gazette de Leyde, No. I, January 2, 1781, Supplement; J. Adams to the President of Congress, January 1, 1781 (Wharton, IV, 219–221); De Vinck (Ostende) to States General, December 27, 1780 (Sparks Dutch Papers).

[2] Franklin to Dumas, January 18, 1781 (Wharton, IV, 240).

[3] Welderen to the States General, December 21 and 29, 1780 (Bancroft MSS., America, Holland, and England).
The causes and motives of George III's conduct were laid before the English Parliament in a message on January 25, 1781. In it, of course, the Dutch were represented as the aggressors, making a rupture with the United Provinces indispensable (Hansard, Parliamentary History, XXI, 960). A short account of the events preceding the rupture was sent by J. Adams to the President of Congress on January 5 and 15, 1781 (Wharton, IV, 228, 229, 234).

[4] Resolution of the States General, January 15, 1781 (Sparks MSS., CIII).

Harris remained firm in his belief that no harm would be done to England by Russia. Great Britain's enemies would never so far mislead Catherine as to make her believe that the support of the United Provinces was a casus foederis of the convention of the Armed Neutrality. The King of Prussia was moving heaven and earth to fix this idea in her mind, and, besides, was offering troops to the Dutch in any number, and money to the Danes in any amount, provided only that they should employ their ships against England.[1] The fact seems to have been that the Empress of Russia, at this time, was favorably disposed toward the Republic, while she was indignant at the attitude of Great Britain.[2] Harris tried every means to thwart the ratification by Russia of the convention with the United Provinces, but without success. He informed his government that he had been more lucky in preventing the immediate evils with which the accession of the Dutch threatened England. He had prevailed on Her Majesty to act only as a well-wisher to both countries, and to show that determination by holding out conditions "by no means dishonorable" to the English.[3]

---

[1] Harris to Keith, January 10/21, 1781 (Malmesbury, Correspondence, I, 376).

Prussia acceded to the Armed Neutrality on May 8, 1781. Thulemeier transmitted a copy of the treaty to the States General in August, 1781 (Thulemeier to Frederick II, August 21, 1781, in Bancroft MSS., Prussia and Holland).

[2] Thulemier to Frederick II, January 12, 1781 (Bancroft MSS., Prussia and Holland); Dumas to the President of Congress, January 23, 1781 (Wharton, IV, 200).

[3] Harris to Stormont, April 13/24, 1781 (Malmesbury, Correspondence, I, 403).

A curious diplomatic blunder of the United States of America should be mentioned here, namely, its request to be admitted to the neutral league. In execution of the resolution of Congress of October 5, 1780, John Adams on March 8, 1781, transmitted a memorial to the States General in which he said that the American Revolution had furnished the occasion of a reformation in the maritime law of nations of vast importance to a free communication among mankind by sea, and that he therefore hoped it might not be thought improper that the United States should become parties to it. Copies of this memorial were delivered by him to the representatives at the Hague of France, Russia, Denmark, and Sweden, and also to the pensionary of Amsterdam (Wharton, IV, 274, 275). Since the object of the convention of the Armed Neutrality was to guard the rights

The verdict which was pronounced by the provincial court of Holland on the action of Amsterdam caused much embarrassment. Van Berckel was acquitted, but the city of Amsterdam was declared guilty and criminal.[1] The French ambassador warned his Dutch friends not to adopt that declaration, because it would justify the hostilities of England, and the city of Amsterdam wrote to the Prince of Orange asking him to oppose the publication of the verdict.[2] Van Berckel sent an address to the States of Holland and Westfriesland in which he defended his honor and asked to have his innocence declared.[3]

The whole Dutch people were in a state of utmost consternation, since they were not at all prepared for war, although it had been threatening for a long time. On January 12, 1781, the States General resolved to distribute letters of marque to privateers and orders to their men of war to seize everything that they could belonging to the English. But there were no privateers ready and comparatively few war vessels,[4] while as early as the end of December, 1780, a great many English privateers had left Liverpool to capture Dutch vessels.[5] Here and there voices were

---

of neutrals against belligerents and the United States was a belligerent power, the American proposition could not be complied with. Vauguyon refused to second Adams without express order from the French government (Vauguyon to Adams, March 14, 1781, in Wharton, IV, 300).

The Gazette de Leyde registered with satisfaction the failure of England to prevent the accession of the United Provinces to the Armed Neutrality (XXVII, April 3, 1781).

[1] J. G. Tegelaar to van der Capellen, March 21, 1781 (Beaufort, Brieven van der Capellen, 225).

[2] Thulemeier to Frederick II, March 27 and 30, 1781 (Bancroft MSS., Prussia and Holland).

[3] Resolutions of the States of Holland and Westfriesland, May 4, 1781; Thulemeier to Frederick II, May 8, 1781 (Bancroft MSS., Prussia and Holland).

[4] Dumas to the President of Congress, January 12, 1781 (Wharton, IV, 200); J. Adams to the President of Congress, January 14, 1781 (ibid., IV, 231).

The States General on January 26, 1781, issued orders forbidding the Dutch to export contraband of war to England or goods for the account of the English king and his subjects (Groot Placaatboek, IX, 109, 110).

[5] Tegelaar to van der Capellen, December 26, 1780 (Beaufort, Brieven van der Capellen, 222).

heard, including that of the government of Zealand, which pleaded for reconciliation with England, but petitions to this effect remained without consideration by the States General.[1]   Others were hopeful that the United Provinces would be victorious in the end, though they might be defeated by Great Britain in the beginning and lose St. Eustatia together with other West Indian possessions.[2]   It was thought throughout the United Provinces that the Republic would receive effective assistance from the neutral league.[3]

The Dutch press was a power of great influence in the Netherlands during the period under consideration and especially during the Dutch-English controversy.[4]   Both parties, the Orangists as well as the Patriots, made the most intense use of it, in order to propagate their respective views.   Its importance in the political development of the country equalled if not exceeded that of the political press of our own time.   There were in existence two classes of literature of this kind, newspapers and sporadically issued pamphlets.   Up to 1780 the Dutch newspapers had only registered the current events in a colorless way, but from then on they served party purposes more or less, their number at the same time increasing considerably.   The majority of them were organs of the Patriots.[5]   Many of the

---

[1] J. Adams to the President of Congress, January 15, 1781 (Wharton, IV, 232).
The Province of Zealand then declared her willingness to take part in the hostilities, but reserved to herself the right of demanding, from the other provinces, compensation for all the cost, losses, and damages which she might experience during the hostilities with England (Van der Spiegel, II, 4-11).

[2] Tegelaar to van der Capellen, December 26, 1780 (Beaufort, Brieven van der Capellen, 220-221).

[3] Gazette de Leyde, No. 1, January 2, 1781, Supplement.

[4] John Adams frequently made use of the Dutch press for furthering the American cause in the United Provinces.   This was possible by the assistance of Cérisier, Dumas and others, without Adams' becoming known as the author (J. Adams to Livingston, September 4, 1782, in Wharton, V, 690-691).

[5] Perhaps one of the oldest Dutch newspapers, still in vogue at the outbreak of war between the United Provinces and England, was the "Nederlandsche Mercurius" (1756-1806).   In a French spirit were published, from 1779, the "Lettres Hollandaises" (Dutch

pamphlets were edited anonymously and, consequently, exhibited a more violent character than the party newspapers, since their authors could not easily be brought to account. The distribution of these pamphlets in the United Provinces was usually effected as secretly as their publication, and they reached all classes of the population. At this period they grew like mushrooms and formed not only a potent factor in party controversies but tended to influence considerably the foreign policy of the Netherlands.

No doubt, the most famous of these pamphlets was the one entitled "Aan het Volk van Nederland" (To the People of the Netherlands).[1] Only recently has the author

Letters), a paper which originated in the French legation at the Hague. One of its editors was A. M. Cérisier, a clever author, entertaining close relations to the French ambassador. Its name was later changed to "Nouvelles Lettres Hollandaises" (New Dutch Letters), and from 1787 to "Le Politique Hollandais" (Dutch Politics), when Cérisier took the editing into his own hands. The most influential Patriot paper was probably "De Post van den Neder-Rhijn" (1780–1787), edited by Pieter 't Hoen, and read in thousands of copies. Van der Capellen and van der Kemp, regents of Amsterdam, and other Patriots contributed to it. To counteract it the Orangist van Goens, with the knowledge and support of the stadtholder, issued the "Ouderwetse Nederlandsche Patriot" (1781–1783). It was well written, but its edition did not exceed seven hundred copies and it had therefore soon to be discontinued (Blok, Geschiedenis, VI, 577; Colenbrander, Patriottentijd, I, 258). One of the most violent Patriot papers was the "Politieke Kruyer," but it was issued only from September, 1782 (Blok, Geschiedenis, VI, 398). A periodical of vast importance which became popular in most European countries on account of its reliability was the "Gazette de Leyde," edited by Etienne and Jean Luzac, who inclined toward France and greatly aided the American cause.

The memory of Jean Luzac was honored by the Holland Society of Philadelphia when, in 1909, it sent as delegate a prominent member, the noted author of various books on Holland, Dr. William Elliot Griffis of Ithaca, New York, to Leyden in order to place there on the house once occupied by Luzac a tablet, bearing this inscription: "In grateful remembrance to Jean Luzac, friend of Washington, Adams, and Jefferson, champion of the truth and justice of the cause of American independence in the Gazette de Leyde. Erected by the Holland Society of Philadelphia, 1909" (Washington Sunday Star, October 24, 1909, Part 2).

[1] This pamphlet is not to be confounded with another one of almost the same title: "Aan't Volk van Nederland" ("of Bewijzen en Consideratien over de voordeelen der Negotie met de Noord Americaanen"), which, though written in favor of the Americans, was rather colorless. A great many of the pamphlets issued about this time were addressed "aan't Volk van Nederland," as, for example,

been discovered to have been van der Capellen, the untiring friend of the American cause.[1] This pamphlet was chiefly directed against the house of Orange, especially against William V, and its services consisted in diminishing the power of the English party, while it advanced the cause of the United States in the Netherlands.[2]

The most important pamphlet coming from the other side was van Goens' "Politiek Vertoog over het waar Systema van Amsterdam" (Political Argumentation regarding the true System of Amsterdam), dated March 11, 1781. It denounced the policy of Amsterdam as selfish, tending

"Antwoord van Pieter Dwars-Doelen Scheepstimmerman op de Werf Vrijheid en Eendracht . . . *aan't Volk van Nederland* in't algemeen en aan de inwoonders der Stad Amsterdam in het bijzonder," a pamphlet written against the English.

[1] Up to 1908 neither the Congress of the United States nor the American people in general had formally recognized the very valuable services which van der Capellen rendered to the struggling American colonies. It is owing to the Holland Society of New York and especially to one of its presidents, Mr. John R. van Wormer, chairman of the committee formed for the purpose, that this debt of honor was paid on June 6, 1908, by placing a commemorative bronze tablet on the walls of the house No. 12 Bloemendal Street, which van der Capellen and his wife occupied until shortly before his death in 1784. The tablet, which was unveiled by Mr. van Wormer on behalf of the Holland Society of New York under the auspices of the Dutch authorities, bears the following inscription: "Erected by the Holland Society of New York A. D. 1908 to Joan Derck van der Capellen tot den Pol, Ridder in de Ridderschap van Overyssel 1741–1784, in grateful recognition of the services rendered by him during the war of the Revolution on behalf of the United Colonies of North America, 1775–1783, which materially contributed toward the establishment of their independence as a nation."

Rev. Dr. William Elliot Griffis of Ithaca, New York, first suggested to the Holland Society the scheme as it was executed. A detailed report on the history of the van der Capellen tablet was published by the Holland Society of New York in 1909.

[2] Its effect is said to have resembled that of an electric shock. On September 25 and 26, 1781, it was spread through the principal Dutch cities and also through the country by van der Kemp, van der Capellen's friend (Adrian van der Kemp came later to America where he founded the town of Barneveldt, now Trenton, N. J., and surveyed the route of the Erie Canal. Griffis, Young People's History of Holland, 266). Although several individuals were employed for this purpose and $2500 offered for the discovery of author and publisher, the names of the author and his associates were not disclosed (Fairchild, van der Kemp, 54–57; Groot Placaatboek, IX, 409).

to make the rest of the country serve the particular interests of the great city. The pamphlet advocated severe measures against Amsterdam, and was originally intended only for a limited circle of readers, especially the regents of Dutch cities, but soon became known to the public in general, which received it in a very unfriendly manner. Amsterdam was praised by the people as the champion of progress, while the stadtholder was called the usurper of the rights of the people.[1] Van Goens became the object of severe attacks and was referred to as the enemy of his country. While his essay had been called forth by two pamphlets by one Hendrik Calkoen, strongly taking sides with Amsterdam,[2] a number of counter publications appeared, the consequence of the " Politiek Vertoog."[3]

Another pamphlet which cleverly represented the English views was the " Rechtsgeleerde Memorie" (Judicial Memorial).[4] The author tried to show that Yorke's accusations were well founded and that the English crown was

---

[1] Colenbrander, Patriottentijd, I, 258, 259.

[2] Q. N., Het Politiek Systema van de Regeering van Amsterdam, in een waar daglicht vorgesteld, en haar gedrag tegens de beschuldiging van den Ridder Yorke, bescheidenlijk verdeedigd in een' Brief aan een Heer van Regeering in Zeeland (The Political System of the Administration of Amsterdam, represented in true daylight, and her conduct modestly defended against the accusation of Sir Joseph Yorke in a letter to a gentleman of the Government in Zealand).

Q. N., Het Waare Dag-Licht van het Politiek Systema der Regeeringe van Amsterdam, uit de Vaterlandsche Historien opgehelderd (The true Daylight of the Political System of the Administration of Amsterdam, explained from the History of the Country).

[3] For instance:—

C. P., Le Voici of Pourtrait en Byzonderheeden, aangaande den Politiek-Vertoog-Schrijver Hijklof Michael van Goens (Behold him, or portrait and peculiarities concerning Rijklof Michael van Goens, the writer of the Politiek Vertoog). In this pamphlet van Goens was called a traitor.

C. P., Supplement de Le Voici, etc. This was a continuation of the foregoing pamphlet.

Brieven van Candidus, Betreffende den Schrijver en inhoud van zeker Geschrift, getiteld: Politiek Vertoog, etc. (Letters by Candidus, concerning writer and contents of a certain pamphlet entitled, etc.).

[4] Rechtsgeleerde Memorie, waarin onzijdig onderzogt word de gegrondheit der Klagten, etc. (Judicial Memorial, in which is impartially examined the justice of the complaints of the King of Great Britain, etc.).

justified in asking the punishment of the burgomasters and pensionary of Amsterdam. Nicolaus Bondt replied with a vigorous pamphlet, including also remarks in refutation of Goens' " Politiek Vertoog," without however producing any new ideas about the latter.[1] Even in England pamphlets appeared in defense of the course taken by Great Britain against the Netherlands. " L'Esprit du Sisteme Politique de la Regence d'Amsterdam, etc." (Spirit of the Political System of the Administration of Amsterdam) is an exemple. These pamphlets were translated into Dutch and distributed over the United Provinces.[2]

---

[1] De Eer der Regeering van Amsterdam verdedigt, etc. (Defence of the Honor of the Administration of Amsterdam).

[2] The title in Dutch was: De Geest van het Politiek Systema van de Regeering van Amsterdam, etc.

Only a few of the immense number of pamphlets which were published on the occasion of the breach between the United Provinces and England have been mentioned here in order to show, from the tone of the more important of them, their influence upon the events under consideration. The Public Library in New York City possesses a large and interesting collection of these pamphlets, the examination of which would form a study in itself, for which the author neither had the time, nor thought it expedient for the present purposes. Many of them seem to be rather absurd, written by incompetent and irresponsible persons.

Regarding the Dutch newspapers, periodicals, and pamphlets see also Blok, Geschiedenis, VI, 395–405.

CHAPTER VII.

The United Provinces and Great Britain as Enemies.

In Great Britain many voices were heard severely criticizing the government for breaking with the United Provinces. In the British Parliament the subject was taken up by the opposition with enthusiasm.[1] The States General, notwithstanding that the indignation of the Dutch at the attitude of the English cabinet was strong and general, were slow even in finding an answer to the complaints of Great Britain, not to speak of active measures. About the middle of February, 1781, the provincial States of Utrecht expressed their surprise at such inactivity, bringing the matter to a discussion in a secret session of the States General,[2] but it was almost the middle of March before a decision was reached. A declaration of the general government was then published and transmitted to every court.[3]

In this counter-manifesto the imputations of the English king were repudiated in a detailed recapitulation of the relations between the two countries since the beginning of the American Revolution. It was vigorously asserted that the United Provinces had remained neutral throughout the contest. They had prohibited the exportation of military stores to the English colonies in America and instructed all Dutch governors and commanders to refrain from acts which might be interpreted as involving an acknowledgment of American independence. The governor of St. Eustatia was called to account when accused of having violated these

---

[1] Debate in the House of Lords on the King's message relative to the rupture with Holland, January 25, 1781 (Hansard, Parliamentary History, XXI, 998–1103; Andrews, History of the War, IV, 119, 125; Fitzmaurice, Shelburne, III, 109–119).

[2] Secret Resolutions of the States General, February 16, 1781 (Sparks MSS., CIII).

[3] Secret Resolutions of the States General, March 12, 1781 (Bancroft MSS., America, Holland, and England).

orders. After the beginning of the Franco-English war, the British ports were filled with Dutch ships, taken and retained by England, although those vessels carried only goods which the treaties declared free. All their remonstrances regarding this breach of treaty had been of no avail. Even the Dutch flag had not been respected by England, as the Fielding-Bylandt incident showed. Neutral territory of the United Provinces, both in Europe and in America, had been repeatedly violated by Great Britain, especially the island of St. Martin in the West Indies,[1] for which offence not the slightest satisfaction had been offered. As Dutch commerce and navigation was thus in danger of being annihilated, the United Provinces acceded to the Armed Neutrality.

Explanations were also given in the counter-manifesto as to why the Dutch had not furnished assistance to England, and why John Paul Jones had been tolerated in Dutch waters. Subsidies were not given because the United Provinces did not find that their treaties with Great Britain compelled them to do so, and no hostile action had been taken by the Dutch authorities against the American sea-captain because existing regulations prevented the States General

---

[1] The governor of St. Eustatia reported, on August 12, 1780, the following incident, brought to his knowledge by a letter which he had received from the secretary of St. Martin, dated August 9, 1780:—

On August 9, 1780, an English squadron belonging to Admiral J. B. Rodney's fleet and consisting of one ship of the line and six frigates under the command of Captain Robinson anchored at St. Martin. Two of the officers visited the commander of that island, informing him that the squadron was charged to seize all North American vessels and their cargoes that might be found in the waters of the island. The commander's remonstrances against such hostile procedure were without avail. The island being literally defenceless, the English squadron found no further resistance in carrying out its orders. No harm was done to the inhabitants of St. Martin. Part of the squadron, on August 11, called also at St. Eustatia. The American vessels, however, which had happened to be there had left as soon as the incident at St. Martin became known, and the English vessels departed without hostilities.

Missive van Representant en Bewindhebberen der Westindische Compagnie, etc., October 10, 1780 (Sparks Dutch Papers) ; Nieuwe Nederlandsche Jaerboeken, 1780, p. 982; Resolution of the States General, November 20, 1780 (Sparks MSS., CIII) ; De Jonge, Geschiedenis, IV, 436.

from passing judgment upon his conduct before his arrival at the Texel. Moreover, the interests of the Republic did not make it desirable for her to meddle in a contest in which she was not obliged to take part. As to the draft treaty, found with Laurens, and the controversy to which it gave rise, the States General had disavowed the act, agreeably to the English desire, but they could not pronounce punishment upon the culprits because, according to the constitution of the United Provinces, this was not within their jurisdiction, but belonged to the province of Holland. Finally, George III had tried every means to prevent the accession of the United Provinces to the Armed Neutrality, and in reality the admission of the Republic to the northern league should be considered the cause of England's wrath.[1]

What made this counter-manifesto most remarkable was its publication at a time when Catherine II of Russia had just offered her services to the two countries for mediation in the interest of a peaceable adjustment of their mutual grievances.[2] However, many people in the United Provinces did not regret the rupture with England, but regarded war as a lesser evil than the continuance of the humiliations which the Republic had been suffering at the hands of Great Britain. They hoped that a future peace would

---

[1] Counter-Manifesto of the States General, March 12, 1781 (Sparks Dutch Papers; Gazette de Leyde, No. XXIII, March 20, 1781; Davies, History of Holland, III, 465).

[2] John Adams to the President of Congress, March 18, 1781 (Wharton, IV, 306-313).
It seems that John Adams misunderstood the situation when, a few days previous, he wrote the following: "They [the Dutch] are furious for peace. Multitudes are for peace with England at any rate, even at the expense and risk of joining them in the war against France, Spain, America, and all the rest. They are in a torpor, a stupor such as I never saw any people in before, but they cannot obtain peace with England on any other terms than joining her in the war, and this they will not, because they cannot do. I sometimes think that their *affections* would lead them to do it if they dared " (J. Adams to Dana, March 12, 1781, in Wharton, IV, 285). The many aggressions of England had little by little estranged most of her friends in the United Provinces, while the followers of France had increased correspondingly. There cannot have existed much affection for England in the United Provinces at this time.

render their country free and independent of foreign influences.[1]

The States General trusted that the northern powers would come to the assistance of the United Provinces. The Dutch plenipotentiaries at St. Petersburg and the envoys, van Lijnden at Stockholm and Bosc de la Calmette at Copenhagen, received instructions to present notes to that effect to the courts to which they were accredited. They were to express the confidence of the States General in the power, magnanimity and fidelity of their allies. The Dutch government had hesitated to join the alliance but had been justified in so doing since England's conduct toward the Republic had changed from the minute the intention became known in Great Britain. It was evident that the accession of the Republic to the Armed Neutrality was the real cause of the rupture between the two countries, and the States General hoped that their allies would make common cause with them. This was necessary because the Dutch navy was not in a condition to cope with that of England. This was due to the employment of such vast numbers of seamen in private bottoms that crews for war vessels were wanting. Prompt and efficient help was urged, especially by furnishing armed vessels to the United Provinces in excess of the ships which the allies had destined for the common defence.[2]

Frederick the Great felt so sure that Catherine would not abandon the United Provinces, but support them efficiently, that he thought he might safely guarantee such an attitude

---

[1] Thulemeier to Frederick II, January 12, 1781 (Bancroft MSS., Prussia and Holland).

[2] Resolution of the States General, January 12, 1781 (Sparks Dutch Papers).

Thulemeier reported that the States General had dispatched a courier to Copenhagen, Stockholm, and St. Petersburg, since they intended to demand the fulfilment of the obligations contracted in articles 6, 7, and 8 of the maritime convention (Thulemeier to Frederick II, January 16, 1781, in Bancroft MSS., Prussia and Holland).

See also Dumas' letter to the President of Congress, January 23, 1781 (Wharton, IV, 200).

of the empress.[1] Harris in St. Petersburg was of a different opinion. He, too, thought that Catherine would fulfil the obligations contracted by the convention of the Armed Neutrality, but that the States General could not claim any assistance from her, since the rupture between Great Britain and the United Provinces had no reference to that act.[2] From dispatches of Count Goertz, the Prussian envoy at St. Petersburg, we learn that the Russian government was much annoyed at the outbreak of war and greatly embarrassed regarding the course to be taken. At the same time, a side light is thrown upon the spirit in which Frederick received the news of the rupture between the two countries. " Because the English want war with all the world, they will have it ! " he exclaimed, and showed the strongest marks of anger and disappointment. Panin, the Russian minister, also was shocked and confessed that he would never have thought England capable of this act. When asked whether Russia would be obliged to render assistance to her new ally, he answered evasively and seemed to be greatly embarrassed. A decision on this subject would be reached when the sentiments of the courts of Denmark and Sweden became known. It was understood, furthermore, that the empress had written to Frederick the Great about the difficulty in which she was placed by Great Britain and had asked him if Prussia would take sides with her, in case Russia should be drawn into war when aiding her ally.[3]

Catherine seems to have soon made up her mind how to proceed in the matter. The British minister at St. Petersburg wrote at the beginning of March that the empress remained firm in her resolution to exclude the United Provinces from the protection which the maritime league would

---

[1] Frederick II to Thulemeier, February 5, 1781 (Bancroft MSS., Prussia and Holland).

[2] Harris to Stormont, February 2/13, 1781 (Malmesbury, Correspondence, I, 385).

[3] Elliot to Stormont, February, 1781 (Malmesbury, Correspondence, I, 383). The English minister told Lord Stormont that these informations were confidentially given to him by a person who had perused Count Goertz's last dispatches.

have afforded them, if they had remained neutral. Beyond assisting the Republic with her good offices, the Dutch ambassadors were to be told that she could do nothing in the present situation.[1] Harris even urged the Russian government to have examined the instructions which were issued to the Russian sea commanders, "lest either wilfully or inadvertently their orders for protection should be extended to the Dutch ships." The Russian minister at the Hague learned that in Catherine's opinion the Dutch demand for assistance was premature.[2] Panin answered the Dutch plenipotentiaries that the United Provinces need not regret having joined the maritime league, but that they must make efforts themselves and not fall asleep. As the Republic was mostly concerned she ought to put herself in a position to effect her own defence, in order to repulse the enemy and to pursue the war with success.[3]

The United Provinces, however, were hopelessly torn by inner political and party strifes, and even now, in the hour of danger, little or no exertion was made for the safety of the Republic. The situation is vividly described by a letter of John Adams which he wrote in March from Leyden:—

"The nation has indeed been in a violent fermentation and crisis. It is divided in sentiments. There are stadtholderians and republicans; there are proprietors in English funds, and persons immediately engaged in commerce; there are enthusiasts for peace and alliance with England; and there are advocates for an alliance with France, Spain, and America; and there are a third sort, who are for adhering in all things to Russia, Sweden, and Denmark. Some are for acknowledging American independence, and entering into treaties of commerce and alliance with her; others start at the idea with horror, as an everlasting impediment to the return to the friendship and alliance with England; some will not augment the navy without increasing the army; others will let the navy be neglected rather than augment the army.

"In this perfect chaos of sentiments and systems, principles and interests, it is no wonder there is languor, a weakness, and irresolution that is vastly dangerous in the present circumstances of affairs. The danger lies not more in the hostile designs and exertions of the English than from seditions and commotions among the people,

[1] Harris to Stormont, February 26/March 9, 1781 (Malmesbury, Correspondence, I, 391).
[2] Thulemeier to Frederick II, March 9, 1781 (Bancroft MSS., Prussia and Holland).
[3] Same to same, March 13, 1781 (ibid.).

which are every day dreaded and expected. If it were not for a standing army, and troops posted about in several cities, it is probable there would have been popular tumults before now; but everybody that I see appears to me to live in constant fear of mobs, and in a great degree of uncertainty whether they will rise in favor of war or against it; in favor of England or against it; in favor of the prince or of the city of Amsterdam; in favor of America or against it."[1]

Frederick the Great was very indignant at the inactivity of the Republic, which he said should rather be called indolence. It was unpardonable to reduce the naval armament to six vessels when it should consist of twenty-one.[2] The state of the Dutch navy, in fact, was most deplorable, and what was worse, there was no hope of having it rebuilt very soon.[3] All Europe was surprised at the idleness of the Dutch, and public opinion gradually turned against them. The Prussian king thought the English party and the Duke of Brunswick responsible for this pusillanimity, which thwarted the best intentions of the government.[4]

During all this time while the Dutch contented themselves with quarreling as to whether the navy or army[5] should be increased, or whether the Duke of Brunswick or the Prince

---

[1] J. Adams to the President of Congress, March 19, 1781 (Wharton, IV, 314).
Great dissatisfaction was reported from Zealand and Friesland. They demanded peace with England on any condition, and even threatened to withdraw from the union (Thulemeier to Frederick II, May 8, 1781, in Bancroft MSS., Prussia and Holland); Resolution of the States General, January 22, 1781 (Sparks MSS., CIII).
On the situation see also Adams' letters of May 16 and 24, 1781 (Wharton, IV, 420, 431–433).
[2] Frederick II to Thulemeier, May 7 and 10, 1781 (Bancroft MSS., Prussia and Holland).
[3] J. Adams to the President of Congress, May 27, 1781 (Wharton, IV, 448–451).
[4] Frederick II to Thulemeier, June 18, 1781 (Bancroft MSS., Prussia and Holland).
[5] It may be mentioned here that petty German sovereigns offered their services to the United Provinces as they had done to Great Britain. The Prussian envoy at the Hague reported that the Duke of Württemberg, the Landgrave of Hesse-Darmstadt, and the Prince Bishop of Fulda had proposed to the States General a subsidy treaty, by which they would be obliged to furnish a certain number of troops to the United Provinces during the war with England (Thulemeier to Frederick II, February 23, 1781, in Bancroft MSS., Prussia and Holland).

of Orange himself was to blame for the pitiful position,[1] the English had been intensely active. They succeeded in making the North Sea and Baltic so unsafe for Dutch navigation that, in 1781, only eleven of their ships sailed through the Sound, while in 1780 about 2058 had passed there.[2] Still they were not satisfied, and looked about for further methods of hostility.

Before the beginning of the war the British government had asked Yorke's advice as to the best means for striking the Republic violently. They thought of destroying the Dutch navy and arsenals at home, but the ambassador dissuaded them from such a step because the shallowness of the coast rendered the Texel, where most of the naval craft of the United Provinces was stationed, and still more the inland waters comparatively secure against an attack. Furthermore it was to be feared that the English name would be hated in the Republic for centuries if the war should be carried into the heart of the country.[3] It would be much more effective to blockade the ports, seize as many as possible of the vessels of the Republic in the open sea and attack her especially in the West Indies, where immediate action should be taken because the West Indian possessions were her gold-mine for the moment, employing the greatest number of Dutch citizens. Yorke recommended the temporary capture of St. Eustatia, in order to cut off the intercourse between Amsterdam and the American rebels. According to rumor, ten or eleven men-of-war were preparing to sail for the West Indies, three of which would remain at St. Eustatia, while the rest were to be dispersed among the other possessions. It would be wise to strike the blow before those vessels should arrive.[4]

---

[1] Many thought that the Republic was approaching destruction, and that it would be wise to sell all private property, because it would in less than ten years lose more than half its value (Thuessink to van der Capellen, in Beaufort, Brieven van der Capellen, 260).

[2] Kampen, Verkorte Geschiedenis, II, 300.

[3] Colenbrander, Patriottentijd, I, 190.

[4] Yorke to Stormont, November 7, 1780 (Sparks MSS., LXXII).

The English cabinet seems to have agreed with Yorke, since George III at the same time that he issued his manifesto, had instructed Admiral Rodney to attack and seize the Dutch possessions in the West Indies. St. Eustatia and St. Martin were to be taken first, since it was thought that large quantities of provisions and other stores were there or upon their way thither. Major-General Vaughan was to assist in the invasion of the islands.[1] Rodney, who was in American waters with his squadron, received this order on January 27 and, assisted by General Vaughan, embarked the English troops immediately, sailing from St. Lucia in the Lesser Antilles on January 30. They arrived at St. Eustatia on February 3, occupying the island and seizing the Dutch man-of-war "Mars," commanded by Captain Bylandt, together with more than 150 vessels of all descriptions, including five American armed ships. Rodney informed the admiralty in London that all the magazines and storehouses

---

[1] George III's order to Rodney, December 20, 1780 (Rodney, Letters from Sir George Brydges, now Lord Rodney, to His Majesty's Ministers, 5).

Rodney's conduct relative to the capture of St. Eustatia was later severely criticized, and he had his correspondence published in order to show "that his Views were invariably directed, during the whole Period of his Command, to the Advancement of the Public Service, and the Glory and Prosperity of his Country." There were even officers in the English navy who were discontented with Rodney's conduct in the St. Eustatia affair from the beginning (Captain W. Young to Middleton, St. Eustatia, March 3, 1781, in Laughton, Letters and Papers of Charles, Lord Barham, I, 95; Middleton's memorandum, ibid., 97 ff.).

In regard to the date of Rodney's orders there seems to be a discrepancy. Reports from St. Pierre, Martinique, dated February 15, 1781, stated that the frigate which brought the directions to Admiral Rodney when at St. Lucia to commence hostilities against Holland had an extraordinarily short passage, his letters being dated the 6th of January (Papers of the Continental Congress, Letters of W. Bingham, J. Parsons, No. 90, Vol. I, 339, in the archives of the Department of State, Washington).

Instructions, similar to those sent to Rodney relative to the West Indies, were sent to the East Indies (Mahan, Influence of Sea Power, 406). But it was the Dutch West Indian possessions which England wanted to strike first, because of the assistance they were giving to the United States of America and France. Besides, there were only a few English men-of-war in the East Indies, while Admiral Rodney with his fleet was already in West Indian waters (Colenbrander, Patriottentijd, I, 191).

at St. Eustatia were filled and even the beach had been found covered with tobacco and sugar. All of this he would ship to England on board the vessels taken in the bay. He reported also that the Dutch islands of St. Martin and Saba had surrendered.[1] There were, however, very few vessels there.[2]

Rodney then directed Sir Samuel Hood with a squadron to attack Curaçao; Rear-Admiral Drake, to seize Surinam; while some frigates were to blockade the mouths of the rivers Demerari and Essequibo.[3] A Dutch convoy of twenty-six merchant vessels, which had sailed from St. Eustatia the night before Rodney's arrival, was captured by Captain Reynolds of Rodney's squadron and taken back to St. Eustatia. The Dutch Vice-Admiral Crul was killed in the action.[4] By not hauling down the Dutch flag at St. Eustatia for some days, Rodney caught several more merchant vessels entering the road of the island in good faith.[5] Samuel Parsons at St. Pierre, Martinique, on learning of the capture of St. Eustatia by the English, bought the fastest vessel in the harbor to convey the news to the United States, in order to prevent American vessels from going to St. Eustatia.[6] More than 2000 American merchants and seamen fell into Rodney's hands at St. Eustatia.[7] He was de-

---

[1] Rodney to Philip Stephens, Secretary of the Admiralty, St. Eustatia, February 4, 1781 (Rodney's Letters, 7) ; Gazette de Leyde, No. XXIV, March 23, 1781 ; De Jonge, Geschiedenis, IV, 462.

Captain Count Bylandt's report to the stadtholder regarding the loss of the Dutch frigate " Mars," February 6, 1781 (Gazette de Leyde, Supplement, March 27, 1781).

[2] Captain W. Young to Middleton, St. Eustatia, February 3, 1781 (Laughton, Barham's Letters, I, 91).

[3] Rodney to Stephens, February 6, 1781 (Rodney's Letters, 11).

[4] Van Beverhoudt to van der Capellen, St. Thomas, February 21, 1781 (Beaufort, Brieven van der Capellen, 239). Tegelaar to van der Capellen, Amsterdam, March 21, 1781 (ibid., 226).

[5] Kampen, Verkorte Geschiedenis, II, 299; Major-General Vaughan to Lord George Germain, St. Eustatia, February 7, 1781 (Remembrancer, or Impartial Repository of Public Events, Part I, Vol. XI, 261).

[6] Samuel Parsons to the Committee for Foreign Affairs, St. Pierre, Martinique, February 15, 1781 (Papers of the Continental Congress, Letters of Bingham and Parsons, No. 90, Vol. I, 339).

[7] Rodney to Stephens, February 10, 1781 (Rodney's Letters, 13).

termined to remain at the island until all the stores captured should be embarked, and "till the *Lower Town,* that Nest of Vipers, which preyed upon the Vitals of Great Britain be destroyed."[1]

The Jews especially were made to feel his wrath. They were forced to give up all the cash and goods which they possessed, and were driven from the island,[2] but the persecution was not confined to the Hebrew race. Rodney ordered all Americans, without exception and distinction, to leave St. Eustatia, which fate was subsequently shared by all Frenchmen and also by all citizens of Amsterdam residing on the island. By a final proclamation the British admiral informed all foreigners of every kind that they must depart, allowing only the settled inhabitants of St. Eustatia to remain. Even English citizens engaged in commerce at the island were not spared, their goods being confiscated, though British merchants were allowed by special acts of Parliament (the Grenada Act, the Tobacco Act and the Cotton Act) to trade with St. Eustatia. Rodney gave as a reason for his proceedings that those Englishmen were supplying the enemies of their country.

All remonstrances, in which even the legislature of the island of St. Christopher took part, against Rodney's behavior were in vain. He shipped the stores which he had seized, partly to the British islands in the West Indies, partly to Great Britain, and the rest he sold at public auction.[3] The reproach was soon made to him that he committed the same crime for which he pretended to punish the people of St. Eustatia, in that he also supplied the enemies of Great Britain. The stores, sold at auction, were pur-

---

[1] Rodney to General Cunningham, Governor of Barbados, February 17, 1781 (Rodney's Letters, 17).

[2] Van Beverhoudt to van der Capellen, St. Thomas, February 21, 1781 (Beaufort, Brieven van der Capellen, 239).

Rodney's own almost boasting account of his treatment of the inhabitants of St. Eustatia is to be found in a letter to Stephens, dated St. Eustatia, March 6, 1781 (Rodney's Letters, 29–31).

[3] "As for the other goods . . . they were sold *sub hasta.* The island . . . became one of the greatest auctions that ever was opened in the universe" (Hannay, Rodney, 155).

chased by the neighboring neutral islands, from which they found their way to America and the French settlements. At the auctions only about one fourth of the value of the merchandise was realized, so that the enemies of Great Britain were supplied by the English government at much lower rates than by the Dutch.[1]

One Dutch man-of-war, the frigate " Eendragt," had been detached by Rear-Admiral Count van Bylandt on January 29, 1781, to sail for the West Indies. When on March 18 it reached the river Berbice, Captain A. de Roock sent Lieutenant Zeegers with an armed sloop to the governor of the Dutch colony. The lieutenant found the fortress burnt down and completely ruined. He then proceeded further up the river, where he met the director of the plantation "Ithaca," G. Hobus, who told him that, on March 7 or 8, letters had arrived from Demerari and Essequibo announcing the capture of those colonies by the English.[2] On the following day, Hobus said, a British war vessel of 36 cannon took Berbice, the crew putting the ammunition of the fortress on board and throwing everything else into the river. They then set fire to the fortress and loaded four ships, which they had taken in the river, with the products of the farm. Captain Roock did not consider his forces strong enough to retake and hold Berbice, so he sailed for the French island Grenada, where Governor Count de Durat informed him of the details of the seizure of St. Eustatia by Rodney. While Roock was at Grenada, a French ship arriving from Martinique brought the news that Rodney had sailed with his fleet from St. Lucia leaving about 1000 troops at St. Eustatia.[3] The English admiral's task on the

---

[1] Debate in the British Parliament on Mr. Burke's motion relating to the seizure and confiscation of private property in the island of St. Eustatia, May 14, 1781 (Hansard, Parliamentary History, XXII, 219–257).

Burke's speech on this occasion is remarkable for its force and beauty, though scarcely exaggerating the facts.

[2] It was also said that St. Eustatia and Curaçao were occupied by the English. Curaçao, however, was successfully defended against the British and remained Dutch (Blok, Geschiedenis, VI, 383).

[3] Report of Captain A. de Roock of the frigate " Eendragt " to the

latter island had been completed. After its capture and
devastation he had continued using it as a trap for catching
Americans. On March 29, he wrote from St. Eustatia to
William Baird[1] that fifty American vessels had been taken
and that their crews would be sent to England.[2] The
island had then been in the possession of the English for
about two months, but it seemed that the fact was not yet
sufficiently known in the United States, for almost daily
American vessels loaded with tobacco would approach St.
Eustatia and fall an easy prey to the British forces.[3]

When the capture of nearly all of their West Indian
possessions became known in the United Provinces it caused
much consternation. Amsterdam's losses at St. Eustatia
were enormous, and consequently the big city was deeply
affected by this severe blow so promptly dealt by England.
"The merchants of Amsterdam," wrote the American agent
at the Hague, " who have a great share in the effects seized
on at St. Eustatia, having resolved to send deputies to the
English ministry in order to have them restored to them,
and having invited the merchants of Rotterdam to join with
them in this deputation, the latter have answered that, with
men capable of acting so ruffianlike, they would rather let
them keep all that they had robbed than debase themselves
by courting the robbers. This noble answer would be still
more so if Rotterdam had lost as much at St. Eustatia as
Amsterdam; there being as for that a very great difference."[4]

Prince of Orange, June 24, 1781, and report of Lieutenant J. B.
Zeegers to A. de Roock, March 18, 1781 (Sparks Dutch Papers).

The surrender to the English of the two Dutch colonies of
Demerari and Essequibo was reported by Rodney to Stephens on
March 17, 1781 (Rodney's Letters, 37).

Davies (History of Holland, VIII, 469, 470) says that Demerari,
Berbice, and Essequibo were delivered up to the English with a
pusillanimity which not even their insufficient state of defence could
excuse.

[1] Baird had belonged to the English Council of the Government of
New York.

[2] Rodney's Letters, 56; Gazette de Leyde, No. XXXIV, April 27,
1781.

[3] Rodney to General Cunningham, Governor of Barbados, March
31, 1781 (Rodney's Letters, 57).

[4] Dumas to the President of Congress, April 2, 1781 (Wharton,
IV, 323).

Of what immense importance St. Eustatia had been to the American cause was recognized by the English to its fullest extent after they occupied the island. Rodney himself declared that had it not been for the "infamous island of St. Eustatia," the American rebellion could not possibly have subsisted.[1] The American agents and other people dealing or connected with the Congress of the United States who were taken prisoners at St. Eustatia were sent to England and subjected to hard treatment there. Franklin in Paris received instructions to pay particular attention to the exchange of these prisoners of war.[2]

Rodney and his country were to enjoy but little of the spoils taken at St. Eustatia! The admiral had dispatched thirty-four of the vessels, taken by him at that island and laden with valuable goods seized there, under the convoy of two English men-of-war to Great Britain. In the Channel this fleet was met by a French squadron under Vice-Admiral de la Motte-Piquet. He captured twenty-two of the Dutch merchant vessels and brought them into Brest.[3] The

[1] Rodney to Rear Admiral Sir Peter Parker, St. Eustatia, April 16, 1781 (Rodney's Letters, 69).

According to the English admiral, the business district of St. Eustatia, or Lower Town, was a range of storehouses of about a mile and a quarter in length. These stores were rented at the enormous sum of twelve hundred thousand pounds sterling a year (Rodney to Stephens, April 27, 1781, in Rodney's Letters, 75).

It is evident what an immense business must have been done at St. Eustatia when during the last stages of the American Revolution trading with the Americans and French allowed the paying of such exorbitant rents.

[2] James Lovell (for the Committee of Foreign Affairs) to Franklin, May 9, 1781 (Wharton, IV, 405, 406).

The prisoners mentioned in this letter were Mr. Samuel Curson, Mr. Isaac Gouverneur, Jr., and Dr. John Witherspoon, Jr.

Among the Dutch prisoners whom Rodney sent to England from St. Eustatia was the governor of the island, de Graaf. The latter's plantations were confiscated in the name of the king of England, "pour se venger de la faveur que ce Gouverneur a accordée selon les ‘idées du Ministère Anglois au Commerce de l'*Amérique-Septentrionale*" (Gazette de Leyde, No. XXXIV, April 27, 1781).

[3] Berkenrode to the States General, May 13, 1781 (Bancroft MSS., America, Holland, and England).

Captain W. Young had advised Rodney to direct the route of the convoy and to inform Lord Sandwich where English cruisers might meet them in European waters, since the immense riches carried by

remaining twelve, according to a letter from Franklin, were soon afterwards taken by French and American privateers, so that not one ship of the convoy arrived in England.[1] St. Eustatia also was soon lost to the English. Rodney's ill health compelled him to leave for England, sailing on August 1, 1781. He had ordered the island always to be protected by several frigates and to have the large sum of money, still at St. Eustatia, sent in Rear-Admiral Hood's squadron to North America for the payment of the British troops there. For some reason or other these orders were not executed.[2]

In the meantime a French fleet of about four hundred sail, amongst which were said to be about thirty vessels of the line,[3] arrived in West Indian waters under the command of Count de Grasse. He was met by the general and commander of Martinique, Marquis de Bouillé, with about 1200 troops on board of three frigates, one sloop, and one brig. An expedition was then led by Bouillé to St. Eustatia,

---

the fleet called for protection (Captain Young to Middleton, in Laughton, Barham's Letters, 94).

It seems that either Rodney did not follow Young's advice, or that the cruisers which were to meet the fleet missed them.

De la Motte-Piquet's capture of the convoy under Hotham raised the spirits of the Dutch " from that unmanly gloom and despondency into which they were thrown by the capture of St. Eustatia, Demerara, and Essequibo " (J. Adams to the President of Congress, May 16, 1781, in Wharton, IV, 419).

[1] Franklin to J. Adams, May 19, 1781 (Wharton, IV, 423).

John Adams thought that the capture of St. Eustatia was the most complete blunder the English had committed during the war because the island was the channel through which British manufactures were carried to North America, and it had furnished provisions and assistance to the English fleets and armies in the West Indies. As the British merchants were permitted by an act of Parliament to trade with St. Eustatia, all who had suffered by its capture were clamoring against the British government and especially against Rodney and Vaughan for illegally seizing their property. These commanders were threatened with as many law-suits as there were losers (J. Adams to the President of Congress, May 29, 1781, in Wharton, IV, 460–461): Andrews, History of the War, IV, 126.

In fact, Rodney was subsequently compelled to pay back all he had gained at St. Eustatia and died a poor man (Hannay, Rodney, 156).

[2] Rodney's Letters, 84.

[3] Samuel Parsons to Committee for Foreign Affairs, St. Pierre, Martinique, March 18, 1781 (Papers of the Continental Congress, Letters of W. Bingham, J. Parsons, No. 90, Vol. I, 343).

which place was reached in the night of November 26. The island was garrisoned by 650 British troops, commanded by Colonel Cockburn. Bouillé was prevented from landing more than 500 men, the sea running high. Of the events which followed this realistic description is given:—

"They [the French] concealed themselves among the Canes, till the Hour at which the Gates of the Fort were usually opened. In the Instant that the Troops came out to perform their Exercise on the Savanna, the Marquis caused the whole of his little army to discharge their Musquets in the air and rush with their Bayonets on the Enemy. It is impossible to conceive the confusion into which this well concerted Stratagem threw the British tho' much superior in Number and in actual position of Battle. Some called for Quarter and others took to their Heels, endeavouring to regain the Fort, which the French took possession of without opposition."[1]

Two hundred and fifty thousand pounds sterling in cash fell into the hands of the French,[2] so that no financial profit at all was derived by the English from their conquest of St. Eustatia. The island, however, had lost its importance. It no longer proved the mère nourricière, either for the United States or for the French,[3] falling back into its former insignificance, never to rise again up to the present day. The trade which had been carried on by way of St. Eustatia henceforth favored the Danish island of St. Thomas in the Lesser Antilles.[4]

---

[1] Samuel Parsons to Committee for Foreign Affairs, St. Pierre, Martinique, December 31, 1781 (Papers of the Continental Congress, Letters of W. Bingham, J. Parsons, No. 90, Vol. I, 331).

The writer dated his letter correctly, at the end, December 31, 1781; at its head it is marked, however, December 31, 1780. This error seems not to have been detected when the letters were arranged in volumes, and this manuscript is consequently inserted in the wrong place.

France kept St. Eustatia as Dutch property for the Republic, not as a French conquest (Kampen, Verkorte Geschiedenis, II, 300).

[2] Rodney's Letters, 84.

[3] Hunt to Middleton, March 17, 1782 (Laughton, Barham's Letters, 149).

When Rodney returned to the West Indies in February, 1782, he learned that the French had not only taken St. Eustatia, but also the British islands of St. Christopher, Nevis, and Montserrat (Fitzmaurice, Shelburne, III, 125). Soon, however, the "tide of war" became again favorable to England, and "her flag was triumphant in every Part of the West Indies" until the conclusion of peace (Rodney's Letters, 175; Wharton, IV, 323).

[4] Colenbrander, Patriottentijd, I, 191.

In the East Indies the English at Madras, when learning of the rupture between Great Britain and the United
Provinces, fitted out an expedition against the principal
Dutch settlement on Coromandel coast, the town and harbor
of Negapatam. An Indian prince, Hyder-Ali, being hostile
to the English, there was danger that he and the French,
with whom he was allied, would make common cause with
the Dutch and use Negapatam as a place of arms. The
command of the expedition was entrusted to Sir Hector
Munro. The English garrisons were much reduced, their
main forces being in the field against Hyder-Ali, and
Munro's detachment, therefore, was comparatively small.
Negapatam, on the other hand, was strongly fortified,
and, besides, had been reinforced by Hyder-Ali, who
foresaw the English attack. Negapatam was thus defended by more than 8000 men, while the English numbered about 5000; nevertheless after a siege of five
days the town surrendered. Everything belonging to the
Dutch government and the Dutch East India Company had
to be delivered to the British.[1] With Negapatam the other
Dutch possessions fell into the hands of the English and
also the important harbor of Trinconomale on the island of
Ceylon. These events in the East Indies took place on
November 12, 1781, and January 15, 1782, respectively.
Another possession of the Dutch, the Cape of Good Hope,
was in danger of being taken by the British Captain John-
stone and his ships. It was saved only by the active intervention of the French, Admiral Suffren covering the Cape
with a squadron.[2] Trinconomale, on September 1, 1782,
was retaken from the English by Suffren, but Negapatam
remained lost.[3]

---

[1] Andrews, History of the War, IV, 239, 240.
    The English author concluded: "The reduction of Negapatam
completed the revolution that had begun to take place in the southern
provinces on the coast of Coromandel. It not only restored the
power and influence of the [English] East India Company in those
parts, but it raised the reputation and dread of the British arms
higher than ever."
    [2] Davies, History of Holland, III, 470; Kampen, Verkorte Ge-
schiedenis, II, 300; De Jonge, Geschiedenis, IV, 470.
    [3] Colenbrander, Patriottentijd, I, 195.

The Dutch at home were startled when they learned the fate of their colonies. It was impossible to render assistance, for the United Provinces had only fifty war vessels which could be considered serviceable, while the construction of new ones made little or no progress. There were, besides, not more than thirty-three vessels in the harbors at home, while the rest were abroad, and of these only eleven were ships of the line. With this small force, not even a convoy to the Baltic was ventured.[1] The aspect became a little brighter when, during the summer, reports arrived in the United Provinces that an encounter had occurred between the Dutch captains Melvill and Oorthuys and the English off Gibraltar. Although Melvill had been compelled to capitulate with his vessel, Oorthuys had not only saved the man-of-war under his command, but forced an English ship to haul down her flag.[2]

A convoy to the Baltic was now decided upon, although a strong British squadron under Admiral Hyde Parker was said to be near, and even to have orders to destroy the small Dutch fleet in the Texel. On August 1, 1781, the convoy, consisting of eight men-of-war, seven frigates, and one cutter under Rear-Admiral Zoutman, sailed from the Texel with seventy-two merchantmen.[3] On Sunday, August 5, between three and four o'clock in the morning, at the Doggersbank in the North Sea, they met Parker with eleven English war vessels and four cutters. The battle began at eight o'clock, and lasted until half past eleven. It was fierce and bloody. Both parties fought as long as their ships

---

[1] Urgent requests were made to the States General by shipowners, freighters, owners of plantations in the West Indies, merchants, etc., at Dordrecht, Haarlem, Amsterdam and Rotterdam for the protection of those Dutch Indian possessions not yet captured by the English. In case a convoy should not be possible, they asked to be granted generous contributions for the arming of their own vessels. This petition was received by the States General on June 7, 1781. It was approved by the Prince of Orange and resulted in a circular letter of the States General, dated June 20, to all the provinces recommending an appropriation of 1,200,000 guilders for the purpose desired (Sparks Dutch Papers); J. Adams to the President of Congress, June 12, 1781 (Wharton, IV, 495–498).
[2] Kampen, Verkorte Geschiedenis, II, 302–303.
[3] Davies, History of Holland, III, 470, 471.

were able to manoeuver. The English withdrew, and soon afterwards the Dutch also left the scene of the battle to repair their vessels as well as they could in order to sail back to the Texel, which they reached safely. Zoutman reported that on all vessels officers and men had shown great courage and had fought like lions.[1] According to Parker's account the Dutch were the first to retire, the British, however, not being able to follow them.[2]

When the news of the battle reached the United Provinces, the whole people were frantic for joy over its result. Van der Capellen wrote that the Dutch with an inferior force had put the English admiral, who commanded nine large vessels, to flight after a most bloody battle, which lasted for four hours. The courage of the Dutch had been so great that even those who had lost an arm or a foot could not be persuaded to leave their posts but insisted on remaining at the cannon.[3] After all the humiliations which the United Provinces had suffered from the hands of Great Britain this indecisive battle at the Doggersbank was exaggerated to a great national feat. John Adams, under the influence of public enthusiasm at Amsterdam, called the encounter a "glorious victory" of the Dutch.[4] The Prince of Orange, in person, presented Zoutman with a memorial coin on a golden chain, while King George III, considering Parker the victor, visited him on board his flagship.[5] There were, however, a few voices heard in the United Provinces judging the Doggersbank incident more soberly. They maintained that the battle could be regarded as a victory

---

[1] Rapport van . . . Schout bij Nagt J. A. Zoutman an Zijne Doorlugtige Hoogheid [Prince of Orange] van de Bataille met een Engelsch Esquader, August 10, 1781 (Sparks Dutch Papers).

[2] J. Adams to the President of Congress, August 18, 1781 (Wharton, IV, 642).

[3] Van der Capellen to Livingston, August 18, 1781 (Beaufort, Brieven van der Capellen, 257).

[4] J. Adams to the President of Congress, August 22, 1781 (Wharton, IV, 649).

[5] Kampen, Verkorte Geschiedenis, II, 301, 302.

William V of Orange publicly directed an address of thanks to all who had taken part in the combat on board of the Dutch vessels (J. Adams to the President of Congress, August 22, 1781, in Wharton, IV, 653, 654).

neither by the one nor by the other party, but that the English had succeeded in compelling the Dutch convoy to discontinue its voyage.[1]

In the meantime efforts to bring about peace were not wanting. Ever since the beginning of the war between Great Britain and the United Provinces attempts had been made to effect a reconciliation between the two powers. The Empress of Russia, Catherine II, made it her duty to try her utmost for such a purpose. At first she considered a joint mediation with Emperor Joseph II. She informed France and Spain of her plan, declaring that the mediation was to include all the belligerents.[2] The prospect of a mediation may perhaps have been one of the causes for the inactivity displayed by the Dutch, as it seemed that the majority of the people in the United Provinces did not think the war would continue long.

Not until the beginning of February were letters of

---

[1] Le Politique Hollandais, No. XXX, September 3, 1781.

As a matter of fact, the owners of the mercantile ships which had returned from the Doggersbank to the Texel later asked for an indemnification because their vessels were compelled to stay in harbor, which caused heavy expenses for equipping, wages, monthly pay, subsistence of crew, etc. (J. Adams to the President of Congress, October 18, 1781, in Wharton, IV, 787, 788).

[2] Harris to Stormont, January 15/26, 1781 (Malmesbury, Correspondence, I, 377).

Catherine's efforts to have Frederick the Great offer his mediation to the United Provinces failed because the Prussian king, it was said, did not want to take a share in the quarrel (Elliot to Harris, February 10, 1781, in Malmesbury, Correspondence, I, 384).

As a fact, however, the king was willing to use his good offices for the Republic, but he feared that his representations might, in the beginning at least, be coolly received in England (Frederick II to Thulemeier, February 12, 1781, in Bancroft MSS., Prussia and Holland). The project of Frederick's mediation was discussed by the Prince of Orange, the Grand Pensionary, and Griffier Fagel. They demanded that Great Britain should not only recognize the independence of the flag of Dutch merchant vessels, but also the validity of the treaty of 1674 with the clause of free ships, free goods (Thulemeier to Frederick II, February 23, 1781, in Bancroft MSS., Prussia and Holland). The king answered now that the Republic would obtain her ends more easily and promptly through Russian mediation. The representations, in order to be effective, should be made through a maritime power. He would therefore try to engage Russia to use all her influence in the interests of the United Provinces (Frederick II to Thulemeier, March 1, 1781, in Bancroft MSS., Prussia and Holland).

13

marque demanded by a privateer from Rotterdam, while Amsterdam refused altogether to take them. Vauguyon, in order to rouse the energy of the Dutch, even offered to furnish French letters of marque to their privateers, but he found no candidates for such favors in the United Provinces.[1] Nevertheless, strong as their desire for peace may have been, owing to the consciousness of their utter feebleness, the States General unanimously rejected a formal proposition of the province of Zealand to open direct negotiations with the court of St. James.[2]

At the beginning of March Prince Gallitzin, the Russian ambassador at the Hague, informed the States General confidentially that the empress, through Simolin, her minister in London, had made urgent representations at the court of St. James for conciliation.[3] This step was attributed to the intervention of Frederick the Great at the Russian court. No results, however, were expected since the principles adopted by the United Provinces and Great Britain respectively regarding the maintenance of the maritime treaty of 1674 were too much opposed.[4] The court of Vienna, having solicited the empress for cooperation in bringing about peace between the belligerents, received the answer that Catherine was willing to accept Joseph's cooperation, but that, first, a reconciliation must be effected between England and the United Provinces.[5] Frederick the Great thought that Catherine's desire to reconcile Great Britain with the United Provinces was sincere. He had even received information from St. Petersburg that, in case England should refuse an

---

[1] Thulemeier to Frederick II, February 6, 1781 (Bancroft MSS., Prussia and Holland).
[2] Thulemeier to Frederick II, February 9, 1781 (ibid.).
[3] Dimitri Prince de Gallitzin to the States General, March 1, 1781 (Sparks Dutch Papers); Secret Resolution of the States General, March 1, 1781 (Sparks MSS., CIII; Bancroft MSS., America, Holland, and England); Dumas to the President of Congress, March 5, 1781 (Wharton, IV, 273); J. Adams to the President of Congress, March 18, 1781 (ibid., IV, 312–313).
[4] Thulemeier to Frederick II, March 2, 1781 (Bancroft MSS., Prussia and Holland).
[5] Frederick II to Thulemeier, March 15, 1781 (Bancroft MSS., Prussia and Holland).

adjustment with the Republic on the basis of the empress' suggestions, she would, together with her allies, openly take sides with the United Provinces.[1] The latter speedily accepted the mediation offered by Russia, but the English court hesitated and made difficulties.[2] Lord Stormont, who favored a general peace, was opposed to it.[3] The British government, therefore, answered that a mediation between England's old enemies, the French and Spaniards, would be acceptable, but not with regard to the Dutch.[4] Catherine was much annoyed at this reply,[5] considering the refusal as a want of confidence and respect, and attributing it to personal aversion to her.[6] Her indignation was still noticeable in the letter by which she informed the States General of England's attitude and in which she stated that "her compassionate heart had been affected with the difficulties formed by the court of London."[7]

Another effort at mediation was made in July, 1781. This time Catherine and Joseph agreed to try together to procure a general pacification between the belligerent powers, and the States General were sounded by them accordingly. The United Provinces again were willing to accept. Even the Patriots advised this course because they apprehended that

---

[1] Frederick II to Thulemeier, March 19 and 26, 1781 (Bancroft MSS., Prussia and Holland). Catherine was offered every inducement by England to draw her away from the United Provinces. A convention between Great Britain and Russia was suggested and Minorca set as prize, but the empress refused on the ground that she would appear to be influenced as mediatrix by one of the belligerents, if she accepted. Harris gave as a commentary on her answer that she was longing to obtain Minorca, but that she had not the courage to subscribe to the means by which it could be had (Harris to Stormont, March 13/24, 1781, in Malmesbury, Correspondence, I, 401, 402).

[2] Dumas to the President of Congress, March 22, 1781 (Wharton, IV, 322, 323); Secret Resolution of the States General, March 23, 1781 (Sparks MSS., CIII).

[3] Thulemeier to Frederick II, April 10, 1781 (Bancroft MSS., Prussia and Holland).

[4] Malmesbury, Correspondence, I, 410.

[5] Frederick II to Thulemeier, April 9, 1781 (Bancroft MSS., Prussia and Holland).

[6] Harris to Stormont, April 9/20, 1781 (Malmesbury, Correspondence, I, 410).

[7] J. Adams to the President of Congress, June 23, 1781 (Wharton, IV, 513).

otherwise the opposite party might continue to recommend suing for peace directly with England.[1] It was proposed that an armistice of one year should be signed and that the United States should be included in this arrangement. Great Britain declined this plan of mediation also, emphasizing the fact that she would not accept the intervention of any power between herself and her colonies.[2]

In the meantime England tried to negotiate with the United Provinces directly, mainly in order to satisfy the opposition in Parliament. On behalf of the British government, Triquetti, the Sardinian consul at Amsterdam, who was in English pay, made the following proposition to the Dutch for an adjustment of the differences between the two powers. The old treaties were to be renewed, with the exception of that of 1674. The article dealing with naval munitions was to be changed according to the English views. Furthermore satisfaction was to be given for the negotiations of Amsterdam with the United States relative to a commercial treaty. Triquetti's efforts failed. Lord North then sent Paul Wentworth, proprietor of plantations at Surinam, and who had some relations with the United Provinces, to Amsterdam to negotiate with Rendorp, one of the burgomasters of that city. Rendorp demanded indemnity for all the Dutch ships captured by the English.

The Duke of Brunswick was for a separate peace with England, but the Grand Pensionary van Bleiswijck, the Princess of Orange, and also the envoys of France and Prussia were opposed to the plan, so the negotiations remained futile.[3] England, now feeling sure that it would not be possible to draw the Republic back to her former ally, would not have made a third attempt for a separate peace with the United Provinces, had it not been for two reasons. The first was that the opposition in Parliament had to be appeased, and the second that Catherine was once more pro-

---

[1] Dumas to the President of Congress, July 4, 1781 (Wharton, IV, 396).
[2] Malmesbury, Correspondence, I, 433.
[3] Colenbrander, Patriottentijd, I, 209 ff.

posing a mediation between England and the Republic.[1]
Harris advised the English king to accept Catherine's proposal this time, because a refusal would be liable to operate
very powerfully on her irritable character, and however
potent and conclusive the reasonings might be, they would
carry no conviction to a mind like hers. He even hinted
that Catherine might join in the war against Great Britain.[2]

On September 11, 1781, England accepted Russia's separate mediation in order to gain Catherine's friendship.[3]
The latter soon opened negotiations, this time at the Hague,
suggesting that all unnecessary formalities be omitted and
that both parties state their conditions of peace. The terms
would then be compared to see if there was any prospect for
a speedy arrangement.[4] The States General also accepted
Catherine's offer,[5] although the large cities like Amsterdam
and Rotterdam seemed little disposed toward a separate
peace with England.[6] These proceedings did not please
France. The French ambassador, Vauguyon, asked the
Grand Pensionary that the Republic should not conclude a
separate peace with Great Britain, and said that the King
of France would like to be informed of any step taken by
the United Provinces in that direction. He was answered
that, although the States General knew of no obligation forbidding them to conclude a separate peace with England,
since there was no alliance, not even a concert with France,
His Majesty the King would be promptly instructed of
everything pertaining to his interests.[7]

---

[1] Colenbrander, Patriottentijd, I, 213.
[2] Harris to Stormont, August 14/25, 1781 (Malmesbury, Correspondence, I, 441).
[3] Stormont to Harris, September 7, 1781 (Malmesbury, Correspondence, I, 446–447). Regarding the text of Stormont's note to
Simolin, accepting Russia's mediation, see J. Adams to the President of Congress, December 13, 1781 (Wharton, V, 43, 44).
[4] Secret Resolution of the States General, November 26 and 27,
1781 (Sparks MSS., CIII).
[5] Secret Resolution of the States General, December 18, 1781
(Sparks MSS., CIII; Sparks Dutch Papers).
[6] Thulemeier to Frederick II, December 4, 1781 (Bancroft MSS.,
Prussia and Holland).
[7] Same to same, December 25, 1781 (Bancroft MSS., Prussia and
Holland).

In January, 1782, the Empress of Russia dispatched Markoff to the Hague to conduct the negotiations. Before his departure from St. Petersburg the English envoy, Harris, tried to influence him favorably toward England, warning him especially against Vauguyon and the King of Prussia. Markoff would see the latter while passing through Berlin on his way to the United Provinces. Harris, according to his own words, gave Markoff "such intelligence on the character and disposition of His Prussian Majesty [Frederick the Great], as might put him on his guard against His very persuasive manner, and almost irresistible eloquence,"[1] which shows how much the English apprehended Frederick's influence in the United Provinces. The kings of Sweden and Denmark also offered their good offices to Great Britain, but their mediation was refused.[2]

Dana, the American agent at St. Petersburg, foresaw that Catherine's last efforts to bring about a separate peace between England and the United Provinces would be as fruitless as before. In his opinion, which finally proved to be correct, there could be no peace in Europe separate from that of the United States, since the latter affected the European systems too sensibly to be overlooked.[3] In the United Provinces the same view prevailed. "A separate peace with England," wrote Livingston, "is now impossible without degrading the character of the nation and exposing it to greater evils than they are threatened with from England. Besides, what advantages are to be derived from such a peace? Can Britain restore her conquests, now in the hands of the French? Can she give back the plunder of St. Eustatia, or the cargoes of the Indiamen divided among the captors? Can she afford them a compensation for the loss of last year's commerce? Or can she draw from her ex-

---

[1] Harris to Stormont, St. Petersburg, January 7/18, 1782 (Malmesbury, Correspondence, I, 480–482).

[2] J. Adams to the President of Congress, December 25, 1781, and January 16, 1782 (Wharton, V, 70, 71, 114, 115); Dana to Ellery, January 17, 1782 (ibid., V, 116); Dana to Livingston, March 5, 1782 (ibid., V, 223).

[3] Dana to Ellery, January 17, 1782 (ibid., V, 116).

hausted purse sufficient sums to defend the barrier against the troops of France, who would certainly avenge herself for such ingratitude?"[1]

In March, 1782, the States General formally communicated their conditions for a separate peace with England to the Russian government, which were that the rights of the Armed Neutrality be saved to them. This meant free navigation.[2] England, on the other hand, demanded that the treaty of 1674 should not be renewed in its old form, thereby denouncing the principle of free ships, free goods. Furthermore, no indemnity for injuries done to Dutch property at sea was mentioned. As to the Dutch colonies occupied by the English, uti possidetis was to be the basis of the settlement. In addition to this, the United Provinces should be obliged to expel the American agents from their territory and to forbid all loans for the United States.[3]

For the purpose of quieting the opposition in Parliament, the English government decided again to send Paul Wentworth secretly to the United Provinces in behalf of a separate peace.[4] His instructions directed him to find out also whether, in case of such a peace being brought about, France was to keep the Cape until a general peace would be concluded. England cared for a separate peace with the Republic only if the French were to abandon the Cape, but even then the obnoxious article regarding "free ships, free goods" would have to be removed from the treaty of 1674. The Prince of Orange, acting upon Rendorp's advice, informed France of England's proposition, adding that the

---

[1] Livingston to J. Adams, March 5, 1782 (Wharton, V, 220).

[2] Secret Resolution of the States General, March 4, 1782 (Sparks Dutch Papers).
The States of Holland passed the measure in February, 1782 (J. Adams to Livingston, February 19, 1782, in Wharton, V, 188).
As early as about the middle of February, 1782, Harris had been privately informed in St. Petersburg that the acknowledgment by England of the principles of the Armed Neutrality would mean immediate peace with the United Provinces (Harris to Stormont, February 4/15, 1782, in Malmesbury, Correspondence, I, 483, 484).

[3] Colenbrander, Patriottentijd, I, 215.

[4] Thulemeier to Frederick II, February 26, 1782 (Bancroft MSS., Prussia and Holland).

United Provinces would not make any arrangements contrary to the principles of the Armed Neutrality. When Wentworth arrived at the Hague pretending that his government had sent him for negotiations on the exchange of prisoners of war, he was told that the United Provinces demanded of England free navigation, return of the Dutch possessions occupied by the British, and an indemnity for the Dutch losses at sea. This was almost equal to a refusal of the English offer, and, in fact, Wentworth had to return to Great Britain without having achieved anything.[1]

On March 30, 1782, Lord North's cabinet fell. Rockingham became prime minister and Fox secretary for foreign affairs. This meant a complete change in the foreign policy of Great Britain. One of Fox's first official acts was to write a letter to the Russian envoy in London in which peace was offered to the United Provinces on the basis of the treaty of 1674 and an immediate truce proposed.[2] Harris was now directed to persuade Catherine to a more active and efficient negotiation.[3] Fox's letter to Simolin, dated March 29, 1782, was transmitted to the States General.[4] The question was now, whether the United Provinces would abandon "France and America, and throw themselves alone upon the Mercy of England."[5] In May, Fox renewed his proposition to the United Provinces,[6] but the latter, in the meantime, had concluded a concert with France for combined naval action, and were consequently not free to accept England's offer.[7]

---

[1] Colenbrander, Patriottentijd, I, 218–220.

[2] Franklin to Livingston, April 12, 1782 (Wharton, V, 300).

[3] Fox to Harris, April 2, 1782 (Malmesbury, Correspondence, I, 493–495); Harris to Fox, April 19/30, 1782 (ibid., 498–500).

[4] Memorie, Exhibitum, April 3, 1782 (Sparks Dutch Papers).

[5] J. Adams to van der Capellen (Beaufort, Brieven van der Capellen, 278).

[6] Dumas to Livingston, May 10, 1782 (Wharton, V, 410); Extract, Secret Resolution of the States of Holland, May 24, 1782 (Sparks Dutch Papers).

Fox's second letter was dated May 4, 1782 (Secret Resolution of the States General, May 13, 1782, in Sparks MSS., CIII).

[7] Concept-Extensie mit kragt der Resolution commissorial van 15 en 24 Mey 1782. Exhibitum 31 Mey 1782 (Sparks Dutch Papers). Secret Resolution of the States General, July 17, 1782 (Sparks

On April 12, 1782, Admiral Rodney won a tremendous naval battle in the West Indies, which lasted almost twelve hours without a moment's intermission. The commander of the French fleet, Count de Grasse, was taken prisoner and his flagship, with four other ships of the line, was seized by the English.[1] Adams said that this success made England so giddy that she would give up the idea of peace for some time.[2] Soon also the attention of the Empress of Russia was drawn to affairs at home, a Turkish war being expected, which prevented her from prosecuting with vigor her plans for mediation,[3] and this practically caused the discontinuance of the negotiations.

Ever since the beginning of the war the United Provinces had stood in reality alone. Their relations with France were scarcely different from those before the war, except that on May 1, 1781, at Versailles a convention had been signed by Vergennes and the Dutch envoy, Lestevenon van Berkenrode, regarding reprisals.[4] Some people thought that an alliance between France and the Republic would occasion a general European war.[5] Frederick the Great warmly recommended an alliance with the French court, but the Prince of Orange, who was still in favor of England, expressed his apprehension that this would mean absolute

---

Dutch Papers), according to which the King of France expressed his satisfaction at the refusal of the Dutch regarding a separate peace.

[1] Rodney to the Lieutenant-Governor of Jamaica. On board the "Formidable," between Guadaloupe and Monserrat, April 14, 1782 (Journals of the Assembly of Jamaica, VII).

[2] J. Adams to Livingston, June 9, 1782 (Wharton, V, 483).

[3] Harris to Grantham, August 5/16, 1782 (Malmesbury, Correspondence, I, 527); same to Lord Mountstuart, October 14/25, 1782 (ibid., II, 4, 5); same to Grantham, November 25/December 6, 1782 (ibid., II, 16).

[4] Van Berkenrode to the States General, May 3, 1781 (Bancroft MSS., America, Holland, and England).

The convention was ratified at the Hague on May 16, 1781, and at Versailles on May 27, 1781 (Sparks Dutch Papers; Wharton, IV, 435). For text of the convention see also Wharton, IV, 435.

[5] J. Adams to the President of Congress, June 15, 1781 (Wharton, IV, 507).

dependence of the Republic upon her powerful neighbor.[1]
The king informed his envoy at the Hague that this answer
seemed to him to be not only superficial but weak. What,
he said, would be the result, if peace was concluded at a
moment when the United Provinces were without allies?
No one would be interested in the fate of the Republic. On
the other hand, if she were an ally of France, that power
would be obliged to secure an honorable and suitable peace
for the Dutch.[2]

In the provinces the idea of an offensive and defensive
alliance with France had many adherents. In November
even a whole province, that of Friesland, proposed it to the
States General.[3] The Patriots, of course, worked also for an
alliance with France. Van der Capellen,[4] however, thought
that the views of France and the other great powers on
this subject should be known before definite steps were
taken. Vauguyon, whom he addressed accordingly, avoided
an answer, thereby arousing van der Capellen's suspicion.
France, the latter wrote to a friend, must find means to
prevent other powers from interfering with the affairs of
the United Provinces. If she could not, or would not do
this, the Patriots would make no further attempts to bring
about an alliance with her. It was true that the Republic
was only a second-class power, not strong enough to defend
herself successfully even against one of the three great

---

[1] Thulemeier to Frederick II, July 20, 1781 (Bancroft MSS.,
Prussia and Holland).

[2] Frederick II to Thulemeier, July 26, 1781, and January 3, 1782
(Bancroft MSS., Prussia and Holland).

[3] Resolution of the States General, November 16, 1781 (Sparks
MSS., CIII) ; Thulemeier to Frederick II, November 23, 1781 (Bancroft MSS., Prussia and Holland).

[4] Van der Capellen, the public sentiment being strongly in his
favor, was in the beginning of 1783 restored to his seat in the
provincial assembly of Overyssel, from which he had been expelled
after his famous speech against the lending of the Scotch Brigade
to Great Britain (above, p. 32). J. Adams, who as American peace
commissioner was temporarily in Paris, sent his congratulations to
van der Capellen by Dr. Wheelock, the president of Dartmouth
College in America, who happened to travel from Paris to the
United Provinces (J. Adams to van der Capellen, February 18,
1783, in Beaufort, Brieven van der Capellen, 369).

powers surrounding her. This would necessitate an alliance of the United Provinces with one or the other of these countries, preferably with the strongest and the one which, by her position, could either benefit or injure the Republic most. This was France.[1] For fear that the latter power might altogether withdraw from the United Provinces and keep the Dutch colonies in her possession the Patriot leader continued to plead for an alliance.[2]

The French court, on the other hand, was not pleased with the various efforts made for a separate peace between Great Britain and the United Provinces, and Vauguyon was very active in his efforts to thwart them. He did not conceal the fact that the court at Versailles would take strong countermeasures in case the Republic should accept conditions from Great Britain incompatible with her dignity and contrary to the interests of the belligerents.[3] How utterly without power and defence the Dutch really were is shown by an incident which, under different circumstances, might have provoked war. The United Provinces, in their controversies during the preceding century with Louis XIV, had obtained the right of keeping garrisons in several barrier fortresses of the Austrian Netherlands, as a protection against French aggressions. Emperor Joseph II now took advantage of the weakness of the Netherlands and forced them to withdraw these garrisons in November, 1781.[4]

Although there was no prospect of a formal alliance between France and the United Provinces, serious preparations were made for a time in the Republic for a combined naval action with France against England. In a secret

---

[1] Van der Capellen to Vauguyon, November 2, 1782; Vauguyon to van der Capellen, November 5, 1782; van der Capellen to Gijzelaar, November 11, 1782 (Beaufort, Brieven van der Capellen, 362 ff., 374).

[2] Van der Capellen to Vauguyon, December 2, 1782 (Beaufort, Brieven van der Capellen, 394, 395); same to Valck, December 15, 1782 (ibid., 419, 420).

[3] Thulemeier to Frederick II, December 21, 1781 (Bancroft MSS., Prussia and Holland).

[4] Wild, Die Niederlande, I, 267; Davies, History of Holland, III, 488, 489; Dumas to the President of Congress, January 30, 1782 (Wharton, V, 139).

session of the States General in the spring of 1782 it was resolved to request the Prince of Orange to confer with the court of France on such a concert.[1] Though he did not consider the Dutch fleet strong enough to furnish convoys, defend the coast, and fight the enemy at the same time,[2] William V carried out the resolution. France willingly entered into the agreement, thereby binding the Dutch to her interests, but answered evasively regarding all active measures which might result therefrom. She had made a secret arrangement with Spain to have the French fleet near Gibraltar, and now kept the United Provinces waiting for the promised combined naval action. This prevented them from accepting Fox's peace offers,[3] which they undoubtedly would have done if France had shown her cards openly.

The Dutch, in their ignorance of the real cause, condemned the Prince of Orange for letting the Dutch war vessels remain in the ports of the Republic instead of having them join the French fleet. Finally a juncture of the fleets at Brest was arranged between the two powers, but the ten Dutch vessels which were designated for this purpose refused to sail and declared that they were not prepared for such a step. This caused a storm of indignation in the United Provinces and violent attacks on the Prince of Orange.[4] An investigation regarding the condition of the Dutch navy and the causes of its inefficiency was instituted, lasting until 1787, but with no practical results.[5]

---

[1] Secret Resolution of the States General, March 4, 1782 (Sparks Dutch Papers).

[2] Thulemeier to Frederick II, February 19, 1782 (Bancroft MSS., Prussia and Holland).

[3] Colenbrander, Patriottentijd, I, 231, 232.

[4] J. Adams to Livingston, September 23, 1782 (Wharton, V, 752); Dumas to Livingston, September 27, 1782, and March 27, 1783 (ibid., V, 777; VI, 347); Davies, History of Holland, II, 447, 474–478; Kampen, Verkorte Geschiedenis, II, 305 ff.
Very ugly accusations were made also against the Duke of Brunswick which finally caused his downfall (Kampen, Verkorte Geschiedenis, II, 305 ff.). When the popular indignation threatened to become an uprising against him, he left the Hague to take up his residence in his own government, Bois-le-Duc (Davies, History of Holland, III, 478).

[5] Blok, Geschiedenis, VI, 391.

CHAPTER VIII.

THE UNITED STATES AND THE UNITED PROVINCES FORM CLOSER RELATIONS.

Van der Capellen wrote in 1779 that the time had not yet come for the public reception of an American envoy by the United Provinces. He advised, however, that Congress should send over a gentleman of distinction and ability, who might, in the beginning, live in the Republic as a private citizen, study the conditions of the country and learn its language, until an occasion for showing his public character should arrive.[1] The United States had sufficient work for such a representative in the United Provinces, since now all correspondence between the two republics had to be directed through the American ambassador, Franklin, at Paris. It seemed that the latter gentleman was already overburdened with work, and that the affairs of America for that reason must suffer, at least as far as the Netherlands were concerned.[2]

Probably acting upon van der Capellen's advice, Con-

---

[1] Van der Capellen to Trumbull, July 6, 1779 (Beaufort, Brieven van der Capellen, 108, 109).

[2] Van der Capellen to Livingston, July, 1779 (Beaufort, Brieven van der Capellen, 115).

Steven Sayre asserted that he had been asked by Franklin whether van der Capellen had applied to Congress to be appointed United States minister to the Netherlands. Sayre answered that if van der Capellen had done this, his only motive could have been the wish to serve America (Sayre to van der Capellen, October 24, 1779, in Beaufort, Brieven van der Capellen, 158). There are no suggestions in van der Capellen's correspondence that he ever desired to be appointed American minister. Probably Dumas saw and misunderstood van der Capellen's letters to Trumbull and Livingston regarding the sending over of an American representative, and informed Franklin erroneously that the Dutch statesman was anxious to receive a commission.

Van der Capellen was indignant and thanked Sayre for defending his character against the "calumny" (Van der Capellen to Sayre, November 16, 1779, in Beaufort, Brieven van der Capellen, 159).

gress in October, 1779, appointed its former president, Henry Laurens, minister plenipotentiary of the United States to the United Provinces.[1] He also received instructions to negotiate a loan of ten millions abroad. But Laurens being delayed in departing for the United Provinces, John Adams, then residing at Paris, was authorized by Congress on June 20, 1780, to enter upon that part of the minister's duties in the Republic.[2] On September 3, following, the vessel "Mercury" in which Laurens had finally sailed for Europe was taken by the English cruiser "Vestal" and the minister himself was made prisoner, his papers, as has been seen, furnishing Great Britain the pretext of her rupture with the Netherlands.[3]

John Adams, arriving at Amsterdam in August, 1780, previous to the receiving of his commission, found his position difficult from the beginning.[4] Not being vested with any political authority, he did not communicate his business to the States General and the Prince of Orange, or even to the magistrates of Amsterdam.[5] He was, however, of opinion that he would be successful, if he had full powers from Congress, in opening a considerable loan in the United Provinces and extending the commerce between the two countries.[6] The Dutch were highly ignorant of American affairs, and it would be necessary to enlighten them before they would risk anything for the United States.[7] While

---

[1] Van Dircks to van der Capellen, November 30, 1779 (Beaufort, Brieven van der Capellen, 165).

[2] Wharton, I, 506; IV, 56, 61. Dana received the same commission, in case Adams should be unable to take Laurens' place (ibid., IV, 62, 63).

[3] Ibid., I, 579.

[4] According to his own words, he entered the United Provinces "a forlorn pilgrim without a letter of introduction." He received his provisional commission for negotiating a loan only on September 19, 1780 (Fairchild, van der Kemp, 65).

[5] J. Adams to the President of Congress, September 24, 1780 (Wharton, IV, 66); Thulemeier to Frederick II, October 13, 1780 (Bancroft MSS., Prussia and Holland).

[6] J. Adams to the President of Congress, August 14 and 23, 1780 (Wharton, IV, 29, 42); October 11, 1780 (ibid., IV, 95); October 14, 1780 (ibid., IV, 98).

[7] J. Adams to the President of Congress, September 25, 1780 (ibid., IV, 67-69).

Franklin felt humiliated by "running about from court to court begging for money and friendship,"[1] Adams saw no reason why they should be ashamed

"of asking to borrow money, after maintaining a war against Great Britain and her allies for about six years without borrowing anything abroad. When England has been all the time borrowing of all the nations of Europe, even of individuals among our allies, it can not be unnatural, surprising, or culpable, or dishonorable for us to borrow money. When England borrows annually a sum equal to all her exports, we ought not to be laughed at for wishing to borrow a sum annually equal to a twelfth part of our annual exports. We may and we shall wade through if we can not obtain a loan; but we could certainly go forward with more ease, convenience and safety by the help of one. I think we have not meanly solicited for friendship anywhere. But to send ministers to every great court in Europe, especially the maritime courts, to propose an acknowledgment of the independence of America and treaties of amity and commerce, is no more than becomes us, and in my opinion is our duty to do. It is perfectly consistent with the genuine system of American policy, and a piece of respect due from new nations to old ones."[2]

Van der Capellen, who had so often before shown his sincere desire of furthering the American cause, offered his services to Adams and recommended a number of friends to him, as Adriaan Valck at Rotterdam, Tegelaar, and the Mennonite minister van der Kemp,[3] who might be employed as correspondents or in any other capacity for promoting Adams' object.

From another side also aid was proposed to Adams. The King of Spain had expressed his willingness to guarantee the payment of the interest and principal of a loan of 150,-000 dollars for the use of the United States. The American commissioners at Paris could not avail themselves of this offer on account of the extensive loans which the French minister of finance, Necker, was about to make. Franklin, therefore, thought that probably the king's promise might have weight in the United Provinces.[4] In this, however, he

---

[1] Franklin to Adams, October 2, 1780 (Wharton, IV, 74).
[2] J. Adams to Franklin, October 14, 1780 (Wharton, IV, 96).
[3] Van der Capellen to J. Adams, October 16, 1780 (Beaufort, Brieven van der Capellen, 199, 200).
Interesting is Adams' letter to van der Capellen of October 17, 1780, in which he informed the latter of the financial condition of the United States (ibid., 195–199).
[4] Franklin to J. Adams, October 20, 1780 (Wharton, IV, 101).

was very much mistaken. The Dutch did not show any inclination at all to loan money to the United States.[1] The latter, disappointed at not being successful in borrowing money either in Spain or the Netherlands, appealed to Louis XVI. A foreign loan of specie, they said, at least to the amount of twenty-five million livres would be indispensably necessary for a vigorous prosecution of the war. The King of France was asked either to advance this sum from his royal coffers or to help Congress to secure it from other sources by acting as security for the payment of interest and principal.[2]

Adams' efforts to raise a loan in the United Provinces were much hampered by similar attempts of the separate American states. Mr. A. Gillon, for example, was active at Amsterdam in his efforts to borrow money for South Carolina at five per cent. interest.[3] Adams attributed his failure to obtain money to the avarice of the Dutch and to their fear that the United States might finally submit to England.[4] Van der Capellen even was somewhat discouraged at the fact that the credit of the United States was so low in the United Provinces. He gave Adams advice as to how the loan could be started, and recommended Tegelaar as a negotiator, or, if he should not suit, J. de Neufville. He mentioned in this connection also the house of Fizeaux, but thought that the fact that its head was related to an English general serving in America should be considered.[5] Adams' answer showed that he had lost almost all hope of ever succeeding in his mission. He would not think it wise or honest to deceive America with any hope of assistance in any

[1] J. Adams to the President of Congress, November 17, 1780 (Wharton, IV, 155); Yorke to Stormont, August 11, 1780 (Sparks MSS., LXXII).
[2] Congress to the King of France, November 22, 1780 (Wharton, IV, 159, 160).
[3] Gillon to van der Capellen, November 25, 1780 (Beaufort, Brieven van der Capellen, 192–194).
[4] J. Adams to the President of Congress, November 25, 1780 (Wharton, IV, 161).
[5] Van der Capellen to J. Adams, November 28, 1780 (Beaufort, Brieven van der Capellen, 208).

way from the Republic. A dispute arose between Adams and van der Capellen regarding the causes of the Dutch attitude, the former attributing it to the fear of the English, and remarking, " The less America has to do with such people, the better it will be for her."[1] Van der Capellen refuted this view, asserting that the bad news from America, the loss of Charleston, the defeat of General Gates, Arnold's desertion, and above all the enormous depreciation of the American paper money had caused the low credit of the United States in the Republic. He assured Adams that the great majority of the Dutch, certainly more than four fifths of them, loved the Americans, and wished sincerely that the United States might be victorious in the end.[2]

In January, 1781, Congress decided to appoint John Adams American minister plenipotentiary to the United Provinces and provided him with credentials to the Prince of Orange.[3] He was instructed not only to negotiate a loan, but also to conclude, if possible, a treaty of commerce and amity with the Republic. His reception by the States General would, of course, involve the acknowledgment of the independence of the United States. Many difficulties were still existing in the United Provinces for such a step. The Prince of Orange especially was hostile to closer relations with the United States. As early as 1778 he had declared that he would retire from the office of stadtholder and with his family leave the country, rather than accede to the acknowledgment of the independence of the United States, because in this case the Republic would be completely delivered to France.[4] Adams seems to have been fully aware of the fact that there was no prospect yet for his obtaining

---

[1] J. Adams to van der Capellen, December 9, 1780 (Wharton, IV, 190). Adams expressed himself similarly to the President of Congress on December 14, 1780 (ibid., IV, 192).
[2] Van der Capellen to J. Adams, December 24, 1780 (Beaufort, Brieven van der Capellen, 209).
See Adams' reply of January 21, 1781 (J. A. Sillem's supplement to Beaufort, Brieven van der Capellen, 46–54).
[3] Huntington, President of Congress, to J. Adams, January 1, 1781 (Wharton, IV, 224, 225).
[4] Nijhoff, Brunswijk, 154, 155.

14

any concessions in the United Provinces. His letters in January and February show that he had not moved one step forward regarding a loan, and that his hopes for being more successful in the near future were very small.[1]

The plan of this loan was to issue one thousand obligations at one thousand guilders each, bearing interest at the rate of five per cent., payable in coupons of twenty-five guilders every six months. This interest was thought more than satisfactory, since it was one per cent. more than was ordinarily paid for bank deposits. The whole amount would be redeemed at the end of the tenth year. The guarantee of all the states combined and of each singly should serve as security for the whole, capital and interest. Their tobacco trade alone, if necessary, would guarantee the restitution of one million guilders in ten years. One objection made in the United Provinces against the loan was that the money could be used to greater advantage at home for furthering Dutch industry. Many Dutch, however, were of the opinion that by gaining free commerce and navigation with the United States, considerable profits could be obtained, since the sending of manufactures there and the bringing back of raw products would not only employ Dutch merchants and shippers, but also Dutch factories.[2]

In the meantime Louis XVI had considered the request of the United States for a loan of twenty-five million livres. Franklin was now told by the French foreign minster that the king was not able to favor the loan in his own dominion, because it would interfere with his obtaining money to continue the war, but that he would turn over to the United States the sum of six millions as a gift exclusive of the three millions which he had secured for Franklin before.[3]

---

[1] J. Adams to the President of Congress, January 4 and 15, 1781 (Wharton, IV, 227, 235) ; same to Franklin, February 15, 1781 (ibid., 256).

[2] Pamphlet, Drie Brieven etc. over het uitgekomen plan van een negotiatie etc., February 25, 27, and 28, 1781 ; Carmichael to the Committee of Foreign Affairs, March 11, 1781 (Wharton, IV, 280).

[3] Franklin to the President of Congress, March 12, 1781 (Wharton, IV, 281).

Part of this gift was to be employed for making purchases in

Adams, still unsuccessful in the Netherlands, did not receive even enough money to discharge the bills of exchange which Congress had drawn upon him and Laurens, but had to depend upon Franklin for their payment. He had no hope that these conditions would change until the independence of the United States should be acknowledged by the Republic.[1] He reported to Congress that people in the United Provinces were as yet so much afraid of being pointed out by the mob or the soldiery as favoring the loan which he had opened that there was no prospect of success for several months, if ever.[2]

In the following month the French foreign minister informed Laurens, the special minister of Congress at Paris, that Louis XVI was going to guarantee a loan of ten millions, to be opened in the United Provinces, in addition to the six millions which he had granted as a gift.[3] France thought that as soon as the Dutch withdrew their funds from England and placed them with the Americans, the resources of the English court would become exhausted. This loan was not to have anything in common with Adams' loan, and Neufville was, therefore, not to be connected with it in any way. The houses of Fizeaux and Grand were given the commission to negotiate it.[4] This loan, however,

France, while the rest was to be sent to the United States for establishing the credit of the government there. Washington alone was authorized to draw bills of exchange in America against this money (Bolles, Financial History, 241).

[1] J. Adams to the President of Congress, April 6, 1781 (Wharton, IV, 352) ; same to Franklin, April 16, 1781 (ibid., IV, 363).

[2] Same to the President of Congress, March 19, 1781 (ibid., IV, 314).

[3] J. Laurens to the President of Congress, April 9, 1781 (ibid., IV, 355).

[4] Vergennes to Vauguyon, April 13, 1781 (Sparks MSS., LXXXIII).

John Jay, before knowing that John Adams was authorized to execute the business which had been committed to Henry Laurens, also made attempts to raise a loan in the United Provinces. As soon as he learned of Adams' commission, he referred the firm of Neufville and Son, with whom he had negotiated, to him, since, he said, " the impropriety of two loans at a time " was evident (Jay to the President of Congress, April 25, 1781, in Wharton, IV, 385, 386). If Jay had not withdrawn, there would have been under consideration three loans for the United States in the Netherlands at the same time, of which none had any prospect of success.

was also a complete failure. The Dutch seemed to have no inclination at all to risk their money in American funds,[1] whereupon Louis XVI decided to supply the ten millions out of his own treasury.[2] The French ambassador at the Hague now asked the States General to guarantee the ten million loan for the United States in the Republic. The Grand Pensionary, however, thought that this step would not be successful, since the dismissal of Necker, which occurred at this time, had struck a mortal blow to the political as well as financial credit of France.[3] The French proposition was then modified. The money was to be loaned to the King of France under the guarantee of the States General at four per cent. interest.[4]

Franklin by this time had grown almost bitter toward the United Provinces, expecting but little from them to the advantage of the United States. Though the Dutch had been in the same situation as the Americans and were then glad to receive assistance from other nations, they did not seem to feel for the United States, or to have the least inclination to help. In his opinion the Dutch lacked magnanimity,[5] but a few days later, Franklin almost apologized for these remarks, saying that he had been out of humor when he made them, because the United States could obtain no loan in the Republic, while England borrowed freely there.[6]

Toward the end of August, the American correspondent at the Hague was able to report that the French loan in the United Provinces for the United States would probably suc-

---

[1] J. Laurens to the President of Congress, May 15, 1781 (Wharton, IV, 416, 417); J. Adams to same, May 16, 1781 (ibid., IV, 420).

Van der Capellen assured Congress again that four fifths of his countrymen were friends of the United States, and that their indifference regarding the American loan was due to bad news from America, etc. (Van der Capellen to Livingston, May 25, 1781, in Beaufort, Brieven van der Capellen, 249–252).

[2] Vergennes to J. Laurens, May 16, 1781 (Wharton, IV, 418); Doniol, Histoire, IV, 559; Bolles, Financial History, 252.

[3] Thulemeier to Frederick II, July 31, 1781 (Bancroft MSS., Prussia and Holland).

[4] Same to same, August 31, 1781 (ibid.).

[5] Franklin to Dumas, August 6, 1781 (Wharton, IV, 625).

[6] Franklin to Dumas, August 10, 1781 (ibid., IV, 627).

ceed, since the States General were going to pass upon it. The latter might open it themselves on their own credit, guaranteeing the payment of the capital and the interest at four per cent. It was still a secret that the loan was intended for the United States.[1] The Prussian envoy at the Hague also learned of the success of this loan, and thought that it would be very helpful to the United States. Great Britain would find in this occurrence a new motive for regretting the inconsiderate rupture with the Netherlands.[2] Franklin, at Paris, was still skeptical about the success of the loan,[3] and in fact Dumas had to admit toward the middle of October that so far as he knew only the provinces of Holland and Friesland had consented to the loan proposed by France.[4] In November Franklin reported that the affair was said to be at last concluded, but it was not yet executed.[5] In reality, however, it had not made much progress, when the news of Cornwallis' surrender reached the United Provinces.

A change in favor of the United States was now expected to take place in the Republic, and, in fact, it began by the depreciation of English securities, with which especially Amsterdam was filled. The consolidated funds, " the true thermometer of the credit of England," fell to fifty per cent., while they formerly had been quoted at one hundred and fourteen.[6] The province of Zealand now also consented to the French loan. Adams' loan, on the other hand, rested as it was.[7] He had received only a few thousand guilders in all, and these he reserved for the relief of Americans

---

[1] Dumas to the President of Congress, August 23 and 30, 1781 (Wharton, IV, 655, 657).

[2] Thulemeier to Frederick II, September 11, 1781 (Bancroft MSS., Prussia and Holland).

[3] Franklin to Morris, September 12, 1781 (Wharton, IV, 704).

[4] Dumas to the President of Congress, October 11, 1781 (ibid., IV, 771, 772).

[5] Franklin to the President of Congress, November 5, 1781 (ibid, IV, 827).

[6] Thulemeier to Frederick II, November 20, 1781 (Bancroft MSS., Prussia and Holland).

[7] J. Adams to the President of Congress, October 15, 1781 (Wharton, IV, 777).

escaping from English prisons.[1] The Dutch firm of John
de Neufville and Son offered to the American commissioners
at Paris a loan of two million guilders, but their conditions
were such that they could not be accepted.[2]

Adams found that there were four persons in the Republic
who had the whole affair of public loans in their hands and
that they refused to sanction a loan to the United States
until peace was restored. These men, he suspected, were·
receiving salaries for opposing American loans, or at least
were being supported by a combination consisting of the
British government, Dutch court, owners of English stocks,
and great mercantile houses, in the interest of the British
ministry.[3] Adams was therefore of opinion that the United
States would not obtain any loan in the United Provinces
until a treaty should be made.[4]

The French loan of five million guilders for the United
States was in the meantime completed in the Republic, but
only a comparatively small part of it remained available for
Congress, most of it being expended for advances made by
France.[5] Van der Capellen thought that the credit of
America was growing considerably in the United Provinces.[6]
Franklin also was better satisfied, saying that there was
some prospect of another loan there;[7] but Adams almost
despaired of success. " I can represent," he said, " my situation in this affair of a loan by no other figure than that
of a man in the midst of the ocean negotiating for his life

---

[1] J. Adams to the President of Congress, December 4, 1781 (Wharton, V, 37). He had ordered a hundred pounds for President Henry
Laurens, who was still imprisoned in the Tower of London. Adams,
solicited by Laurens' daughter for further supplies, referred her to
Franklin (ibid., V, 37).
[2] Franklin to J. Adams, December 14, 1781 (ibid., V, 46–48).
[3] J. Adams to Franklin, January 25, 1782 (ibid., V, 131) ; Bolles,
Financial History, 253.
[4] J. Adams to Livingston, February 14 and 19, 1782 (Wharton,
V, 163, 187) ; Bolles, Financial History, 254.
[5] Thulemeier to Frederick II, December 21, 1781 (Bancroft MSS.,
Prussia and Holland) ; Livingston to General Green, January 31,
1782 (Wharton, V, 142).
[6] Van der Capellen to J. Adams, May 2, 1782 (Beaufort, Brieven
van der Capellen, 291).
[7] Franklin to Jay, April 24, 1782 (Wharton, V, 327).

among a school of sharks. I am sorry to use expressions which must appear severe to you, but the truth demands them."[1]

In the next month, however, he was able to report upon negotiations which he was conducting with three firms regarding the opening of a loan.[2] These houses were Wilhem and Jan Willinks, Nicholas and Jacob van Staphorst, and De la Lande and Fynjé. The loan was to bear five per cent. interest, which, according to Adams, was a moderate rate, since, as he said, France gave as much and other powers much more. The whole amount of the loan was to be five million guilders, but Adams did not expect to obtain that sum for a long time. By Christmas, he said, he might obtain about one million and a half, but hardly more.[3] The contract was sent to Congress for ratification, and Adams hoped to receive thirteen to fourteen hundred thousand guilders upon the receipt of the ratification.[4] Congress approved the contract of the loan and ratified it in September. Adams was admonished to try his utmost to have the whole amount raised, since the United States would need the money in any event. In case the war should continue, it would be essential for further exertions of the Americans, and if peace should be brought about, it would be greatly needed for discharging the army.[5] However, in July of the following year but three thousand of the obligations of the loan had been sold, which, Adams said, was due to the scarcity of money in the United Provinces. The loan was completed only in 1786.[6]

---

[1] J. Adams to Livingston, May 16, 1782 (Wharton, V, 420).
[2] Same to same, June 9, 1782 (ibid., V, 482).
[3] Same to same, July 5, 1782 (ibid., V, 594, 595).
[4] J. Adams to Livingston, August 18, 1782 (ibid., V, 665).
[5] Livingston to J. Adams, September 15, 1782 (ibid., V, 728, 729).
[6] J. Adams to Livingston, July 28, 1783 (ibid., VI, 608).
On August 7, 1783, van der Capellen wrote also that the American loan of five million guilders was not yet filled (Beaufort, Brieven van der Capellen, 653). During the year 1784, 1,488,000 guilders were received; in 1785, 134,000; and in 1786, 118,000 guilders; making it in all five millions, as had been stipulated (Bayley, National Loans, 17). This loan was not repaid until 1797.

A final French loan of six million livres was granted to the United States by resolution of September 14, 1782, bearing five per cent. interest.[1] In Spain also efforts were made to borrow money for the United States, but only a small sum was secured. The amount issued in 1781 was a trifle more than $174,000.[2] Although various other European countries were invited to assist the Americans with loans, no funds were received from the old world besides those mentioned.

John Adams had thus executed one part of his orders, that is, the arranging of a Dutch loan. True, he had experienced many failures before he reached the goal, but the money was now needed by the United States as much as ever. He was not less successful in executing the rest of his instructions. Early in 1781, the province of Friesland had resolved to acknowledge the independence of the United States. Adams thought it now opportune to disclose his public character to the States General and open, if possible, the negotiations between the two republics. In this matter he approached the French ambassador at the Hague, soliciting his assistance.[3] He addressed, on April 19, 1781, a long memorial to the States General, in which he informed them of his appointment as minister plenipotentiary of the United States "to reside near" them and of his instructions to negotiate a treaty of commerce and amity with the United Provinces. At the same time he explained in detail why such a treaty should be concluded as being in the interest and to the advantage of both countries.[4] A shorter note of the same tenor was directed to the Prince of Orange,

---

A number of loans were taken up in the United Provinces by the United States after peace was restored; this continued until 1794. Their discussion, however, would be beyond the scheme of this essay. See De Knight-Tillman, History of the Currency, 31 ff.; Bayley, National Loans, 17 ff.

[1] De Knight-Tillman, History of the Currency, 31.
[2] De Knight-Tillman, History of the Currency, 30.
[3] J. Adams to de la Vauguyon, March 1 and April 16, 1781 (Wharton, IV, 270, 271, 364).
[4] Wharton, IV, 370-376; pamphlet, "Adams' Memorial;" A Collection of State Papers, pamphlet 1; Vaterlandsche Historie, XXVIII, 33.

expressing also the American minister's desire to be received by the stadtholder for the delivery of the credentials.[1]

Adams' memorial caused much discussion as to whether closer relations with the United States would be advantageous to the United Provinces. For many reasons, one anonymous author said, it was to the interest of the Dutch to conclude a commercial treaty with the United States. Many products of America, in his opinion, were suitable for Europe, and this trade could be greatly increased after the hostilities had ceased. Agriculture was very extensive in the United States, the products of which could be exchanged in Europe for manufactured articles. There was a large importation of tobacco from Virginia, rice and indigo from Carolina, grain from Pennsylvania, etc. In return for these goods the Dutch could send to the United States linen and cloth (lakens), the products of the United Provinces, and cotton and wool, imported from the Dutch colonies; while silk, which was much bought in America, could be provided from Germany and France. The articles of the East India Company, tea, china, etc., were also much in demand with the Americans. The author concluded, therefore, that the United Provinces in gaining the American trade would not only further Dutch navigation, since the carrying of the goods from and to the United States would almost wholly be effected in Dutch bottoms, but Dutch industry and commerce would be promoted as well. There was danger, however, that American commerce might seek other channels, and a treaty should now be concluded with all possible speed, especially since the equality of both republics, their freedom of politics and religion invited to closer relations.[2]

Another Dutch writer tried to prove that a treaty with the United States would be utterly disadvantageous to the United Provinces. As the Americans, he declared, had no

---

[1] J. Adams' Memorial to the Prince of Orange, April 19, 1781 (Wharton, IV, 377).

[2] Pamphlet: Memorie wegens het commercieele belang etc. van commercie met de Vereenigde Staaten van Nord-Amerika.

navy worth mentioning and only a few privateers, they could not render any assistance to the Republic, either in the West Indies or in Europe; otherwise they would have defended St. Eustatia in their own interest. Besides, Dutch commerce could not gain during the war; on the contrary it was cut off by the war and especially by the capture of St. Eustatia. It would be folly to think of a direct trade with the United States, because it would require continual convoys and a large fleet on the American coast. Indirect trade, however, was precluded as well, since St. Eustatia, Berbice, Essequibo, and Demerari were taken. Of the two remaining Dutch colonies, Surinam was not convenient as a staple place and Curaçao could be of no use at present. How unsafe and unprofitable the American trade was, the author stated, was fully shown by the fact that the French mercantile vessels were almost all captured either on their way to America or coming back. Of many hundreds of vessels only twenty-five to thirty had reached France again. He then set forth what the result of a treaty with the United States would be after peace had been restored, mentioning three possibilities: America would either be victorious, or defeated and subdued, or it might be divided up between England, France, and Spain. If such a division should occur, the United Provinces, by a treaty, would be prevented from sharing in it. In case the Americans should be subdued by England, they would not be able to fulfil their treaty obligations toward the United Provinces. It was improbable, he continued, that the United States would be victorious, since England would never recognize the independence of her former American colonies. But even if the Americans should gain independence and the United States have the most advantageous treaty with them (which, however, very likely France would have), the American trade would prove injurious to the Dutch. The exchange of Dutch products for money or goods was very small. On the other hand their principal business, the carrying trade, would not profit from the independence of

America, since the Americans, having no sound or channel to pass through, would become formidable competitors. They could sail with all winds and in all seasons. Furthermore the United States would not buy through the United Provinces what they could obtain directly from France, Spain, or England. No treaty, he said, would induce American merchants to do so. For trade with America remained then only the few goods which were sent down the rivers Rhine and Maas from Germany to the United Provinces, but these might easily be fetched by the Americans in their own vessels. From all these considerations this author drew the conclusion that a treaty with America would do the Dutch harm rather than good. The Americans would preserve English institutions, especially with regard to legal matters and courts, since their language was the same; and they would, therefore, also remain in closer commercial relations with England than with any other nation.[1]

John Adams again suggested to Vauguyon that the United Provinces should be invited to join the French-American alliance,[2] while the Prussian envoy at the Hague thought that the French ambassador was taking up this project. Thulemeier, however, doubted that a treaty between the two republics could be brought about, since the Prince of Orange had discussed the subject with him in a manner which proved the strong opposition of the stadtholder to such a measure.[3] The French ambassador thought it not even advisable yet for Adams to deliver his credentials. When the latter disclosed to Vauguyon his intention of doing so, the Frenchman said that he had no instructions from his government to express an opinion about the matter, but that privately he did not think the present moment favorable for the step.[4]

[1] Pamphlet, Consideration op de Memoria etc., 19 April 1781 (August L. Schlözer, Briefwechsel meist historischen und politischen Inhalts, 130–149).

[2] Wharton, IV, 397 ff.

[3] Thulemeier to Frederick II, April 20, 1781 (Bancroft MSS., Prussia and Holland); same to same, April 24, 1781 (ibid.).

[4] Vauguyon to Vergennes, April 21, 1781 (Sparks MSS., LXXXIII).

Adams, however, did not heed Vauguyon's advice. At the beginning of May he had a conference with the Grand Pensionary, who told him that his recognition as American minister might be difficult, since the United Provinces had not yet acknowledged the independence of the United States. Although Adams had thus received little encouragement, he tried, on the following days, to deliver his credentials to the Dutch officials. All declined more or less politely to receive them. The Grand Pensionary who was to have a copy of the original said that it was not customary to deliver the paper to him but that it would be better to hand it to the griffier of the States General. The president of the latter body, to whom Adams went next, refused to accept the papers on the ground that such an act implied an acknowledgment, the responsibility for which he could not take upon himself. The president, however, promised to report the case to the States General. Thereupon Adams tried to deliver his memorial to the Prince of Orange through the latter's privy counsellor, but received the envelope back unopened with "a polite excuse from the prince that he could not receive it till after their high mightinesses should have resolved if, and when, he was to be admitted in the character which he had set forth with them."

Adams now published his memorial in English, French, and Dutch. All the public papers in the United Provinces inserted it, and Dumas reported that it was generally known, and that it both pleased and puzzled everybody. The president of the States General kept his promise and forwarded Adams' request. As a result the deputies of all seven provinces demanded and received copies of the report, in order to transmit them to their regencies for deliberation and decision. When the American minister told Vauguyon of the steps which he had taken, the latter repeated his former remark that he did not think the time favorable for such a measure, but that, personally, he would support it.[1] The French government approved of the ambassador's attitude. He was instructed not to take any steps toward the admission of Adams' credentials, but rather to try to convince him that the present circumstances were not favorable to his measure. Vergennes added that Vauguyon would probably not change Adams' intention, but that the ambassador's words would at least serve to justify the French proceedings if the American minister should place France under the necessity of making them known to Congress.[2] Vauguyon was also directed not to hesitate to tell the Dutch authorities that he did all in his power to dissuade Adams from delivering his credentials. In case the latter should again approach the French ambassador for advice in the matter, Vauguyon was to persuade him to withdraw his credentials quietly until circumstances should permit the States General to accept them.[3]

When this letter was written, Vauguyon had already informed the Dutch ministers that Adams had acted without the approbation of the court at Versailles. The ambassador said he deemed this measure necessary in order to show that his government did not mean to contribute to the embarrassment of the States General.[4] Vergennes now commissioned the French minister in the United States, de Luzerne, to inform Congress of the attitude and conduct of

---

[1] Dumas to the President of Congress, May 2, 4, 11, and 16, 1781 (Wharton, IV, 393, 394); J. Adams to the President of Congress, May 3, 7, and 16, 1781 (ibid., IV, 398, 401–403, 419); Resolution of the States General, May 4, 1781 (Sparks MSS., CIII); Thulemeier to Frederick II, May 15, 1781 (Bancroft MSS., Prussia and Holland).

Thulemeier thought that Adams would not be admitted yet because the Dutch government did not want to irritate England, and also because neither the northern powers, nor the court of Vienna, nor even Spain had recognized the independence of the United States (Thulemeier to Frederick II, May 8, 1781, in Bancroft MSS., Prussia and Holland).

The Prussian envoy also reported that Adams had given the Grand Pensionary to understand that a refusal of the Dutch government might cause the United States later to decline commercial relations with the United Provinces (Thulemeier to Frederick II, May 11, 1781, ibid.).

[2] Vergennes to Vauguyon, May 6, 1781 (Sparks MSS., LXXXIII).
[3] Vergennes to Vauguyon, May 11, 1781 (ibid.).
[4] Vauguyon to Vergennes, May 11, 1781 (ibid.).

France in this case. The French Foreign Secretary said that he was convinced that Adams would be censured for "his very awkward precipitation."[1] The prospect of the American cause in the United Provinces was thus not very bright, and it was even said that the States General had decided to refuse the admission of a minister from Congress.[2] The Prince of Orange also was still opposed to closer relations with the United States.[3]

The first opinion expressed openly in favor of a treaty with America and published in the United Provinces was that of Baron van der Capellen van de Marsch, who pleaded for an alliance with both France and America. Baron de Nagel, of Zutphen, also said that he would rather acknowledge the independence of the United States than form an alliance with France.[4]

About this time Adams received instructions and a commission from Congress with full powers to "confer, treat, agree, and conclude" a treaty of alliance between France, the United Provinces, and the United States.[5] The American minister communicated the news to Vauguyon, suggesting that they confer together on the subject. There were three ways, he said, to propose the treaty to the United Provinces. The French ambassador might open the negotiations in the name of his royal master, or both Adams and

---

[1] Vergennes to Vauguyon, May 17, 1781 (Sparks MSS., LXXXIII).

Adams was later asked "with friendly and patriotic anxiety" by Livingston to report about the motive which had prompted him to make the proposition of May 4, 1781, and to print the memorial. He gave then a vivid and detailed account of his reasons (J. Adams to Livingston, February 21, 1782, in Wharton, V, 193–199). The subsequent events showed that Adams was a better judge of affairs than Vauguyon.

See on this subject also Doniol, Histoire, IV, 562, 563; V, 48–57.

[2] Thulemeier to Frederick II, June 12, 1781 (Bancroft MSS., Prussia and Holland).

[3] Thulemeier to Frederick II, July 3, 1781 (Bancroft MSS., Prussia and Holland).

[4] J. Adams to the President of Congress, November 1, 1781 (Wharton, IV, 813, 814; A Collection of State papers, pamphlet 2).

Baron van der Capellen van de Marsch strongly supported also Adams' demand of an answer (Wharton, V, 246, 247; A Collection of State Papers, pamphlet 5).

[5] Resolves of Congress, Comprising the Instructions to John Adams, August 16, 1781 (Wharton, IV, 636–638).

Vauguyon might do so jointly, or, finally, Adams alone might propose the treaty as a consequence of his former suggestion of a similar treaty.[1]

Adams' instructions had been accompanied by a report of Cornwallis' surrender, and he remarked to Franklin how easy a thing it would be to bring the war to a happy conclusion, if only Spain and the United Provinces would cooperate with the United States and France with the sincerity of the latter power.[2] The American minister apparently had great hopes for the conclusion of an alliance between the United States, France, and the United Provinces against England. He informed Jay, the American commissioner in Spain, that there would probably soon be a proposal of such a triple alliance, and if Spain would join and make it quadruple, it would be so much the better.[3] When, at the beginning of December, Adams acknowledged the receipt of the instructions to Congress, he was not so hopeful regarding the conclusion of a treaty with the United Provinces. "The Dutch," he said, "are so indolent, so divided, so animated with party spirit, and above all so entirely in the power of their chief, that it is very certain that they will take the proposition ad referendum immediately and then deliberate upon it a long time." The news of Cornwallis' defeat, however, he continued, had made a great impression upon the Dutch, so that his proposition, if made immediately, would have a great effect. This he could not do, because he was compelled to wait for the approval of the French court.[4] So far, Vauguyon had only referred to the American proposition as "very well considered."[5]

About the middle of December, Adams was able to write to Congress that the first public body in the United Provinces had proposed an alliance with the United States. It was the quarter of Oostergoo. This, the minister said, was only a

---

[1] Adams to Vauguyon, November 25, 1781 (Wharton, V, 3, 4).

[2] J. Adams to Franklin, November 26, 1781 (ibid., V, 7, 8).

[3] J. Adams to Jay, November 28, 1781 (ibid., V, 32).

[4] J. Adams to the President of Congress, December 4, 1781 (ibid., V, 36, 37).

[5] Adams to Jay, November 26, 1781 (ibid., V, 10, 11).

part of one branch of the sovereignty, but the whole Republic must follow. " It is necessitated to it by a mechanism as certain as clock work; but its operations are and will be studiously and zealously slow. It will be a long time before the measure can be completed."[1]

The French ambassador at the Hague grew more communicative now. He called on Adams in Amsterdam and suggested that the latter should go to the Hague and demand an answer from the States General regarding his former proposition. After that the American minister, according to Vauguyon's advice, was to visit the cities of Holland, and apply to their regencies.[2] Adams went to the Hague on January 8, and, on the following day, called upon the president of the States General, demanding verbally a categorical answer to his memorial regarding a treaty of commerce and amity and the presentation of his credentials. The president, van der Sandheuvel, reported Adams' request to the States General and the matter was again taken ad referendum.

Not a single province had so far answered the minister's memorial. The Grand Pensionary, Bleiswijck, was ill and could not be seen by Adams. The latter then visited the deputies to the States General from all the cities of the province of Holland, who without exception received him very kindly, but were unable to make definite promises.[3] Van der Capellen tot den Poll, who had just shown again his love for the United States by offering twelve thousand florins to Adams' loan in preference to that guaranteed by

---

[1] J. Adams to the President of Congress, December 14, 1781 (Wharton, V, 49, 50) ; A Collection of State Papers, pamphlet 3.

[2] J. Adams to the President of Congress, December 18, 1781 (Wharton, V, 55).

Count de Vergennes approved of this course to be taken by Adams (Vauguyon to Adams, December 30, 1781, in Wharton, V, 79, 80).

[3] Adams to the President of Congress, January 14, 1782 (Wharton, V, 97–99) ; A Collection of State Papers, pamphlet 4; Resolution of the States General, January 9, 1782, and Resolution of Holland and Westfriesland (Sparks Dutch Papers) ; Thulemeier to Frederick II, January 11, 1782 (Bancroft MSS., Prussia and Holland) ; Vaterlandsche Historie, XXIX, 127.

France, was furious at the slow advance of the American cause in the United Provinces, and even exclaimed that he was ashamed to be Dutch. Van der Capellen, too, had suggested that Adams should demand a categorical answer from the States General to his memorial, since many people in the Republic desired an alliance with America.[1] Adams himself found his office more and more distasteful and wished "every hour in the twenty-four" that he was back in the United States again.[2]

About a week after Adams had written in such despairing terms the province of Friesland publicly acknowledged the independence of the United States. Several cities of the province of Holland and the whole Republic were expected soon to follow this example.[3] Adams now began to think of transferring his residence from Amsterdam to the Hague, in order to be in closer touch with the Dutch government. For this reason he purchased a "large and elegant house in a fine situation on a noble spot of ground" at the Hague for about sixteen thousand guilders.[4] It caused surprise in the

[1] Van der Capellen to Adams, January 6, 1782 (Beaufort, Brieven van der Capellen, 264, 265).
Regarding Adams' answer see Beaufort, Brieven van der Capellen, 266, 267. He said that the time was approaching very fast when the Republic must decide.
Van der Capellen tot den Poll to van der Capellen van de Marsch, January 17, 1782 (ibid., 266).
[2] J. Adams to Franklin, February 20, 1782 (Wharton, V, 189).
[3] Vaterlandsche Historie, XXIX, 129.
[4] J. Adams to Livingston, February 27, 1782 (Wharton, V, 206, 207).
This was the first legation building which the United States ever owned. Adams took the title in his own name, since the United States was not yet recognized by the United Provinces. As soon as this should be done and Congress approve of the transaction, the title was to be transferred to the United States. Adams could not pay the whole amount. He took for first payment the money of his loan and some cash which he had brought from America, in all ten thousand guilders. The rest was to be furnished by Franklin or to be borrowed from a friend. The American legation, or "Hôtel des Etats-Unis de l'Amérique," as it was officially called, was situated upon the Fleweele Burgwal, a canal street (J. Adams to Livingston, May 16, 1782, in Wharton, V, 420).
Besides the United States, only France and Spain owned legation buildings at the Hague, while all the other nations represented there rented houses for their ministers (Dumas to Livingston, April 4, 1782, in Wharton, V, 293).

United Provinces that Adams should take this step with the intention of establishing himself in his quality as American minister to the United Provinces before the States General had attributed this character to him.[1]   In the beginning of March the deputies of Friesland proposed to the States General the admission of Adams as "minister of the Congress of North America."[2]   As the Friesians were said to carry through everything that they undertook, it was generally thought that a treaty with the United States would soon be perfected.   Adams himself did not share in this opinion.[3]

Neither did the French court think the acknowledgment of American independence by the Dutch in the near future probable, because there was nothing which rendered such a step necessary.   The Foreign Secretary at Paris informed the French ambassador to the United Provinces that it was most important for France not even indirectly to promote such a measure.   She could not wish, he said, to guarantee the consequences to the Republic which might result from the recognition of the United States.[4]   Strange to say, Amsterdam was now opposed to closer relations with America.   Van der Capellen attributed this to intrigues. He had also heard that Vauguyon was dissuading the Dutch from recognizing the United States, but this rumor, he declared, was without foundation.   He would regret extremely if the United Provinces should neglect this opportunity

---

[1] Thulemeier to Frederick II, February 26, 1782 (Bancroft MSS., Prussia and Holland).

[2] Resolution of the States General, March 5, 1782 (Sparks MSS., CIII).

Friesland played a prominent part for the American cause by its enthusiasm for liberty.   The students of the University of Franeker held a grand festival, celebrating the future of the young republic. Then the province was leading in the recognition of the independence of the United States and the admission of Adams as American minister.   When finally the United States was recognized by the States General, the "Society of Citizens" at Leeuwarden, on May 8, 1782, resolved to have a medal struck in commemoration of the event (Griffis, Brave Little Holland, 231; Collection of State Papers, pamphlet 24).

[3] J. Adams to Livingston, March 11, 1782 (Wharton, V, 234–236).

[4] Vergennes to Vauguyon, March 7, 1782 (Sparks MSS., LXXXIII).

for furthering their commerce, navigation and industry.[1]
Many petitions from Dutch manufacturers and merchants,
and also from the municipalities of cities, such as Dort and
Leyden, were directed to the authorities of the separate
states and even to the States General, demanding closer commercial relations with the United States and the admission
of Adams.[2] The growing popular sentiment in favor of
America was now soon to prompt a decision in the United
Provinces.

The second province which urged the States General to
admit Adams as minister plenipotentiary of the United
States was Holland and Westfriesland. The provincial assembly passed a resolution to this effect on March 29, 1782,[3]
and communicated it immediately to the States General, at
the same time making it known to Adams through the Grand
Pensionary. Adams thanked that official very warmly and
expressed the hope that the other provinces would soon
follow the example given by Friesland and Holland.[4] In a
little more than three weeks this was accomplished. Overyssel followed on April 5,[5] Zealand on April 8, Groningen

---

[1] Van der Capellen to Valck, March 13, 1782 (Beaufort, Brieven
van der Capellen, 272) ; same to A. M. Jansen, March 14, 1782 (ibid.,
275).

[2] J. Adams to Livingston, March 19, 1782 (Wharton, V, 248 ff.;
A Collection of State Papers, pamphlets Nos. 6 ff.) ; Vauguyon to
Vergennes, March 15, 1782 (Sparks MSS., LXXXIII) ; Thulemeier
to Frederick II, March 22, 1782 (Bancroft MSS., Prussia and
Holland).

[3] Wharton, V, 258; Sparks MSS., CIII; A Collection of State
Papers, pamphlet 17; Dumas to Livingston, March 29, 1782 (Wharton, V, 276) ; Thulemeier to Frederick II, March 29, 1782 (Bancroft MSS., Prussia and Holland).

[4] J. Adams to van Bleiswijck, March 31, 1782 (Wharton, V, 289).
About this time extracts from van der Capellen's correspondence
with the Americans were published in the Courant and caused great
surprise and excitement in the United Provinces. The author was
proud that his efforts for the American cause had not been without
result. Still, he said, what could the friends of the United States
have done if Adams had not been in the United Provinces? That
the latter had been appointed by Congress minister plenipotentiary
to the United Provinces, van der Capellen attributed to his letters
to Trumbull and Livingston, in which he had recommended the
sending over of an American envoy (Van der Capellen to Valck, in
Beaufort, Brieven van der Capellen, 284).

[5] Van der Capellen to J. Adams, April 6, 1782 (Beaufort, Brieven
van der Capellen, Aanhangsel, 59).

on April 9, Utrecht on April 10, Guelderland on April 17, and the States General finally resolved upon the admission of John Adams on April 19.[1]　On April 22 the latter presented his credentials to the Prince of Orange, on which occasion nothing remarkable happened.　Adams in his address to William V emphasized the friendly feelings existing in America for the United Provinces, and the prince answered in such a low and indistinct way that the American minister understood only the statement that the stadtholder had put no difficulty in the way of the reception.[2]　A few days later Adams presented a memorial to the president of the States General, in which he formally proposed the conclusion of a treaty of amity and commerce between the United States and the United Provinces, and asked that a commission be appointed with full powers to negotiate with him on the subject.[3]　The deputies for foreign affairs, thereupon, were instructed by the States General to confer with the American minister, which they did, receiving from him a draft of the treaty.　Copies were sent to all the provinces for deliberation, and, at the same time, the original draft was referred to the deputies for naval matters for examination.　After this committee should have obtained the advice of the col-

---

[1] Collection of State Papers, pamphlets Nos. 18 ff.; Sparks MSS., CIII, under dates of April 8 to 22, 1782; J. Adams to Livingston, April 19, 1782 (Wharton, V, 315–319).

The resolution of the States General of April 19, 1782, was in the following terms: " Deliberated by resumption upon the address and the ulterior address made by Mr. Adams the 4th of May, 1781, and the 9th of January of the current year to the president of the assembly of their high mightinesses, to present to their high mightinesses his letters of credence, in the name of the United States of North America, and by which ulterior address the said Mr. Adams has demanded a categorical answer to the end to be able to acquaint his constituents thereof; it has been thought fit and resolved that Mr. Adams shall be admitted and acknowledged in quality of envoy of the United States of North America to their high mightinesses as he is admitted and acknowledged by the present " (Wharton, V, 319).

[2] J. Adams to Livingston, April 22, 1782 (Wharton, V, 319, 320); Thulemeier to Frederick II, April 23, 1782 (Bancroft MSS., Prussia and Holland).

[3] J. Adams to Livingston, April 23, 1782 (Wharton, V, 325); Resolution of the States General, April 23, 1782 (Sparks MSS., CIII).

leges of the admiralty, a full report was to be presented to the States General for final decision.[1]

A perfect revolution had thus taken place in the inner politics of the United Provinces, the English party having lost ground completely, and the Prince of Orange being compelled to yield to public sentiment, which had grown decidedly anti-English. The Duc de la Vauguyon said that the Dutch nation had avenged itself " of all the political and other evils which the English have done them since Cromwell." The Spanish envoy expressed himself similarly in declaring that Adams " had struck the greatest blow which had been given in Europe for a long time."[2]

Adams thought now that it was time to do something for the men who had been especially helpful to him in bringing about the success of the American cause in the United Provinces and who hitherto had not received the reward they deserved. He mentioned, above all, Dumas, the American correspondent, whom he recommended ˙for an appointment as secretary of legation and chargé d'affaires at the Hague. Then he called the attention of Congress to Mr. Thaxter, a gentleman whose " indefatigable application to the affairs of the United States, and whose faithful friendship " to Adams recommended him to the favor of Congress. Next, Edmund Jennings of Brussels was lauded, having " honored " the American minister " with his correspondence," and having been often serviceable to the United States. Finally Adams praised M. A. M. Cerisier, " one of the greatest historians and political writers in Europe, author of the ' Tableaux de l'Histoire des Provinces Unies des Pays Bas,' " and of the " Politique Hollandois." His pen, the minister said, had erected a monument to the American cause more glorious and more durable than brass or marble. " I have had no money," Adams concluded, " but my salary, and that has been never paid me without grudging. If I have friends in Europe, they have not most certainly been made

---

[1] Secret Resolutions of the States General, April 26, 1782 (Sparks Dutch Papers).

[2] Dumas to Livingston, May 10, 1782 (Wharton, V, 409).

by power, nor money, nor any species of corruption, nor
have they been made by making promises, or holding out
alluring hopes. I have made no promises, nor am I under
any obligation but that of private friendship and simple
civility to any man, having mentioned such as have been
my friends because they have been friends to the United
States, and I have no other, in Europe at least, and recommended them to the attention of Congress, as having rendered important services to our country, and able to render
still greater."[1]

In the meantime the deputies for naval matters had deliberated upon the projected treaty with the United States,
and considered the advice of the colleges of the admiralty.
They proposed some slight changes in Adams' draft, which
had to be submitted to the latter for examination and approval.[2]   Since all the provinces had to pass upon the treaty
bill, the American minister thought that it would be three
months before the treaty itself would be signed.   An alliance
between the two republics had not yet been proposed by him,
since he waited for the advice of the French ambassador,[3]
who apparently was not in a hurry to give it.[4]   In a conference with the Grand Pensionary Adams suggested that the
United Provinces should send an ambassador to Congress,
and consuls at least to Boston and Philadelphia.   Mr. van
Bleiswijck answered that it was difficult to find a man who
was able to act as ambassador and at the same time willing
to undertake such a long voyage.[5]   Adams became now the
recipient of many attentions in the United Provinces.   The

---

[1] J. Adams to Livingston, May 16, 1782 (Wharton, V, 420–423).
  Dumas was not proposed to Congress as American chargé d'affaires, Livingston establishing the principle that a foreigner should
not act as regular representative of the United States abroad, and
that such positions must be filled by Americans (Livingston to the
President of Congress, September 12, 1782, in Wharton, V, 719).
[2] Resolution of the States General, May 21, 1782 (Sparks Dutch
Papers).
[3] J. Adams to Livingston, June 9, 1782 (Wharton, V, 482).
[4] The French court was against the alliance, preferring not to have
their hands bound (Adams to Livingston, September 6, 1782, in
Wharton, V, 706).
[5] J. Adams to Livingston, June 15, 1782 (Wharton, V, 495).

merchants of the city of Schiedam sent a deputation inviting him to an entertainment in his honor and sending congratulations to Congress.[1]

At about the middle of August, the treaty of amity and commerce was passed by the provinces, and the States General proposed final conferences with the American minister.[2] At last, on October 8, 1782, the treaty and a convention concerning recaptures were signed by both parties at the Hague and sent to America for the ratification of Congress.[3] Both documents were signed by Congress on January 23, 1783,[4] and returned to the United Provinces, where they arrived in May. In the absence of Adams, who had been commissioned to Paris in order to take part in the peace negotiations there, Dumas, acting for the American minister, exchanged the ratifications with the States General of June 23. On the same day van Berckel, burgomaster of Rotterdam and brother of the pensionary of Amsterdam,[5] having been appointed minister plenipotentiary of the States General to Congress, set sail for the United States.[6]

The conclusion of the treaty with the United Provinces was a signal success for the United States. The Dutch Re-

---

[1] J. Adams to Livingston, July 5, 1782 (Wharton, V, 595–597).
[2] Dumas to Livingston, August 16, 1782 (ibid., V, 662).
[3] J. Adams to Livingston, October 8, 1782 (ibid., V, 803, 804); Secret Resolution of Holland and Westfriesland, October 17, 1782 (Sparks Dutch Papers).
[4] They are printed under this date in the Journal of Congress (Wharton, V, 805). The ratification by the States General is dated December 27, 1782 (Sparks Dutch Papers).
[5] Davies, History of Holland, III, 479.
[6] J. Adams to Livingston, May 30, 1783 (Wharton, VI, 457); Dumas to the States General, June 5, 1783 (ibid., VI, 476, 477); Dumas to Livingston, June 23, 1783 (ibid., VI, 502).
Regarding the appointment of a Dutch envoy to the United States see also: Adams to Livingston, June 15, 1782 (Wharton, V, 495); Resolution of Holland and Westfriesland, December 12, 1782 (Sparks Dutch Papers); Dumas to Livingston, December 12, 1782 (Wharton, VI, 130); same to same, January 11, 1783 (ibid., VI, 204); same to same, January 20, 1783 (ibid., VI, 221); same to same, March 14, 1783 (ibid., VI, 271).
For the reception of van Berckel by Congress see: Secret Journal of Foreign Affairs, October 25, 1783 (Wharton, VI, 714) and van Berckel's reports of October 20 and November 4, 1783, both received by the States General on December 22, 1783 (Sparks Dutch Papers).

public was the first nation, after France, to enter into closer relations with America. There was, however, a vast difference between the two agreements. With France, the treaty was in some degree an act of charity and had been felt as such by the United States, but with the United Provinces the parties had negotiated as equals. Furthermore the recognition of American independence by the Dutch and the conclusion of the treaty between the two republics established the value of the United States in the eyes of the world, thereby marking a step forward in the independent national life of the new commonwealth.[1]

---

[1] Trescot, Diplomacy of the Revolution, 89-91.

The United Provinces were soon to discover that this treaty with America was not of material advantage to them. The United States proved to be rivals rather than customers of the Dutch Republic. By 1786 they had taken away from the Dutch a considerable portion of the trade to China. American merchants also established a flourishing though illicit commerce with the Dutch West Indian colonies, Surinam, and the Cape of Good Hope, thereby greatly decreasing the trade between the United Provinces and their colonies (Davies, History of Holland, III, 479, 480).

CHAPTER IX.

PEACE.

Not having succeeded in concluding a separate peace with the United Provinces, England tried to sever France from the rest of her enemies by offering a separate peace to her. In case this should not be feasible, England proposed a general peace.[1] The Duc de Vergennes flatly declined to enter upon negotiations regarding separate peace and declared that it would be the privilege of France and her allies to make the propositions for peace which they considered acceptable.[2] The Dutch, hoping that France, while negotiating for a general peace, would also defend their interests, asked Louis XVI to make assurances in this respect. He answered evasively that he made it an unalterable law to guard carefully the interests essential to the dignity and prosperity of the United Provinces.[3] When it was understood that Great Britain had authorized Mr. Oswald and the English ambassador at Paris, Fitzherbert, to treat with the four powers at war with her,[4] the States General chose Mr. de Brantzen as special minister to support the Dutch minister at Paris, Lestevenon de Berkenrode,[5] in negotiating for peace.[6] The two plenipotentiaries of the Republic were to negotiate with England on the basis, first of all, that the Dutch, in conformity with the principles of the Armed Neutrality, as a conditio sine qua non, were " in

[1] Secret Resolution of the States General, May 21, 1782 (Sparks MSS., CIII).
[2] Berkenrode (Dutch envoy at Paris) to the States General, May 26, 1782 (Bancroft MSS., America, Holland, and England).
[3] Berkenrode to the States General, July 14, 1728 (Bancroft MSS., America, Holland, and England).
[4] J. Adams to H. Laurens, August 15, 1782 (Wharton, V, 662); same to Dana, September 17, 1782 (ibid., V, 732).
[5] J. Adams to Livingston, August 18, 1782 (ibid., V, 665).
[6] J. Adams to Jay, August 17, 1782 (ibid., V, 664).

full possession and indisputable enjoyment of the rights of
the neutral flag and of free navigation;" that naval stores
should henceforth be regarded as free merchandise and not
contraband; that all Dutch possessions taken by the English were to be restored to the United Provinces; and that
losses, "unjustly" caused by Great Britain, should be indemnified by the latter.[1] Of the other powers the Count
d'Aranda was to represent Spain in the peace negotiations
at Paris; Franklin and Jay, the United States.[2] When Berkenrode and Brantzen, however, handed a copy of their
credentials to Fitzherbert, he declared that he did not yet
have sufficient instructions from his government,[3] and it
soon became evident that England would not be inclined to
réstore all of her conquests of Dutch territory. Count de
Vergennes had sent a special ambassador, M. de Rayneval,
over to Great Britain, in order to sound the English ministry
regarding the sincerity of their desire for peace. This
diplomat reported that Lord Shelburne had declared that
England would keep the Dutch fort Trinconomale on the
coast of Ceylon because it suited her well.[4] Difficulties were
also encountered with another of the conditions of the
United Provinces. Vergennes told their plenipotentiaries
that a failure of the negotiations, or at least a long delay,
would be likely if the States General insisted on free navigation according to the principles of the Armed Neutrality
as a conditio sine qua non. England would most certainly
not grant it, since, in this form, it would involve a general
law. He proposed, therefore, that the Dutch should merely
mention free navigation as one of their conditions for peace,
without adding to it the obnoxious clause regarding the
treaty of the Armed Neutrality.[5] In fact, Fitzherbert, a

---

[1] Wharton, V, 665, 666; Secret Resolution of the States General,
August 19, 1782 (Bancroft MSS., America, Holland, and England).
[2] J. Adams to Livingston, September 23, 1782 (Wharton, V, 751).
[3] Berkenrode and Brantzen to the States General, September 19,
1782 (Bancroft MSS., America, Holland, and England).
[4] Conferences of M. de Rayneval with Lord Shelburne, October,
1782 (Wharton, V, 821).
[5] Berkenrode and Brantzen to the States General, November 7,
1782 (Bancroft MSS., America, Holland, and England).

few days later, received information from his government
that the Dutch conditio sine qua non would not be considered.[1] The English ambassador also hinted to the Dutch
plenipotentiaries that the conditions of the States General,
as they were now, would never be accepted by Great Britain, and recommended their modification before they should
be formally presented to him.[2] This advice, however, was
not heeded, and the conditions remained practically un-
changed, even the article concerning free navigation, on the
ground that full enjoyment of free navigation according to
the principles of the Armed Neutrality had been proposed
to the United Provinces in an official letter which the English secretary of state, Fox, had addressed to Simolin, the
Russian ambassador at London, on May 4, 1782.[3]

In the meantime John Adams had joined Franklin and
Jay in Paris to take part in the peace negotiations. At the
beginning of December Adams verbally informed the Dutch
plenipotentiaries that the preliminaries, as far as the United
States and Great Britain were concerned, had already been
signed on November 30, 1782,[4] but that definitive peace
was only to be concluded in concurrence with the other belligerent powers. In a confidential appendix to their report
regarding this conversation with Adams, Berkenrode and
Brantzen stated that Louis XVI had promised to restore to
the States General all Dutch territories which should be in
the possession of France at the conclusion of peace.[5] The
fear of the Dutch that they might eventually lose one or the
other of their colonies which had been recaptured by the
French from Great Britain was thus removed, but the

---

[1] Berkenrode and Brantzen to the States General, November 18,
1782 (Bancroft MSS., America, Holland, and England).

[2] See statement dated November 29, 1782, in Sparks MSS., XL.

[3] Articles presented by Berkenrode and Brantzen to Fitzherbert
on December 6, 1782 (Sparks MSS., XL; Bancroft MSS., America,
Holland, and England).

[4] J. Adams' Journal, December 3, 1782 (Wharton, VI, 103-105).

[5] Berkenrode and Brantzen to the States General, December 3,
1782 (Bancroft MSS., America, Holland, and England); van der
Capellen to Valck, December 15, 1782 (Beaufort, Brieven van der
Capellen, 418).

negotiations did not proceed as the States General wished.
In the first interview which Berkenrode and Brantzen had
with Fitzherbert after the presentation of the Dutch peace
conditions, the Englishman flatly rejected the indemnity
claims of the States General for losses at sea.[1]   He confined himself to a discussion of this article, but it was to be
expected that in the succeeding conferences he would deal
with the other articles in a similar way.   In the United
Provinces the Dutch peace conditions were not generally
approved.   Van der Capellen thought it a mistake to demand free navigation as a sine qua non, since Great Britain
had not even acknowledged to Russia the principles of the
Armed Neutrality, and could not be expected to act differently toward the United Provinces.   What then, he asked,
was the use of insisting on a condition which would never be
accepted?[2]   France and England now reached an agreement
also; and there was only one point of difference left between Spain and Great Britain,[3] so that little remained as
far as these powers were concerned except the settling of
the forms.   Even France feared that the negotiations between the United Provinces and England might cause delay
and embarrassment.[4]   John Adams actively assisted the
Dutch plenipotentiaries in Paris, whenever he could.   He
supported especially their claims regarding free navigation,
as may be seen from his own words:—

"Unnecessary, however, as any exertions of mine have been, I
have not omitted any opportunity of throwing in any friendly suggestions in my power where there was a possibility of doing any
good to our good friends the Dutch.   I have made such suggestions
to Mr. Fitzherbert.   But with Mr. Oswald I have had several very
serious conversations upon the subject.   So I have also with Mr.
Vaughan and Mr. Whitefoord.

"To Mr. Oswald I urged the necessity of Great Britain's agreeing
with the Dutch upon the unlimited freedom of navigation, from a
variety of topics, some of which I may explain to you more particularly hereafter.   Thus much I may say at present, that I told him

[1] December 6, 1782 (Sparks MSS., XL).
[2] Van der Capellen to Hooft, December 5, 1782 (Beaufort, Brieven
van der Capellen, 410–412).
[3] J. Adams' Journal, December 5, 1782 (Wharton, VI, 109).
[4] Vergennes to Luzerne, the French envoy to Congress, December
19, 1782 (Wharton, VI, 152).

that it was impossible for Great Britain to avoid it; it would probably be insisted upon by all the other powers. France and Spain,
as well as Russia, Sweden, Denmark, Prussia, the Emperor, and
Portugal, as well as Holland, had already signed the armed neutrality. The United States of America had declared themselves
ready to sign, and were ready. The combination being thus powerful, Great Britain could not resist it. But if she should refuse to
agree to it with Holland, and the other powers should acquiesce,
and Holland should make peace without it (which would never,
however, be the case), yet all would be ineffectual, for Holland
would forever be able to make use of other neutral bottoms, and
would thus enjoy the benefit of this liberty and reality, though
denied it by treaty and in appearance. It would, therefore, be
more for the honor and interest of Great Britain to agree to it with
a good grace in the treaty with Holland. Nay, the wisest part she
could act would be to set on foot a negociation immediately for
signing herself the treaty of the armed neutrality, and then admit-
ting it into the treaty with Holland would be a thing of course. At
one of these conversations Dr. Franklin was present, who supported me with all his weight; at another, Mr. Jay seconded me
with all his abilities and ingenuity. Mr. Oswald has several times
assured me that he had written these arguments and his own
opinion, in conformity with them, to the King's ministers in London, and I doubt not they will be adopted."[1]

When Fitzherbert at last replied officially to the memorandum of the Dutch plenipotentiaries of December 6, the
answer was such that it cast a gloom over the whole nation.
Free navigation in conformity with the articles of the
Armed Neutrality was rejected. It was admitted that Fox
had proposed free navigation, but the question at stake had
then been a separate peace between the two nations. The
proposition of Mr. Fox was now void, since the Dutch had
refused it. Great Britain, Fitzherbert stated, would return
to the United Provinces all Dutch possessions in the hands
of England at the conclusion of peace except Trinconomale
on the island of Ceylon. Losses at sea, he declared further,
could not be indemnified by Great Britain, because she had
been compelled to make war upon the Republic and had not
begun the hostilities deliberately.[2] On January 20, 1783,
the preliminary articles of peace were signed by the representatives of England on the one hand, and France and

---

[1] J. Adams to Dumas, January 1, 1783 (Wharton, VI, 191–192).
[2] Berkenrode and Brantzen to the States General, January 5, 1783
(Bancroft MSS., America, Holland, and England); Lord Grantham
to Fitzherbert, December 18, 1782 (Sparks MSS., XL).

Spain on the other. At the same time the cessation of hostilities was arranged by the ministers of these powers, to which measure the United States, through Franklin and Adams, also acceded.[1] The United Provinces were not yet ready to sign preliminaries,[2] but were included in the armistice.[3] That France had not delayed the signing of the preliminary treaty until the negotiations between the United Provinces and England were also concluded was bitterly resented by the Dutch, who now considered themselves abandoned by the French and delivered over to the hatred or mercy of Great Britain.[4] Vergennes assured the Republic again, that France would not conclude peace with England definitely, unless the United Provinces were included. The preliminary treaty, he said, had been necessary, because the United States were exhausted and had asked through Franklin for twenty millions to be able to carry the war through another campaign. France, however, was not in a position to grant this loan. Taxes, he further explained, could not be increased in America, since this might cause an insurrection and jeopardize everything. Spain was also exhausted and absolutely demanded the conclusion of the preliminary agreement.

The only important point which the Dutch, so far, had gained during the negotiations was that England had renounced Trinconomale, but she demanded Negapatam instead. The States General, however, were decided not to grant this, and still insisted upon free navigation.[5] The negotiations had thus arrived at a dead-lock. The States

[1] English Commissioners' Declaration of the Cessation of Hostilities, January 20, 1783 (Wharton, VI, 223, 224).

[2] Franklin to Livingston, January 21, 1783 (Wharton, VI, 225).

[3] Vergennes to Luzerne, January 22, 1783 (Doniol, Histoire, V, 278); Berkenrode and Brantzen to the States General, January 23, 1783 (Bancroft MSS., America, Holland, and England). George III proclaimed the cessation of hostilities on February 14, 1783, including the United States, France, Spain, and the United Provinces (Wharton, VI, 251, 252); Groot Placaatboek, IX, 159.

[4] Van der Capellen to Jansen, January 29, 1783 (Beaufort, Brieven van der Capellen, 496–499); same to Tegelaar, February 13, 1783 (ibid., 516, 517).

[5] Dumas to Adams, February 4, 1783 (Wharton, VI, 235, 236).

General now thought of eliminating the question of free navigation from the peace conferences by proposing to France, Spain, and the United States a separate joint convention on the principles of the Armed Neutrality. Their High Mightinesses tried to secure the cooperation of the American ministers in Europe, who were willing to aid the States General as much as their instructions allowed,[1] but the whole plan failed. Meanwhile the negotiations made no progress, the United Provinces not yet being willing to make concessions of importance. In February the States òf Holland and Westfriesland passed a resolution, according to which new instructions should be sent to Berkenròde and Brantzen.[2] The States General approved of it, though the provinces of Friesland, Zealand, and Groningen had not yet consented, which made the resolution unconstitutional.[3] Conferences were now held not only between the Dutch and English plenipotentiaries at Paris, but Brantzen seht his secretary, Mr. For, to England in order to negotiate there directly with the Foreign Secretary, Fox. Still no agreement was brought about at either place.[4]

As an expedient England was said to have proposed to France that the latter should cede to Great Britain the French island of Tabago in the West Indies, in which case England would restore Negapatam to the Dutch. It would be left to the French, then, to obtain a suitable compensation from the United Provinces, but Louis XVI, it was asserted, declined to turn Tabago over to Great Britain. "France,"

---

[1] Dumas to J. Adams, January 24, 1783 (Wharton, VI, 229, 230); same to same, January 28, 1783 (ibid., 232); J. Adams to Dumas, January 29, 1783 (ibid., 232, 233); Dumas to J. Adams, January 30, 1783 (ibid., 233, 234); same to same, February 4, 1783 (ibid., 235); J. Adams to Dumas, February 5, 1783 (ibid., 236); Dumas to Adams, February 18, 1783 (ibid., 255, 256); same to same, March 6, 1783 (ibid., 273); Dumas to Livingston, April 18, 1783 (ibid., 384); Livingston's Memorandum of June 3, 1783, etc. (ibid., 473, 474); Report of a Committee of Congress, June 12, 1783 (ibid., 482, 483).
[2] Resolutions of Holland and Westfriesland, February 21, 1783 (Sparks Dutch Papers).
[3] Dumas to J. Adams, March 4, 1783 (Wharton, VI, 272).
[4] Dumas to Livingston, May 8, 1783 (Wharton, VI, 416).

said van der Capellen, "in rejecting this proposition, gives evidence, that she does not consider the friendship of the Republic worth a small and deserted island."[1]   The leader of the Patriots also mentioned these rumors to the French chargé d'affaires at the Hague, who said he did not believe in them.   Bérenger defended the attitude of his country toward the Republic.   France, he said, was by no means indifferent toward the friendship of the United Provinces, in whose prosperity and independence she took the most sincere interest.[2]

Toward the end of July, the situation relative to the Dutch-English negotiations was not materially changed. The following letter of the American minister at the Hague, who had returned from Paris after the preliminaries were signed and his business terminated there, describes excellently the state of affairs as far as the United Provinces were concerned:—

"It is the general opinion here, both among the members of the States and at the Hôtel de France, that the delays of the definitive pacification are contrived by the court of London in order to set all their instruments at work in this Republic to induce it to renew its ancient connexions with Great Britain, particularly their alliance, offensive and defensive, by which each power was bound to furnish the other, if attacked, a certain number of ships and troops. Against this the patriotic party is decided, and they are now very well satisfied with the grand pensionary, Bleiswick, because he openly and roundly takes their side, and the court is said to be discontented with him for the same reason. There is, no doubt, an intelligence and correspondence between the two courts of London and the Hague to bring about this point. The grand pensionary told me yesterday that the court of London desired it, and there were persons here who desired it, and he knew very well who they were; but that most certainly they would not carry their point. Van Berckel, Visscher, and Gyselaer all assured me of the same, and added that the fear of this had determined them not to send a minister to London, but to go through with the negociation at Paris, although they were all highly dissatisfied with the conduct of France, and particularly with that of the Count de Vergennes.

[1] Van der Capellen to Jansen, May 30, 1783 (Beaufort, Brieven van der Capellen, 606).
[2] Bérenger to van der Capellen, June 6, 1783 (Beaufort, Brieven van der Capellen, 609).
Doniol (Histoire, V, 283 ff.) tries to show in detail that France was very much occupied with the welfare of the United Provinces and anxious to obtain as favorable a peace for them as was possible under the circumstances.

"They all say he has betrayed and deserted them, played them a very bad trick (tour), and violated his repeated promises to them. They do not in the least spare M. Bérenger and M. Merchant, who conduct the French affairs here in the absence of the Duc de la Vauguyon, but hold this language openly and freely to them. These gentlemen have sometimes found it hard to bear, and have winced and sometimes even threatened; but their answer has been more mortifying still: 'Do as you please, drive the Republic into the arms of England if you will. Suppress all the friends of France, if you chose it.' And some of them have said. 'We will go to America.' They all say that France had the power to have saved them; that the acquisition of Tobago was no equivalent to France for the loss of the Republic, etc., etc., etc. They are all highly pleased with the conduct of their own ambassador, Brantzen, with his activity, intelligence, and fidelity. They all say that they would send a minister to London to negociate there, if they were sure of. being able to carry an election for a man they could depend upon. But the court here would have so much influence in the choice that they would run a risk of sending a man who would insensibly lead them into a revival of the old ties with England, which they say is enslaving the Republic to that kingdom.

"I learn here from all quarters a confirmation of what I had learned before at Paris from M. Brantzen and the Duc de la Vauguyon, viz., that the Duke of Manchester had given them no answer, nor said a word to them for six weeks, in answer to the propositions they had made; among which was an offer of an equivalent for Negapatnam. They offered some establishments in Sumatra and Surat. Lately the Duke of Manchester has received a courier, and has given an answer that a real equivalent might be accepted. No answer is given to any other point, and this is vague; so that another courier must go to London and return. Parliament is now up, and perhaps the ministers may now be more attentive and less timorous."[1]

The belief, general in the Republic, that France had failed to put pressure upon Great Britain in favor of the Dutch and would finally conclude a separate peace with England, caused great apprehension to her adherents in the United Provinces.[2] It was evident that French influence was rapidly decreasing and that the Orangist, that is, English, party, was gaining correspondingly. The latter endeavored to detach the Republic entirely from France and to restore, by a revival of the alliance of 1674, the former friendly relations with England. Adams thought that the apparent change in the French policy was a blunder of Vergennes,

[1] J. Adams to Livingston, July 25, 1783 (Wharton, VI, 596, 597).
[2] Same to same, August 3, 1783 (ibid., VI, 632, 633); van der Capellen to Racer, August 5, 1783 (Beaufort, Brieven van der Capellen, 648–650); van der Capellen to Baron de Breteuil, September 1, 1783 (ibid., 655–665).

who did not know how to negotiate with free nations. "He can not enter into the motives," the minister said, "which govern them; he never penetrates their real system, and never appears to comprehend their constitution."[1]

With Vergennes' support the Dutch plenipotentiaries tried again to save Negapatam for the United Provinces, but their efforts were in vain. They offered to Great Britain the Dutch establishments on the west coast of Sumatra. England, however, refused on the ground that those territories would not be of the least use to her. She insisted on the cession of Negapatam and, besides, demanded unlimited free navigation in the East, that is to say, among the Dutch East Indian possessions. Furthermore, an agreement was to be made between the two nations relating to the commerce on the African coast. Berkenrode and Brantzen then offered an equivalent in money for Negapatam. For two months they did not receive an answer, and when it arrived it was a refusal. George III promised that Negapatam should be returned to the Dutch later, if a suitable compensation would be found. Seeing that England was decided not to make peace, unless Negapatam was ceded, the Dutch plenipotentiaries yielded in this point. They asked, however, that the conditions concerning free navigation in the eastern seas should be dropped, as well as the article regarding the salute to the English flag, which had also been demanded. The sea, the Dutch pleaded, was free and there was therefore no reason why a particular dominion over the sea should be recognized. The British negotiator still insisted on his conditions, although Vergennes now actively supported the Dutch ministers. Since all the other treaties were ready to be signed, the latter asked the States General for speedy instructions.[2]

Toward the end of August Vergennes informed Berkenrode and Brantzen that the court of Great Britain was urging the powers concerned to designate a day for the signing

---

[1] J. Adams to Livingston, July 31, 1783 (Wharton, VI, 623, 624).
[2] Berkenrode and Brantzen to the States General, August 13, 1783 (Sparks Dutch Papers).

of the definitive treaties. He said that he could not delay the conclusion of the final agreement any longer. France as well as Spain, he continued, was now compelled to keep a large quantity of troops in the field, which was a heavier strain on the finances of both countries than they could afford, while the uncertain political situation greatly damaged French commerce. In his opinion, all these evils were due to the delay of the negotiations caused by the indecision of the United Provinces. The Dutch plenipotentiaries protested, asserting that the delay had not been their fault and that the States General should be given sufficient time for deliberation. Thereupon the third of September was fixed as the day for the signature.[1]

The States General now instructed their plenipotentiaries again to represent to the English peace commissioner the injustice and unfairness of the British conditions, and to try all means to obtain better terms. Berkenrode and Brantzen were also to remind Vergennes of Louis XVI's promise not to separate his cause from that of the Republic, and to request his active cooperation for the sake of the United Provinces. The plenipotentiaries were authorized only in case all these efforts should fail, to comply with the English conditions, namely, the cession of Negapatam, free navigation in the eastern seas and the salute to the English flag on the high seas, but to concede only as much as was absolutely necessary in order to avoid an exclusion of the Dutch from general peace.[2]

After receiving these directions, Berkenrode and Brantzen called upon Vergennes, who informed them that he had already asked the British government to grant more moderate conditions to the Dutch, but that his request had not been complied with. He then called the attention of the commissioners to the services which France had ren-

[1] Berkenrode and Brantzen to the States General, August 25, 1783 (Bancroft MSS., America, Holland, and England).
[2] Secret Resolution of Holland and Westfriesland, August 26, 1783 (Sparks Dutch Papers); Secret Resolution of the States General, August 28, 1783 (Bancroft MSS., America, Holland, and England).

dered to the United Provinces in the saving of the Cape of
Good Hope to the Dutch, in the recapture of their possessions in the East and West Indies, and other matters.   The
United Provinces, he said, had not been fortunate in
their measures and the enemy, naturally, now took advantage of it.   In 1763 France had been in the same position
and had been compelled to accept the hard terms stipulated
by Great Britain.   Vergennes declared that he tried to delay
the signing of the treaties, by informing England of the determination of Louis XVI not to make peace, unless the
United Provinces were included.   Nevertheless, circumstances made it necessary to come to a conclusion and to
fix the date for the signatures.

The Dutch plenipotentiaries then had a conference with
the Duke of Manchester, the special English peace commissioner at Paris.   No understanding, however, could be
reached.   In order to have the Dutch-English preliminaries
signed before the other powers concluded their definitive
treaties, Berkenrode and Brantzen, on September 2, sent
their treaty project to the Duke of Manchester.[1]   It was
immediately signed by the latter and by both Dutch plenipotentiaries.[2]   The definitive treaty of peace between Great
Britain and the United Provinces was concluded at Paris on
May 20, 1784, being subsequently ratified at St. James on
June 10, and at the Hague on June 15 of the same year.

The treaty contained eleven articles, of which the following were of importance: Article two stipulated that the
vessels of the Republic should salute those of Great Britain
in the same manner as before the war.   According to article
four the States General had to cede to England the city of

---

[1] Berkenrode and Brantzen to the States General, September 3,
1783 (Bancroft MSS., America, Holland, and England).

[2] Projet d'Articles Praeliminaires de Paix entre Sa Majesté le Roi
de la Grande Bretagne et Leurs Hautes Puissances les États Généraux des Provinces Unies des Pais-Bas.—A la Haye.   Chez Isaac
Scheltus etc., 1783.

They were signed by the plenipotentiaries at Paris on September
2, 1783; by the respective governments at St. James on September
10, 1783, and at the Hague on September 26, 1783 (Sparks Dutch
Papers).

Negapatam, but the latter was to be restored to the United Provinces, in case an equivalent should be offered. Article five provided for the restitution to the United Provinces of all their possessions that Great Britain or the English East India Company had conquered during the war. In article six the States General promised not to hinder the navigation of the subjects of England in the eastern seas. Article seven arranged that commissioners should be named to settle the difficulties between the English African Company and the Dutch West India Company regarding navigation on the coast of Africa.[1]

Concerning the United Provinces Great Britain had thus absolutely made her own conditions, to which the former, not being able to carry on the war alone, were compelled to submit. It was different with the other powers. The United States were recognized as an independent nation whose boundaries should be the Mississippi River on the west, Florida on the south, and the southern boundary of Canada on the north. Furthermore the Americans should have the right of fishing on the coast of Newfoundland and in the Gulf of St. Lawrence, while the coasts of the United States would not be open for fishing to English subjects. France received back her possessions in the East Indies, as well as Tabago in the West Indies and Senegal in Africa.[2] Spain regained Florida and the island of Minorca.

The United Provinces by accepting England's conditions suffered permanent and very painful losses. Ceylon and the Moluccas had, in fact, been wrenched from them by Great Britain: the possession of Negapatam, together with free navigation among the Molucca islands, enabled England to establish there a flourishing smuggling trade in spices, thus enjoying all the advantages of this commerce while in no wise contributing to the expenses of keeping up the planta-

---

[1] Traité de Paix entre Sa Majesté le Roi de la Grande Bretagne et Leurs Hautes Puissances les États Généraux des Pais-Bas.—A la Haye. Chez Isaac Scheltus, etc., 1784 (Sparks Dutch Papers).
[2] France had paid dearly for this success, since the war cost her 1250 million livres (Pfister, Die amerikanische Revolution, II, 350).

tions.   The obligation of saluting the English flag was also considered very humiliating by the Dutch.[1]

The United Provinces, which had proved themselves the benefactors of the United States and France during the gigantic struggle just terminated, must then be considered the real and only victims of the American Revolution.   Both abroad and at home was this true, for party dissensions in the United Provinces during the contest widened to such a degree that reconciliation became hopeless, and a revolution unavoidable.   When this catastrophe a few years later really occurred, England with the aid of Prussia seized the opportunity to subdue the Republic still further, and her dependence upon her British neighbor became complete.

---

[1] Van der Capellen to Baron de Breteuil, September 1, 1783 (Beaufort, Brieven van der Capellen, 658).

INDEX.